INSTRUMENTS

IN THE

REDEEMER'S
HANDS

Resources for Changing Lives

A series published in cooperation with
THE CHRISTIAN COUNSELING AND EDUCATIONAL FOUNDATION
Glenside, Pennsylvania

Susan Lutz, Series Editor

Available in the series:

Edward T. Welch, *When People Are Big and God Is Small: Overcoming Peer Pressure, Codependency, and the Fear of Man*

Paul David Tripp, *Age of Opportunity: A Biblical Guide to Parenting Teens*

Edward T. Welch, *Blame It on the Brain? Distinguishing Chemical Imbalances, Brain Disorders, and Disobedience*

James C. Petty, *Step by Step: Divine Guidance for Ordinary Christians*

Paul David Tripp, *War of Words: Getting to the Heart of Your Communication Struggles*

Edward T. Welch, *Addictions—A Banquet in the Grave: Finding Hope in the Power of the Gospel*

Paul David Tripp, *Instruments in the Redeemer's Hands: People in Need of Change Helping People in Need of Change*

David Powlison, *Seeing with New Eyes: Counseling and the Human Condition through the Lens of Scripture*

INSTRUMENTS

IN THE

REDEEMER'S
HANDS

PEOPLE IN NEED OF CHANGE
HELPING PEOPLE IN NEED OF CHANGE

PAUL DAVID TRIPP

PUBLISHING
P.O. BOX 817 • PHILLIPSBURG • NEW JERSEY 08865-0817

Page design by Tobias Design
Typesetting by Michelle Feaster

Printed in the United States of America

Library of Congress Cataloging-in-Publication Data

Tripp, Paul David, 1950–
    Instruments in the Redeemer's hands : people in need of change helping people in need of change / Paul David Tripp.
        p.   cm.—(Resources for changing lives)
    Includes bibliographical references and index.
    ISBN 978-0-87552-607-2 (pbk.)
    1. Peer counseling in the church. I. Title. II. Series.

BV4409.T75 2002
253—dc21

                                                                    2002028537

To Tedd.
Thanks for leading the way.

CONTENTS

ILLUSTRATIONS

PREFACE

What God has ordained for his church is both wonderful and sobering. It is wonderful because he is a jealous and determined God. His work in his people will not fail, but will continue until it is completed. It is sobering because this work follows an "all of my people, all of the time" model.

Many of us would be relieved if God had placed our sanctification in the hands of trained and paid professionals, but that simply is not the biblical model. God's plan is that through the faithful ministry of every part, the whole body will grow to full maturity in Christ. The leaders of his church have been gifted, positioned, and appointed to train and mobilize the people of God for this "every person, everyday" ministry lifestyle.

The paradigm is simple: when God calls you to himself, he also calls you to be a servant, an instrument in his redeeming hands. All of his children are called into ministry, and each of them needs the daily intervention this ministry provides. If you followed the Lord for a thousand years, you would still need the ministry of the body of Christ as much as you did the day you first believed. This need will remain until our sanctification is complete in Glory.

That is what this book is about: how God uses people, who are themselves in need of change, as instruments of the same kind of change in others. This book's goal is not just that people's lives would be changed as they give help and receive it. The goal is to help change the church's very culture.

I am persuaded that the church today has many more consumers than committed participants. Sure, Joe and Sheila may volunteer for a specific activity like VBS or a diaconal project, but this frequently falls woefully short of the "everyone, all the time" model of the New Testament. Our tendency toward ecclesiastical consumerism has seriously weakened the church. For most of us, church is merely an event we attend or an organization we belong to. We do not see it as a calling that shapes our entire life.

But consider this: we could never hire enough paid staff to meet the ministry needs of the average local church. The "passive body that pays the professionals" culture of the modern evangelical church must be forsaken for the ministry model God has so wisely ordained. To that end this book has been written.

As always when I come to the end of a project like this, I am aware of how privileged I am. To be released for six months from normal ministry responsibilities to focus on writing is an amazing gift. My thanks goes out to John Bettler, the faculty and staff of the Christian Counseling and Educational Foundation, and to all of God's people who have sacrificially given to make this work possible. I must extend my thanks as well to Sue Lutz. Sue, your editing ability is outstanding. Thank you for being willing to turn my thoughts into words that make sense, and thank you for being willing to give me the "bad news" when you are convinced it will make the book better.

Finally, as you read, some of you may wonder why this book doesn't have a chapter-by-chapter study guide. The reason is that this material has been developed as discipleship curriculum for local churches. The *Instruments of Change* curriculum contains twelve lessons with both leader's guide and student manuals available. Each lesson has a threefold focus: concepts you need to know, how those apply to you personally, and how they set an agenda for your relationships and ministry.

The *Instruments of Change* course is the first piece of the *Changing Hearts, Changing Lives Curriculum*. This curriculum will also include courses entitled, *How People Change* and *Change and Your Relationships*. The *Changing Hearts, Changing Lives Curriculum* is an expression of the Christian Counseling and Educational Foundation's commitment to do all it can to assist the local church to train, equip, and mobilize God's people for personal ministry.

If you would like to know more about the *Instruments of Change* curriculum or CCEF, you can log onto our website, www.ccef.org or call 215-884-7676.

I must thank my family. Luella, you are my helper and greatest supporter, but more than that you are my closest friend. I have benefited from your ministry day after day for over thirty years. Justin, Ethan, Nicole, and Darnay, thank you for being patient with a dad who is still learning how to live what he has been called to teach.

To you, the reader, may God richly bless you as you take up his call to be part of the most important thing happening in the universe: redemption.

Paul David Tripp

1 | THE BEST OF NEWS: A REASON TO GET UP IN THE MORNING

What is the best news you can imagine? What is your "If only . . ." dream? Is it becoming a multi-millionaire and buying the house of your dreams? Perhaps it would be the job you have always wanted. Maybe your spouse would suddenly become the person you always hoped for, or your child would finally turn out all right, living responsibly and married to a wonderful person. What would be your best news?

Let's ask the question another way. What is your reason for getting up in the morning? What moves and motivates you through the day? What is so worthwhile that you are willing to give it your time, talents, and energy? What is so significant that you will build your whole life around it?

This book is about the best news a human being could ever receive. It is about something so significant that it makes everything we do worthwhile, even though we are just flawed people in a broken world. This news has nothing to do with fantasies, dreams, or unrealistic expectations. It is rooted in historical facts and present realities. It penetrates the harshest human situation with life-altering hope. It is the only thing really worth living for! It is *the* good news!

TO "GET" THE NEWS YOU HAVE TO UNDERSTAND THE STORY

For a brief period of time when God created the world, perfect people walked through a perfect world in perfect union with God.

1

The environment was lush and rich, with a menagerie of animals that inhabited the air, land, and sea. Every physical and spiritual need was fully met. There were no unfed stomachs or diseases to be feared. The gardens were free of weeds and thorns.

Man and woman, Adam and Eve, lived in perfect union with each other. There was no unhealthy competition, no power struggle, no vengeance or recrimination. There were no secret plots or harsh words, no fear, guilt, shame, or rebellion against authority. There was understanding, communication, and love.

There was no struggle with identity, anxiety, depression, or addiction. There was no painful personal history to overcome. There was no fear of what might happen next, no mixed motives, no struggle with inordinate desire. There was no temptation to sin.

With God, too, there was a perfect union. People loved, worshiped, and obeyed as they were created to do. In the cool of the day they actually walked with God in the Garden, enjoying perfect fellowship with their Maker. They were God's resident managers, placed there to govern what he had made, and they did their job well. God had no reason to confront them, and they had nothing to confess. All was right, day after day. Life was better than anything we can imagine from our sin-scarred vantage point.

But sadly, it didn't last long. In the most significant rebellious act ever committed, man and woman stepped outside of God's ordained plan. In a second it all came crashing down. All of the amazing beauty of that world was deeply and permanently scarred.

In an instant, fear, guilt, and shame became standard human experiences. People who once lived in perfect harmony now accused, deceived, and fought for control. Weeds and disease became daily concerns. People began to desire what was evil and do what was wrong. Rather than submit to God's authority, they lived as their own gods. The world that once sang the song of perfection now groaned under the weight of the Fall.

Sin altered every thought, desire, word, and deed. It created a world of double-mindedness and mixed motives, self-worship and self-absorption. People desired to be served, but they hated serving. They craved control and nurtured delusions of self-sufficiency. They forgot their Creator, but worshiped his creation. Rather than loving people and using things to express it, people loved things and used people to get them. Humanity's second generation even committed murder. They began to lie, cheat, hide, and deny. People suffered at the hands of others, from momentary thoughtlessness to unspeakable acts of physical and sexual abuse. For the first time, people wept from grief within and suffering without.

God now saw his world ravaged by sin. He was unwilling for it to stay this way, so he devised a plan. It would take thousands of years. It would mean harnessing the forces of nature and controlling the course of human history, but he could do it. From the moment of the Fall, for generation after generation, he controlled everything so that someday he could fix what had been so horribly damaged. Into this world, at just the right moment, he sent his one and only Son.

NOW FOR THE BEST OF NEWS

The initial announcement of this good news is so brief that it would be easy to overlook. It comes at the beginning of the Gospel of Mark, just a few sentences in one little verse. Yet it was a fitting summary of Jesus' reason for coming.

Mark records Jesus' words this way: "The time has come. The kingdom of God is near. Repent and believe the good news!" (Mark 1:15). It is tempting to think that this is merely Jesus' way of introducing himself, but his announcement is more than that. It gives all of us who endure the harsh realities of the Fall the only valid reason to get up in the morning. It offers hope that is wonderfully practical and intensely personal.

The news begins with these words: "The time has come." Jesus is saying, "This is what God has been working on. All of history has been moving toward this one moment." God had not forgotten or lost interest in humanity. Since that horrible first fall into sin, he had been bringing the world to this day. What looked pointless and out of control was, in fact, the unfolding of God's wonderful story of redemption, which reached its crescendo with the coming of Christ.

Think about it: every good and bad thing that the Old Testament records had a purpose. All of the battles, journeys, trials, kingdoms, revelations, and miracles; all of the political and personal intrigue, were part of a careful plan to bring the world to this point. Long before the words in Mark were spoken, God had been telling his people that he would restore what was broken. But they rarely understood. Jesus begins his ministry by saying, "Do you understand what is finally taking place? This is the day spoken about by the prophets, when cloudy hope becomes a bright reality. The time has come!"

The question is, "The time has come for *what?*" Jesus is announcing the nearness of the kingdom of God. It is a quiet way of saying, "I am the King of Kings, and I have brought the power of my kingdom with me." Elsewhere Christ makes it clear that this kingdom is not a political, earthly rule. He calls it a "within you" kingdom (see Luke 17:20–21). God's redemptive solution would not come by political revolution or physical war. The primary battle would be fought and won in human hearts.

In our self-absorbed culture, we need to see the grandeur of this kingdom. We cannot shrink it to the size of our needs and desires. It takes us far beyond our personal situations and relationships. The King came not to make our agenda possible, but to draw us into something more amazing, glorious, and wonderful than we could ever imagine. Perhaps the best way to understand these grand purposes is to eavesdrop on eternity. In Revelation 19:6–8, the great multitude of the redeemed stands before the throne and, like the roar of rapids, exclaims:

> "Hallelujah!
>   For our Lord God Almighty reigns.
> Let us rejoice and be glad
>   and give him glory!
> For the wedding of the Lamb has come,
>   and his bride has made herself ready.

Fine linen, bright and clean,
  was given her to wear."

Think about what they are singing. It is not, "I got that job! My marriage was fantastic! I was surrounded by great friends and my kids turned out well." It is not, "I defeated depression and mastered my fears." Two things capture the hearts of the assembled throng. The first is that Christ has won the final victory. His will has been done, his plan accomplished, and he reigns without challenge forever. God has gathered a people who have a passion for his glory and find ultimate comfort in his rule. They are people who followed by faith and obeyed at great cost, who sacrificed and suffered, but with no hint of regret. They have found lasting satisfaction in the person and rule of the Redeemer.

The second glorious thing is that the ultimate celebration has finally come, the wedding of the Lamb. A thunderous shout goes out as the multitude realizes that they haven't just been invited to the wedding—*they* are the bride! They stand clothed in the finest of linen. All the scars and blemishes of sin are gone. All the rags of iniquity have disappeared. They are finally and forever clean. They stand before the Groom, pure and holy.

As we listen to eternity, we realize that the kingdom is about God radically changing people, but not in the self-absorbed sense our culture assumes. Christ came to break our allegiance to such an atrophied agenda and call us to the one goal worth living for. His kingdom is about the display of his glory and people who are holy. This is the change he came, lived, died, and rose to produce. This is the life and work he offers us in exchange for the temporary glories we would otherwise pursue. This kingdom agenda is intended to control our hearts and transform our lives.

Notice that Christ connects the good news to a call to repentance. The Bible defines repentance as a radical change of heart resulting in a radical change in the direction of one's life. It is only possible if there is power to change. How cruel it would be to call sin-paralyzed people to repent without giving them the power to do so! This is where the message gets most exciting. Jesus is saying, "Because I have come, lasting heart change *can* take place." Yes, the world is terribly broken, but the King has come, bringing the power and glory of his kingdom with him!

Maybe you are gripped by a particular sin that you have never been able to defeat. Maybe you are part of a community that seems hopelessly divided. Maybe your own marriage has fallen far short of God's good plan. Maybe you are lugging around painful relics of your own history wherever you go. Perhaps you are tired of good intentions gone sour, broken promises, and shattered hopes and dreams. Our need for change is around us and inside us.

The sin that grips our hearts makes everything more difficult. It morphs love into selfish lust. It takes the God-ordained safety of home and makes it a place where the deepest human hurts can occur. It corrupts the workplace, robs government of its good, and even stains the church. And at the end of the day, it results in death.

You cannot escape sin because it dwells within you. All the things you learn get twisted by its power. You can't outsmart it or buy your way out of it. You can't move to escape it. This is why the coming of the King is the best of news.

Change is possible! You can stand amid the harshest realities of sin and have hope that will never disappoint you (Rom. 5:1–5). That marriage can change. That teenager can change. That church can change. That friendship can change. That bitterness can be put to death. That compulsion can be broken. That fear can be defeated. That stony heart can be made soft, and sweet words can come from a once-acid tongue. Loving service can come from a person who once was totally self-absorbed. People can have power without being corrupt. Homes can be places of safety, love, and healing. Change is possible because the King has come!

In all of this, God's ultimate goal is his own glory. Christ came to restore people to the purpose they were made for: to live every aspect of their lives in worshipful, obedient submission to him. He accomplishes this by breathing life into dead hearts so that we grasp our need for him. He lives sinlessly, keeping the law on our behalf. He lays down his life as a penalty for sin, so that we can be fully forgiven. He adopts us into his family, giving us all the rights and privileges of his children. He daily conforms us to his own image. He enables us by his grace to do what is right. His Spirit lives inside us, convicting of sin, illumining truth, and giving us the power to obey. He places us in the body of Christ where we can learn and grow. He rules over every event for his glory and our good. He makes us the objects of his eternal, redemptive love.

The Bible calls this change *redemption*. We are not only changed, we are restored to God. This is what makes all other change possible.

OUR NEWS MUST BE THE GOOD NEWS

When Jesus commissioned his disciples to minister in his name, this is the message he told them to proclaim. As we face our own struggles with sin and minister to people who seem trapped by things they cannot overcome, this must be our message too. We must faithfully proclaim, "Hope is only to be found in Jesus Christ, the King of Kings. In him, lasting, personal heart change is possible." Any other message encourages false hope.

People struggling with life in a fallen world often want explanations when what they really need is imagination. They want strategies, techniques, and principles because they simply want things to be better. But God offers much more. People need to look at their families, neighbors, friends, cities, jobs, history, and churches, and see the kingdom. They need imagination—the ability to see what is real but unseen. This is what Paul fixed his gaze on (2 Cor. 4). They need to look at a city and see the glorious company of the redeemed being gathered, amidst a brutal spiritual battle, to live in union with God. They need to look at their children and see a Redeemer pursuing their hearts for his own. They need to scan history and see God accomplishing his purpose. People need to see the shining hope of human existence: people can know, love, and serve God. They can commune with him forever and form a community of love that is possible no other way. All of this is possible because the King has placed his love and grace on them.

As sinners, we have a natural bent to turn away from the Creator to serve the creation. We turn away from hope in a Person to hope in systems, ideas, people, or possessions. Real Hope stares us in the face, but we do not see him. Instead, we dig into the mound of human ideas to extract a tiny shard of insight. We tell ourselves that we have finally found the key, the thing that will make a difference. We act on the insight and embrace the delusion of lasting personal change. But before long, disappointment returns. The change was temporary and cosmetic, failing to penetrate the heart of the problem. So, we go back to the mound again, determined this time to dig in the right place. Eureka! We find another shard of insight, seemingly more profound than before. We take it home, study it, and put it into practice. But we always end up in the same place.

The good news confronts us with the reality that heart-changing help will never be found in the mound. It will only be found in the Man, Christ Jesus. We must not offer people a *system* of redemption, a set of insights and principles. We offer people a *Redeemer.* In his power, we find the hope and help we need to defeat the most powerful enemies. Hope rests in the grace of the Redeemer, the only real means of lasting change.

This is what separates believers from our culture's psychology. Because it has fundamentally turned its back on the Lord, the world can only offer people some kind of system. It reduces hope to a set of observations, a collection of insights, or steps in a process. We, on the other hand, meet people as they desperately dig and lovingly ask for their shovels. We gently turn them away from the mound, and joyfully turn them to the Man, Jesus Christ. This is the essence of personal ministry.

But our inclination to replace the King with a thing does not die easily. It rears its ugly head even when we search for answers in Scripture. We approach the Bible with a "where can I find a verse on _____" mentality. We forget that the only hope the principles offer rests on the Person, Jesus Christ. And we forget that the Bible is not an encyclopedia, but a story of God's plan to rescue hopeless and helpless humanity. It's a story about people who are rescued from their own self-sufficiency and wisdom and transported to a kingdom where Jesus is central and true hope is alive.[1]

We cannot treat the Bible as a collection of therapeutic insights. To do so distorts its message and will not lead to lasting change. If a system could give us what we need, Jesus would never have come. But he came because what was wrong with us could not be fixed any other way. He is the only answer, so we must never offer a message that is less than the good news. We don't offer people a system; we point them to a Redeemer. He *is* hope.

WHY HOPE RESTS ON A PERSON

If you are going to help someone, you need to know what is wrong and how it can be fixed. You go to your auto mechanic because he can determine why your car is malfunctioning and get it running again. Any trustworthy perspective on personal change must do the same. It must correctly diagnose what is wrong with people and what is necessary for them to change.

This is where our culture gets it completely wrong. In rejecting a biblical view of people, the world eliminates any hope of answering the "what is wrong?" question accurately. And if it wrongly answers this question, how can it possibly provide a proper solution?

Why do people do the things they do? Is my problem fundamentally an informational one? Will a well-researched, logical set of insights provide the solution? Or is my problem fundamentally experiential? Will dealing with my past solve my problem? Is my problem fundamentally biological? Will helping me achieve chemical balance solve my problem? Or is there something beneath all these things that is more deeply wrong with me? Scripture's answer to this last question is a clear, resounding, "Yes!"

Scripture would agree that my problem is informational, in that I don't know what I need to know. It also affirms the impact of our experiences, though it maintains that our core problem precedes our experience and goes deeper. The Bible also acknowledges the complex interaction between our physical and spiritual natures, but it never locates our core problem in our biology. In this way, the Bible is radical compared to our culture.

The Bible says that our core problem, the fundamental reason we do what we do, is *sin*. What is being said here? Scripture is defining sin as a *condition* that results in *behavior*. We all *are* sinners, and because of this, we all *do* sinful things. This is why I said that our core problem precedes our experience. David captures it well in Psalm 51: "Surely I was sinful at birth, sinful from the time my mother conceived me" (v. 5). David is saying, "I was born with a fundamental problem. I had it long before my first experience. Something is wrong with my inner self that fundamentally affects the way I operate as a human being." This has thunderous implications. Because sin is my nature as a human being, it is inescapable. It marks everything I think, say, and do. It will guide my cravings, my response to authority, and my decision making. It will alter my values, direct my hopes and dreams, and shape every interpretation I make.

If you are going to deal with your own difficulties or assist others who want to deal with theirs, you must correct wrong thinking. Yes, you must deal with the suffering of the past and ways the body isn't properly functioning, but you must do more. You must help them conquer the sin that distorts all these experiences. Consider two examples.

Pamela came from a very abusive home. The worst time of day was when her dad got home from work. Pamela would try to be out of the house or safely hidden in her room in order to stay out of harm's way. These were powerfully influential experiences. We should weep with Pamela, and we should be angry at the wrongs done against her. But we should do more.

As you examine Pamela's current struggles, you realize that her problem is not just her experience, but how she has dealt with it. Pamela is extremely controlling, so she is hard to work with or befriend. She is constantly arguing, always demanding to be affirmed as right. She is obsessed with what people think of her, which shapes every interaction she has with others. Her personal mantra is "What's in it for me?" She is critical and judgmental, seldom giving anyone the benefit of the doubt.

But when Pamela talks with you, she portrays herself as one who suffers deeply. She talks of feeling constantly rejected and alone. She is mystified that people find her intimidating. She feels like no one respects her opinion.

What is going on with Pamela? Are all her present issues the result of her past? It is clearly more than that. Pamela is not only struggling with the horrors of her past, but with how she has dealt with them. This is where Scripture always leads us. If sin is part of our nature, we will always be dealing not only with our history, but with how sin distorts the way we handle it. Help will only come as we deal with our past *and* own our sin. This is essential because *sinners tend to respond sinfully to being sinned against.*

This is why the only hope for Pamela (and for us) is a Redeemer. We cannot step out of our sinfulness. We need more than love and encouragement, information and insight. We need rescue. Anything less will not address what is really wrong with us.

Consider a second person, Jack. Jack's dad was an active elder in their church, and his mom was committed to ministry. He was raised in a fine Christian home where family worship was a daily, shared experience. Jack's dad worked hard and was very successful. His parents had a solid relationship and communicated fairly well with their children. Jack went to a Christian school, and his parents could afford to send him to a fine college. Yet all is not well with Jack.

By the time you talk to Jack, he has had a string of short-term jobs and been married twice. He is palpably angry. Jack complains that he lives in a world of jerks who have no time to listen to someone who knows what he's doing. He says he has lost his jobs because his bosses were intimidated by the fact that he knew more about their businesses than they did. He views his ex-wives as emotionally weak, unable to live with someone who was confident and had his "act together."

Is Jack's present life influenced by his family of origin? Of course!

But once again, there is more going on. Jack is fundamentally struggling with *Jack*. Sin not only causes me to respond sinfully to suffering, it causes me to respond sinfully to blessing. The smart kid teases
the dumb kid. The athlete makes fun of the kid with two left feet.
Something is so wrong inside us that we can't even handle blessing
properly.

Jack needs more than insight. He needs to be rescued from himself, and for this he needs a Redeemer. This is why we cannot simply
offer people a system or give advice on how to deal with their past. We
must point them to a powerful and present Redeemer. *He* is our only
hope. He has conquered sin on our behalf! He willingly offers us his
heart-transforming, life-altering grace!

This is why Paul writes so pointedly in Colossians 2:8, "See to it
that no one takes you captive through hollow and deceptive philosophy, which depends on human tradition and the basic principles of
this world and not on *Christ*." The world's philosophy is deceptive because it cannot deliver what it promises. It may be well researched
and logically presented, but it is not centered on Christ. Because sin
(the condition) is what is wrong, true hope and help can only be
found in him. Any other answer will prove hollow.

WHAT SIN DOES TO US

Sin is the ultimate disease, the grand psychosis. You cannot escape it or defeat it on your own. Look around and you will see its mark
everywhere. Sin complicates what is already complicated. Life in a
fallen world is more arduous than God ever intended, yet our sin
makes it worse. We deal with much more than suffering, disease, disappointment, and death. Our deepest problem is not experiential, biological, or relational; it is moral, and it alters everything. It distorts
our identity, alters our perspective, derails our behavior, and kidnaps
our hope. As Moses noted when he described human culture before
the flood, "The LORD saw how great man's wickedness on the earth
had become, and that every inclination of the thoughts of his heart

was only evil all the time" (Gen. 6:5). This is what sin does to us. It is the ultimate disease!

Our first child was an incredibly active baby. He spent his days grabbing, clinging, and climbing on my wife, Luella, as if she were the ultimate jungle gym. Then, at eight-and-a-half months, this little boy took his first steps. Before long he was moving through our house with amazing speed. I remember thinking that it did not seem natural. He wasn't supposed to be walking, but he was!

When a baby begins to walk, he needs protection from a whole new set of household perils. One way to protect your child is to get down on your knees, look him in the face, and warn him about specific dangers. You take him around the house, pointing out the things to be avoided. It seemed like a huge waste of time at his age, but I went ahead and warned my little boy about the electrical sockets in every room. I told him, "Don't touch them, and don't ever stick anything in them. It could kill you!" He looked at me with a blank stare, while one finger fidgeted with his t-shirt and the other traveled halfway up his nose. I asked him if he understood, he nodded his little head unconvincingly, and off he stumbled to his next toddler adventure. I was sure I had accomplished nothing.

A couple of afternoons later, I was reading in the living room when out of the corner of my eye I saw our baby peeking at me. He glanced at me and then at the wall, then back at me, repeating the cycle several times. When he thought I was sufficiently distracted, he made a beeline for the wall socket. But just before he gave it that first exhilarating touch, he did something that left me amazed. He stopped, looked back to see if I was watching, and then reached for the socket as I leaped to his rescue.

That final glance demonstrated that he *had* understood my toddler-sized lecture, that he *knew* he was acting against my will, that he was trying to hide his rebellion, and that he was inexplicably drawn to what had been clearly forbidden. At least three of sin's devastating elements are clearly displayed in this little vignette.

The first thing sin produces is *rebellion*. This is more than breaking a few rules; it is a fundamental flaw in my character. It is not something I learn; I was born with it.

I did not have to teach my little boy to desire what was prohibited, to look for an opportunity to skirt around authority, and to reach for the "forbidden fruit." I do the same thing myself, and so do you. Whether it's parking in the no parking zone, fudging on income taxes, running away from Mommy in the toy store, refusing to submit to the counsel of an elder, or indulging in secret lust, rebellion is present in each one of us.

Rebellion is the inborn tendency to give in to the lies of autonomy, self-sufficiency, and self-focus. It results in a habitual violation of God-given boundaries. Autonomy says, "I have the right to do what I want when I want to do it." Self-sufficiency says, "I have everything I need in myself, so I don't need to depend on or submit to anyone." Self-focus says, "I am the center of my world. It is right to live for myself and to do only what brings me happiness." These are the lies of the Garden, the same lies Satan has whispered in generation after generation of willing ears. They deny our basic makeup as human beings. We were not created to be autonomous. We were designed to be in daily submission to God and to live for his glory. Living outside this design will never work.

This rebel spirit affects the way we approach difficulty and blessing. Independence, self-sufficiency, and self-absorption lead us to think of ourselves first and to climb over the fences between ourselves and our desires. We want control and hate being controlled. We want to make up the rules and change them whenever it suits us. Essentially we want to be God, ruling our worlds according to our own will. No matter what else we are rebelling against, our rebellion is ultimately directed at God. We refuse to recognize his authority, robbing him of his glory and usurping his right to rule.

Sin also produces *foolishness* in us. Foolishness believes that there is no perspective, insight, theory, or "truth" more reliable than our own. It buys into the lie that we know better. It causes us to distort reality and live in worlds of our own making. It is as if we look at life through a carnival mirror, convinced that we see clearly.

My little boy had been warned of danger, but in his foolishness he thought he knew better. Foolishness controls the man who is open to no one's counsel and the person who sees little need to study God's Word. This foolishness distorts our sense of identity, destroys relationships, retards growth, and derails change.

Foolishness convinces us that we are okay, and that our rebellious, irrational choices are right and best. Foolishness is a rejection of our basic nature as human beings. We were never created to be our own source of wisdom. We were designed to be revelation receivers, dependent on the truths God would teach us, and applying those truths to our lives. We were created to base our interpretations, choices, and behavior on his wisdom. Living outside of this will never work.

When David says in Psalm 14:1, "The fool says in his heart, 'There is no God,' " he gets to the foundation of foolishness. Our foolishness is a rejection of God, an inborn desire to replace God's wisdom with our own. Beneath it all, we want to be our own gods, revealing to ourselves all the "truth" we need.

Finally, sin renders us *incapable* of doing what God has ordained us to do. This *inability* colors every situation and relationship of our lives. It is not just that I don't want to do God's will, or that I think my way is better, it's that even when I have the right intentions, I can't pull it off. I always fall short of God's standard.

Have you ever prepared yourself for a difficult conversation with a friend? You rehearse your lines and anticipate the other person's possible responses. You try to identify where the conversation could go wrong, and you prepare yourself not to say something you will regret. You don't want to "lose it" this time. But when you have the conversation, in the middle of it, something happens. The other person hurts you, the emotional temperature spikes, and you let him have it. In the aftermath, you can't believe it! You did exactly what you had decided not to do!

The apostle Paul powerfully captures this experience in Romans 7: "For what I do is not the good I want to do; no, the evil I do not want to do—this I keep on doing." Haven't you been there too? Paul continues, "So I find this law at work: When I want to do good, evil is right there with me. For in my inner being I delight in God's law; but I see another law at work in the members of my body, waging war against the law of my mind and making me a prisoner of the law of sin at work within my members" (vv. 19, 21–23). Paul says in effect, "Even when I desire to submit to God's authority and listen to his wisdom, I end up doing what is wrong! I fail despite my best intentions!"

It is not just that we are rebels and fools. Sin makes us moral quadriplegics. We are fundamentally *unable* to do what is right. Which of us could say that our anger toward our friends has always been righteous? What husband could say he has always loved his wife as Christ loves the church? What person consistently loves his neighbor as himself? We fail at these things even when we desire to do right, because our moral muscles have been atrophied by sin. We simply cannot do the good we were created to do. This is one of the most tragic results of the ultimate disease, sin.

As human beings, we cannot walk through life on our own. We need rescue, healing, and forgiveness. In short, we need God. We need the good news, the news of the King who has come, making lasting change possible. This alone is our personal hope and the basis of our ministry to others.

The good news of the kingdom is not freedom from hardship, suffering, and loss. It is the news of a Redeemer who has come to rescue me from *myself*. His rescue produces change that fundamentally alters my response to these inescapable realities. The Redeemer turns rebels into disciples, fools into humble listeners. He makes cripples walk again. In him we can face life and respond with faith, love, and hope. And as he changes us, he allows us to be part of what he is doing in the lives of others. As you respond to the Redeemer's work in your life, you can learn to be an instrument in his hands.

2 | IN THE HANDS OF THE REDEEMER

Sam called me in a panic. It had been an ordinary day: get up, go to work, and do his job until quitting time. But as he was rushing home, he was approached by a desperate man. The man said that his life was a mess; he didn't even know where he was going to sleep that night. Sam could tell that he wasn't a seasoned street person. Hoping to be a conduit of help, Sam took him home and called his pastor—me. "Paul," he said, "I came across this guy who lost his job, had a terrible fight with his wife, and was thrown out on the street. I thought I'd bring him over to your house so you could give him the help he needs. Is now okay?"

Before Sam could say anything else, I responded, "Isn't God's love amazing? God cares about this man and put one of his children in his path. God cares about you and has given you an opportunity to be an instrument in his hands. I am persuaded that God never gets a wrong address, and he intends to use *you* in this man's life. Let me pray for you right now, that God will fill your heart with his love and your mind with his wisdom." When I finished praying, Sam said, "But I don't think I am able. . . ." I interrupted, "I will continue to pray for you tonight, and I will call you in the morning. I am so encouraged by your ministry to this man." I said goodbye and hung up the phone.

For the next several weeks, I stood alongside Sam, determined not to take over for him, as he learned how to love his desperate friend. He learned how to be a tool God could use to encourage change in someone's life. In the process, God changed Sam and his wife in some significant ways as well. I had pushed Sam out of the nest, but not because he lacked compassion. His problem was that he lacked courage. Sam had assumed that whatever this man needed was way beyond what he could offer. He didn't see himself as one of God's instruments, only as one of God's conduits—a passive channel connecting one thing to another. An instrument is a tool that is actively used to change something, and God has called all of his people to be instruments of change in his redemptive hands.

Embedded in the larger story of redemption is a principle we must not miss: *God uses ordinary people to do extraordinary things in the lives of others.* What mission board, what ministry, what local church would use the people God used in Scripture? There was Moses (an exiled murderer), Gideon (fearful and hiding), David (the shepherd boy with no military training), Peter (who publicly denied Christ), and Paul (persecutor of the church), to name a few. Along with these are untold numbers of little people God used in big ways to fulfill his plan on earth. God never intended us to simply be the objects of his love. We are also called to be instruments of that love in the lives of others.

MANY TOOLS IN THE TOOLBOX

When you think of personal growth and change, what comes to your mind? Are you like Sam, immediately assuming that you need the help of your pastor, an elder, or a professional counselor? This is what our culture assumes is required to bring about change. Clearly, God raises up particular people for formal ministry roles, but the Bible's circle of helpers includes all of God's people. What's more, the Bible's view of personal change is radically different from our culture's. Scripture declares that personal transformation takes place as our hearts are changed by God's grace and our minds are renewed by the Holy Spirit. We don't change anyone; it is the work of the Redeemer. We are simply his instruments.

The problem is that most of us think that God is carrying around a very small toolbox! A successful carpenter uses many tools, each one designed for a particular job. God has a huge toolbox, and his principal tools are his children. Sadly, many people in the church do not see themselves this way. They think of ministry as something for the paid professional. When they think of their own involvement, they don't think very far beyond saying a prayer or making a meal. Yet their adoption into the family of God was also a call to ministry, a call to be part of the good work of the kingdom.

The overall biblical model is this: *God transforms people's lives as people bring his Word to others.* Our instinct is to ask, "Who are the people God uses, and what are their qualifications? Does God only use certain people? Why some and not others? Am I one of them?" These questions are answered in Ephesians 4:11–16.

> It was he [Christ] who gave some to be apostles, some to be prophets, some to be evangelists, and some to be pastors and teachers, to prepare God's people for works of service, so that the body of Christ may be built up until we all reach unity in the faith and in the knowledge of the Son of God and become mature, attaining to the whole measure of the fullness of Christ.
>
> Then we will no longer be infants, tossed back and forth by the waves, and blown here and there by every wind of teaching and by the cunning and craftiness of men in their deceitful scheming. Instead, speaking the truth in love, we will in all things grow up into him who is the Head, that is, Christ. From him the whole body, joined and held together by every supporting ligament, grows and builds itself up in love, as each part does its work.

The only metaphor that captures God's plan for the church is the metaphor of a body. Christ has given his church leaders, not to bear the full ministry load of the body of Christ, but to equip each member to join in God's work of personal transformation. Remember: no local church could hire enough staff to meet all the ministry needs of a given week! In the biblical model, much more informal, personal ministry goes on than formal ministry. The times of formal, public ministry are meant to train God's people for the personal ministry that is the lifestyle of the body of Christ. Reflect on your own life. Isn't it true that change has not come *only* through the formal ministry of the Word? Hasn't God also used ordinary people to change your heart and transform your life?

To say that God has given us each other to help us mature still doesn't do justice to the body metaphor Paul employs. A body only grows as *each part* does its work. Think of all the interdependencies implied by this image. No change can take place in you that involves only one part of the body.

I was recently reminded of this fact when I began to feel pain in my left shoulder. Whether it was bursitis, arthritis, or the sad encroachment of old age, I suddenly became aware of how much I use that joint. I had never thought much about my shoulders before, but I suddenly gained a new appreciation for how the body works. It is a system of intricately interdependent parts.

The body metaphor also points to careful design. Think of how different a hand is from an eye, or a shoulder joint from a liver! The human body is a picture of intelligent, intentional design. Each part has been carefully crafted and placed to do its work. So is the body of Christ. Not all of God's people are the same. Each of us has been gifted, called, and positioned to do our part in God's kingdom work. Our histories, personalities, abilities, and maturity levels differ, which is how the Redeemer intends it. He is sovereign over it all.

Most of the time, we are oblivious to this. We are too easily captivated by our self-centered little worlds. But Ephesians 4 propels us beyond a life consumed by personal happiness and achievement. Your life is much bigger than a good job, an understanding spouse, and non-delinquent kids. It is bigger than beautiful gardens, nice vacations, and fashionable clothes. In reality, you are part of something immense, something that began before you were born and will continue after you die. God is rescuing fallen humanity, transporting them into his kingdom, and progressively shaping them into his likeness—and he wants you to be a part of it.

Your life is bigger than you ever imagined. You live in one moment in time, yet you stand hand-in-hand with Enoch, Noah, Joseph, Moses, Joseph, Abraham, Isaac, Jeremiah, Ezekiel, Matthew, Peter, Paul, Augustine, Calvin, Luther, and generations of unknown believers who understood their place in the kingdom and did their part in its work. Only as you keep this huge world in view will you be able to live and serve effectively in the small world where God has placed you.[1]

BUT THERE IS MORE

Let's focus now on the second half of the statement: *God transforms people's lives as people* **bring his Word to others**. The changes God produces in his people are directly connected to the ministry of the Word. Again, this is radically different from the way our culture (and sometimes even the church) thinks about personal growth and change. Too often the philosophy of ministry that guides the pulpit and the private conversation are very different. For example, why does it seem right to say "preach the Word" but odd to say "counsel the Word"? From a biblical perspective, both public and personal ministries base their hope for change on the Word of God. They are simply different methods of bringing the Word to people in different contexts.

In personal ministry, I want to bring more than a heart of compassion, a willingness to listen, and a commitment to help bear someone's burden. Though these are the sweet fruit of Christian love, I want to offer more. I want to bring the heart-changing truths of Scripture to people in the midst of their situations and relationships. Personal ministry is about people loving people, but in a way that includes bringing them God's Word. This is the "truth in love" model Paul describes in Ephesians 4. The combination of powerful truth wrapped in self-sacrificing love is what God uses to transform people.

If it is true that there is more informal ministry than formal ministry in any given week, then surely we should evaluate the quality of our counsel in those informal moments. Suppose your neighbor tearfully tells you that she found a pornographic magazine in her son's book bag. Maybe your golfing buddy says he's been thinking about leaving his wife. Perhaps you observe a volunteer behaving inappropriately toward the girls in the youth group. No matter what you do next, your response will be personal ministry or counseling. Yet we usually approach such situations much more casually than we do formal, public ministry.

If you were asked to teach a Sunday school lesson, preach a sermon, or lead a Bible study, you would immediately ask yourself, "Do I have the time I need to prepare?" Yet we often respond to our neighbor, golfing buddy, or church volunteer with little preparation, reflection, or prayer. Why do we spend hours preparing to teach while we offer important personal direction without a second thought? We forget that God uses those interactions to apply the transforming power of Scripture to people's hearts. We forget that God's Word is our primary tool of change. Instead, we come up with a little personal wisdom and personal experience and let the words fly.

This is why the second part of our model is so vital. God is placing people next to people to create a system of intricate interdependencies, but he has also ordained what we are to give each other in those relationships.

GOD'S MONSOON

I have visited northern India several times. For most of the year this part of the world is extremely dry and hot. (I once endured a temperature of 127 degrees in New Delhi!) During the dry season, northern India looks parched and barren, but Indians know that change is on the way. Hope comes from the south as the torrential seasonal rains called monsoons make their way up the continent. When the rains finally reach northern India and satiate its parched ground, it is as if someone flicks a switch: the earth explodes into bloom. In a matter of days, northern India is alive with exotic leaves and flowers.

The transformational power of God's Word is no less dramatic. Personal ministry brings the monsoon of God's Word to the parched terrain of the heart. Though a complete transformation will not take place overnight, our lives will burst forth in new beauty of character and new fruitfulness of life. Isaiah 55:10–13 captures this dynamic well.

> As the rain and the snow
>   come down from heaven,
> and do not return to it
>   without watering the earth
> and making it bud and flourish,
>   so that it yields seed for the sower and bread for the eater,
> so is my word that goes out from my mouth:
>   It will not return to me empty,
> but will accomplish what I desire
>   and achieve the purpose for which I sent it.
> You will go out in joy
>   and be led forth in peace;
> the mountains and hills
>   will burst into song before you,
> and all the trees of the field
>   will clap their hands.
> Instead of the thornbush will grow the pine tree,
>   and instead of briers the myrtle will grow.
> This will be for the LORD's renown,
>   for an everlasting sign,
>   which will not be destroyed.

God's Word changes people this dramatically. The rain that soaks the parched land always has an effect. It bathes soil, which feeds roots, which nourish plants, which produce flowers. So it is with the Word of God. It changes what it touches, producing beauty and fruitfulness in people's lives. These changes point to two wonderful realities. First, we are, in fact, God's covenant children. He has promised to be our God, to be with us and to bless us. Second, these changes point us to his glory. The flowers and fruit that the rain produces give glory to the One who sent it. As we bring God's Word to one another, we are all signs pointing to his glory.

What is the hope here? It is the hope of the kingdom. The King has come and sent his children to one another with his life-changing Word. People who were lost find their way; people once paralyzed with discouragement walk in hope; alienated people live in community as broken relationships are restored; confused minds think in ways that are true, pure, and right; and the person who once lived for his own power now rests in God's. God's rain waters the roots of the heart, and the person's life bursts forth with new fruitfulness. This is the way of the Lord, the hope and work of his kingdom.

ANSWERS, ENCYCLOPEDIAS, AND OUTLINES

Isaiah 55 should instill a great deal of hope in us, but it also raises a question. What is the best way to minister biblically to another person? How can we best bring the power of Scripture to another person's life?

Many Christians simply don't understand what the Bible is. Many think of it as a spiritual encyclopedia: God's complete catalog of human problems, coupled with a complete list of divine answers. If you turn to the right page, you can find answers for any struggle. A more sophisticated variation views the Bible as a systematic theology textbook, an outline of essential topics you must master to think and live God's way. In either case, we tend to offer each other isolated pieces of Scripture (a command, a principle, a promise) that seem to fit the need of the moment. What we think of as ministering the Word is little more than a spiritual cut-and-paste system.

This kind of ministry rarely leads to lasting change because it does not bring the power of the Word to the places where change is really needed. In this kind of ministry, self is still at the center, personal need is the focus, and personal happiness remains the goal. But a truly effective ministry of the Word must confront our self-focus and self-absorption at its roots, opening us up to the vastness of a God-defined, God-centered world. Unless this happens, we will use the promises, principles, and commands of the Word to serve the thing we really love: ourselves. This may be why many people read and hear God's Word regularly while their lives remain unchanged. Only when the rain of the Word penetrates the roots of the problem does lasting change occur.

In personal ministry, there is often a lot of pressure to handle Scripture topically. Usually, you are talking with someone facing some personal, relational, or situational difficulty. You want to find out what the Bible has to say on the subject and apply it to the person's life. So you get out your concordance or topical Bible, scan all the verses on the topic, pick the passages that seem most relevant, and share them with the struggling person. Unfortunately, you are misunderstanding what the Word is and how it is to be used.

Let's say that you are talking with a wife who is in the midst of an all-out war with her husband. Everything in their lives has become a contest for control. They say remarkably unkind things to each other. He has buried himself in his work, and she has found refuge in her children. They spend time with each other only when duty demands it. What is wrong with this marriage? Would you agree that their problems run deeper than communication, role division, work, parenting, and time management? These issues are the fruit of a much more deeply rooted set of problems. The surface chaos will only change as the transforming power of the Word is brought to those roots. Anything less will keep the rebellious, foolish, powerless self at the center, unmoved and unchanged.

What the wife wants is a sweeter, more attentive husband. What the husband wants is a kinder, more content wife. These things are not bad, but God wants more for them—more than a better marriage, and more than the spouse of their dreams. Need-driven, self-focused, solution-defined ministry may *use* the Bible, but it is not truly biblical. It distorts what the Bible was meant to do. This error can rob the body of Christ of its vitality and productivity, relegating many true believers to lives of long-term immaturity. We must opt for something better.

TELL ME THE OLD, OLD STORY

The Bible makes a poor encyclopedia. If that's what God had intended, Scripture would have been arranged differently and included many volumes. As it is, there are many issues that the Bible doesn't address in a topical fashion. The Bible has nothing explicit to say, for example, about schizophrenia, A.D.D., teenagers, family television viewing, or sexual techniques for married couples. If you try to use your Bible as God's encyclopedia, you will either conclude that it has little to say about some crucial issues of modern life or you will bend, twist, and stretch passages to suit your purposes. Either way, you are not getting from the Word what God intended. This misunderstanding underlies the frustration many people feel with Scripture. We secretly wish that God had made it simpler and just arranged it topically!

The Bible does in fact have powerful and important things to say about all the topics listed above, but it does so in a form very different from what we might expect. For example, the Bible never uses the word "teenager," but it does speak with wisdom and practicality to the struggles of this period in life. Without speaking explicitly about many issues I face every day, God in his Word gives me everything I need to be who he wants me to be and do what he wants me to do.

However, if you want God's full perspective on a particular subject, you cannot limit yourself to the Bible passages that specifically focus on it. The couple immersed in the battle for control will not learn how to break out of their endless cycle of turmoil by studying the standard Scripture passages on marriage. Without the perspective of the rest of the Bible, those marital passages will offer little help. In fact, they can be used for purposes that are more about what I want than what God has ordained.

That is how Scripture differs from an encyclopedia. When I use an encyclopedia, I do not need to read other articles to understand the one I am reading at the moment. One article has no connection to another; there are no overarching themes. In the Bible, however, every passage is dependent on the whole, and the whole Bible is held together by interdependent themes that run through every passage like rebar, the steel rods that reinforce concrete. If I handle Scripture topically, I will miss the overarching themes at the heart of everything else God wants to say to me. These themes give me a sense of identity, purpose, and direction that will fundamentally alter the way I think, desire, speak, and act. They will go to the root of my problem, producing change that lasts.

The sad fact is that many of us are simply not biblical in the way we use the Bible! Being biblical does not mean merely quoting words from within its pages. Being truly biblical means that my counsel reflects what the entire Bible is about. The Bible is a narrative, a story of redemption, and its chief character is Jesus Christ. *He* is the main theme of the narrative, and he is revealed in every passage in the book. This story reveals how God harnessed nature and controlled history to send his Son to rescue rebellious, foolish, and self-focused men and women. He freed them from bondage to themselves, enabled them to live for his glory, and gifted them with an eternity in his presence, far from the harsh realities of the Fall.

This overarching story reflects the fact that our problem as human beings is deeper than the individual sins we commit each day, creating the specific problems that complicate our lives. Our deepest problem is that we seek to find our identity outside the story of redemption. If the entire goal and direction of our lives are wrong, we need much more than practical advice on how to do the right thing in a particular situation. We need a message big enough to overcome our natural human instinct to live for our own glory, pursue our own happiness, and forget that our lives are much, much bigger than this little moment of life. Every day, in some way, we buy the lies of autonomy and self-sufficiency, worshiping the creation rather than its Creator.

It is because our sin problem is so pervasive and so deeply ingrained that we need more from Scripture than insight, principles, understanding, or direction. An encyclopedic, problem-solving approach to Scripture is totally inadequate for the true depth of our need. We need something that will change us from the inside out—

we need Christ! Only his person and work can free us from our slavery to self and our tendency to deify the creation. Only as we see our story enfolded in the larger story of redemption will we begin to live God-honoring lives. Lasting change begins when our identity, purpose, and sense of direction are defined by God's story. When we bring this perspective to our relationships, we will have a dramatically different agenda. It will take the principles and commands of Scripture and use them as God intended. We will see how each principle, promise, and command finds its meaning and fulfillment in Christ. Separate them from Christ and they lose their God-intended meaning and get hijacked by other agendas.

For example, what do you learn from the story of the Exodus and the crossing of the Red Sea? Do you see a hero named Moses and a call to be like him? Principles for dealing with difficulty? Keys to leading a rebellious people? Hints for crossing large bodies of water? The seven habits of highly effective nomads? You've probably heard sermons or Sunday school classes to that effect. But they all forget what the Exodus story is ultimately about. The Exodus is but one chapter in the larger story of redemption. It points to our need for a Christ who delivers us from slavery, defeats the Enemy, and leads us in the way we should go. If you learn how to take that identity to your marriage, it will help you understand the passages that directly discuss God's plan for marriage.

The Exodus story has much to say to the warring couple. It can tell them about who they are, why they are struggling, and where hope and help can be found. The themes that run through the Exodus story also run through every marriage passage, because the marriage passages apply God's story of redemption to one of the most important relationships of life. But those marriage passages will not be fully understood if they are divorced from the themes that run through the rest of God's Word. We cannot use the Bible as a divine self-help book! We will always try to use it to get the things our hearts are set on, though this is precisely the bondage that sabotages our relationships. The Redeemer lived, died, and rose again so that we would no longer live for ourselves but for him and his glory (2 Cor. 5:14–15).[2]

GOD'S REBAR

When builders lay a huge slab of concrete, they reinforce it with rebar, metal rods that run horizontally and vertically through the center, adding strength and stability. Similarly, the grand themes of God's story run through every passage of Scripture, producing a stability in my life that I can find nowhere else. Only in the context of these themes will the pieces of my story make any sense.

Let's consider three grand themes of the story of redemption. Embedded in each is a practical comfort, as well as a clear call to wise and godly living. The first is the theme of God's *sovereignty*. Nebuchadnezzar offered one of the best single summaries of this theme after God had taken away his sanity and then restored it.

> His dominion is an eternal dominion;
>   his kingdom endures from generation to generation.
> All the peoples of the earth
>   are regarded as nothing.
> He does as he pleases
>   with the powers of heaven
>   and the peoples of the earth.
> No one can hold back his hand
>   or say to him: "What have you done?" (Dan. 4:34–35)

From the rise and fall of governments to tomorrow's weather to the exact location of every human being, the universe is under God's control. He has the power and authority to do exactly what pleases him, anywhere he chooses to do it. God's sovereignty is not only about power and position, but also about a plan. Scripture clearly teaches that God has a plan for his world and the people in it. God is calling a people to himself, forming them into his likeness, and preparing them for an eternity with him. This is his overarching plan of the ages, revealed in history, present in current events and in the lives of everyone who has ever lived. At any moment in time, the right answer to the question, "What is God doing?" is, "Accomplishing his plan."

This theme is meant to be a great practical comfort to us. Look around—don't things often seem to be out of control? Doesn't it often look like the bad guys are winning? Haven't you cried, "Why me?" or wept at the suffering of another? Don't you sometimes feel lost in the crowd, the custodian of a small and relatively meaningless life? Don't you daily face your powerlessness to even change yourself?

In response to humanity's deepest, heartfelt questions, God sweetly speaks of his sovereignty. "Take heart, I am in complete control. I am the definition of holiness and love. All of my ways are right and true, all of my decisions are best, and I will not rest until my plan has been completed."

There is comfort in your moment of greatest mystery. There is encouragement in your time of greatest confusion, and hope in your moment of greatest discouragement. Your world is not a world of constant chaos controlled by impersonal forces. Your destiny is not in your hands or in the hands of other people. You are held in the hands of your heavenly Father, who rules everything! You are a child of the King of Kings and you live under the shadow of his wing. You are part of his plan. That means that the exercise of his power and authority is for your blessing.

You and I can rest in the middle of deep and personal mysteries. We can press on when little around us makes sense. There is reason in the mystery and order in the chaos, because behind it all stands the One in control of it all.

What does this mean for each of us? It means peace when my brain is unable to put it all together. A Christian's inner peace is never based on his ability to take the teachings of Scripture and figure it all out. Our peace always rests on the presence, power, and character of the Lord. Because he rules heaven and earth according to his wise plan, I need not live in anxiety and fear. God's absolute sovereignty guarantees the fulfillment of each of his promises to every one of his children. This includes you!

King David understood this in one of his darkest moments. His son Absalom had plotted to take his throne. Imagine having to flee the palace for fear of your own son! (This was a monarchy in which the throne passed from father to son only at death.) At one point David is hiding in a cave, surrounded by a loyal band of soldiers. They come to David and essentially ask, "What's going to happen now?" According to Psalms 3 and 4, David responds with a perspective that should be true for all of us. "Lord, when I think about you, my heart is filled with joy. This joy is greater than when the harvest and new wine is bountiful [the happiest time of the year for an agricultural society]. Yes, I am in this cave, but my life is not in the hands of Absalom. My life is where it has always been, in your sovereign hands. So I will not give in to fear. I will not assault my mind with questions I cannot answer. I will sleep in peace, for you alone, O Lord, make me dwell in safety" (Selected verses from Pss. 3–4, author's paraphrase).

Every time you love your enemy, you are resting in the sovereignty of God. Every time you speak lovingly and softly in the face of someone else's anger, you are choosing to rest in the sovereignty of God. Every time you resist the temptation to win an argument at all costs, you are resting in God's sovereignty. Because he rules, nothing you do in obedience to him is ever futile. Your life has meaning and purpose because you are included not only in the plan of the One who rules it all, but also in his family!

Imagine how this rest could change the marriage of the couple we have been considering. Their constant war of words, competition for power, and mutual condemnation are rooted in a deeper battle about who or what will rule their lives. Marriage exposes their controlling desire to get what they want. When my hope is in my ability to rule the day, my spouse becomes a constant threat rather than an intimate companion. This destroys any hope of experiencing the loving, self-sacrificial unity at the heart of any good marriage. All of the Bible's marital passages rest on this theme. Each of them calls me to entrust my mate and myself to the Lord, and to joyfully do what he says is right and best, knowing that my hope rests in his power, not mine.

AMAZING GRACE

The second grand theme is God's *grace*. This theme confronts and encourages me at the deepest personal level, diagnosing the problems that infect my relationships and giving me the only reliable reason to press on.

In all the drama of the story of redemption, one reality repeatedly bursts to the surface: we live in a world where there is grace to be found. God is not only sovereign, he is also abounding in grace. Immediately after Adam and Eve disobeyed him, God made it clear that he was going to do more than punish them. He would send the seed of the woman (Christ) to defeat the Enemy and provide redemption for his people (see Gen. 3:15). God's response to the willful rebellion of his creatures was grace! This grace justifies, providing complete forgiveness and unwavering acceptance with God. This grace adopts, welcoming us into his family with all the rights and privileges of true sons and daughters. This grace enables, empowering me to think, say, and do things I could not do in my own strength. This grace transforms, radically changing every aspect of my life.

Grace is the thick rod of rebar that courses through the concrete of the biblical story. From the first moments of the Fall, to the call of Abraham, to the liberation of the Exodus, to the provisions of the wilderness, to the victories of the Promised Land, to David, Solomon, Isaiah, Jeremiah, and Amos, to the preaching of John the Baptist, to the miraculous pregnancy of Mary, to the earth-bound ministry of the Messiah, to the cross and the empty tomb, to the faithful ministry of the apostles, to the resilience of the church under persecution, to the expectant children of God waiting for his return, this story is a story of grace. Grace defines the story and gives it direction.

The story tells me in a thousand ways that God has made a way to deal with my deepest problem, sin. It reminds me that my life need not be imprisoned by my own rebellion, defeated by my own foolishness, or paralyzed by my own inability. God's grace is most powerful and effective at the moment of my greatest weakness.

How practical and life changing is this? Think of our couple again. One of the most significant problems in their relationship is that there is no *economy of grace*. With all their obvious difficulties, what is most shocking is the profound gracelessness of their marriage. There is no willingness to look within and confess deep-seated sins, so they never find sweet forgiveness. There is no vertical hope to carry them in dark and discouraging times. There is no rest that comes from entrusting each other to the God of grace. There is no faith that he will give them all they need to respond to each other in godly ways. As a result, their relationship is reduced to human demands, human performance, human failure, human judgment, and human punishment. There is no hope or power for change. And because they are not daily soaking in the fountain of God's grace, they do not extend it to one another.

All of their marriage books, communication skills, and attempts at reformation will fail, because their only true hope is God's heart-transforming, relationship-revolutionizing grace. When they begin to rely on that grace and extend it to each other, the foundations of their present economy will crumble, and a foundation of grace-infused, God-empowered love will grow. Only in the economy of grace can the biblical principles for healthy marital relationships bear lasting fruit.

IT'S NOT YOUR PARTY

In 1978 I did one of the most courageous things in my life: I became a kindergarten teacher! Along with a few other brave souls, I had founded a Christian school and begun functioning as its principal. Since our budget and staff were limited, I agreed to temporarily function as the kindergarten teacher.

One Monday afternoon, the mother of one of my novice academics asked if she could have a birthday party for her daughter in the classroom on the following Friday. The day came, and after the mother's frenetic preparation, we all entered the room. She had turned our little classroom into a birthday kingdom! The walls and table were lavishly decorated; multi-colored streamers hung from the ceiling, and a balloon within a balloon was tied to the back of each chair. At each seat was a ribbon-tied cellophane bag of party favors. The only exception was the birthday girl, who was surrounded by a huge pile of beautifully wrapped gifts.

At the far end of the table sat Johnny. Johnny kept doing the same thing over and over. He would look at his little bag of party favors, then at the birthday girl's mountain of gifts, fold his arms, stick out his lower lip, and let out an audible *humph!* Each time, the look on his face got more ugly and his *humphing* more audible. Before long he had become the center of attention and was well on his way to spoiling the party. Then one of the mothers walked over and knelt beside him. She turned his chair so that Johnny was looking directly into her face, and she spoke these profound words: "Johnny, it's not your party!"

Johnny wasn't *supposed* to be the center of attention. He wasn't supposed to have a huge pile of gifts. It was Susie's birthday, and everything was rightly focused on her. Johnny would never enjoy his inclusion in the event if he demanded to be at the center.

So it is with the grand story of the Bible. With all of its locations and people, with all of the dramatic events of nature and history, at the center of the story is the Lord. It is *his* story. Paul summarizes the story this way, "For from him and through him and to him are all things. To him be the glory forever! Amen" (Rom. 11:36).

We were made for his glory, and we are called to display his glory in everything we do. This theme of *glory* is the last of our three overarching themes. Sin makes us glory thieves. There is probably not a day when we do not plot to steal glory that rightfully belongs to the Lord. When we compete with one another for glory, we fail to experience the unity that can only be found when we join together to live for him.

At the bottom of a broken marriage, a shattered family, or a forsaken friendship you will always find stolen glory. We crave glory that does not belong to us, and we step on one another to get it. Rather than glorifying God by using the things he has given us to love other people, we use people to get the glory we love. Sin causes us to steal the story and rewrite it with ourselves as the lead, and with our lives at center stage.

But there is only one stage and it belongs to the Lord. Any attempt to put ourselves in his place puts us in a war with him. It is an intensely vertical war, a fight for divine glory, a plot to take the very position of God. It is the drama that lies behind every sad earthly drama. Sin has made us glory robbers. We do not suffer well, because suffering interferes with our glory. We do not find relationships easy, because others compete with us for glory. We do not serve well, because in our quest for glory, we want to be served.

But the story of Scripture is the story of the Lord's glory. It calls me to an agenda that is bigger than myself. It offers me something truly worth living for. The Redeemer has come so that glory thieves would joyfully live for the glory of Another. There is no deeper personal joy and satisfaction than to live committed to his glory. It is what we truly need. Living for God's glory would revolutionize the marriage of the couple we have been considering by completely redefining their agenda.[3]

A LIFE WORTH LIVING

The central work of God's kingdom is change. God accomplishes this work as the Holy Spirit empowers people to bring his Word to others. We bring more than solutions, strategies, principles, and commands. We bring the greatest story ever told, the story of the Redeemer. Our goal is to help one another live with a "God's story" mentality. Our mission is to teach, admonish, and encourage one another to rest in his sovereignty, rather than establishing our own; to rely on his grace rather than performing on our own; and to submit to his glory rather than seeking our own. This is the work of the kingdom of God: people in the hands of the Redeemer, daily functioning as his tools of lasting change.

3 | DO WE REALLY NEED HELP?

Emily was twelve years old, bright and gifted, but more and more things were making her afraid. She didn't want to play sports any more. She cried each morning about going to school. Her mother Sara didn't know what to do.

Over their regular weekly lunch, Jean told Crystal about her on-going struggles with her husband. Crystal managed to mumble some heartfelt words of comfort, but she really didn't know what else to say.

Frank loves leading his small group, except when it comes to the prayer time. Each week someone shares something that Frank knows he should follow up on, but he doesn't know how to minister to people who haven't really asked for his help.

Fred and Ellen enjoy their relationship with the Smiths, but the Smith kids are driving them crazy. They know the Smiths are struggling as parents, and they have talked together about it. They know they should do more—but what?

Since her husband's death, Mary has had little desire to do much of anything. She spends hours in front of a television she isn't even watching. She would love to talk to a friend about what is happening, but she doesn't think anyone could really help.

Andy's struggle with lust is spinning out of control. He can barely look at a woman without impure thoughts. He has begun to live a secret life, and in his rational moments, he is scared. He would love to talk with someone, but who? He fears that he would be judged and his life would get trashed.

Drew's anger toward his parents grows daily. When he's not at school or work, he is holed up in his bedroom. He has talked to his friends about leaving home, but they seldom say anything helpful. He can't imagine finding an adult he could confide in.

Richard's life is dominated by his work, and his friend George can see its effect on Rich's spiritual life and his family. When George brings up the topic, Rich is prickly and defensive. George knows it's wrong to back off, but he doesn't know what else to do.

Bob loves being a pastor. He loves preparing sermons and he loves to preach. He enjoys organizing church programs that help people grow. What he doesn't love is when someone drops a crisis in his lap. Bob feels tremendous pressure to be a miracle worker, to wave his pastor's wand and make everything all right. A knot forms in the pit of his stomach, and he wonders what the next few weeks are going to be like.

In each of our lives the drama of sin and suffering plays itself out. It may be a secret struggle that is growing more difficult. It may be a relationship that is increasingly conflicted. The horrors of the past may have reared their ugly heads.

Honesty compels us to admit that we are people who need help, surrounded by people in the same situation. You see it in your friends, your family, your neighborhood, your workplace, and your church. You see it in yourself, in moments of candid self-reflection. There are things inside of us that simply don't go away. We do wrong things, feel regret, confess them, resolve not to repeat them, but, in the heat of the moment, go on to do exactly what we promised ourselves we wouldn't!

How does God help us, and how does he use us to help others? We know that God has called us to be part of his kingdom work, but he hasn't given us a neat formula to follow. He hasn't given us "seven steps to personal and relational perfection." Instead, he has told us to place our hope in the presence and work of Jesus the Redeemer. Both the helper and the person needing help depend on his power and wisdom for change.

What does this look like? How do we actually become tools that God can use? To answer this question, we need a biblical understanding of people and their need for help, and a biblical perspective on how change takes place.

Scripture looks at human beings from three angles: Creation, Fall, and Redemption. This sweeping perspective provides the foundation we need for personal ministry. When we start with the Bible's big picture and learn to see with biblical eyes, we will be equipped to be part of God's ongoing work of transformation.

THE BEST PLACE TO START IS AT THE BEGINNING

As we've seen, there is clearly a biblical mandate for personal ministry. What may surprise you is the fact that the need was present even in Genesis 1.

> Then God said, "Let us make man in our image, in our likeness, and let them rule over the fish of the sea and the birds of the air, over the livestock, over all the earth, and over all the creatures that move along the ground."

> So God created man in his own image,
>   in the image of God he created him;
>   male and female he created them.

> God blessed them and said to them, "Be fruitful and increase in number; fill the earth and subdue it. Rule over the fish of the sea and the birds of the air and over every living creature that moves on the ground." (Gen. 1:26–28)

Because this passage is so familiar, it is easy to miss its radical view of people. Properly understood, it will change your life and the way you respond to others.

The account of Creation has a cadence to it, a beat. God creates light, declares that it is good, and there is evening and morning, the first day. God creates heaven and earth, land and water, declares that it is good, and there is evening and morning, the second day. God creates something, declares that it is good . . . and the beat goes on—until he decides to create people. All of a sudden the rhythm is interrupted. God does something with Adam and Eve that he has not done with anything else. His actions demonstrate why personal ministry is necessary for all of us. Immediately after creating Adam and Eve, God *talks* to them. He didn't do this with anything else he created. He simply rested and moved on. When the cadence is broken and God does something different, you should ask yourself why. Why did God talk to them?

God knew that even though Adam and Eve were perfect people living in perfect relationship with him, they could not figure out life on their own. They were created to be dependent. God had to explain who they were and what they were to do with their lives. They did not need this help because they were sinners. They needed help because they were human.

This is the first instance of personal ministry in human history. The Wonderful Counselor comes to human beings and defines their identity and purpose. Why couldn't Adam and Eve live without this? What made them different from the rest of creation? There are three reasons.

First, Adam and Eve were created to be *revelation receivers*. They were given communicative abilities that no other creature was given. They were created with the ability to hear, understand, and apply God's words to their lives. These abilities were not given primarily to encourage human relationships. They were given so that we could know God and understand him.

The rest of creation doesn't need these abilities to live for God's glory. You and I instinctively know this, which is why we don't have religious discussions with the oak trees in our back yards! The oak tree brings glory to God simply by raising its limbs toward heaven. Its presence and form bring glory to its Creator. But human beings need God's words to live fully for his glory.

Our culture tends to think that we need help because of something we did or something that was done to us—the result of either bad biology or bad personal chemistry. But Genesis 1 confronts us with the fact that our need for help preceded sin. We were created to be dependent.

Trying to live without God's help is to assign myself a sub-human existence. It is to live like an animal, as if I were something other than what I am. Vast numbers of people attempt to live this way, but it is an act of irrationality. They deny their identity, subvert their own lives, and crush their own hope. Human beings were created to live on the platform of God's revelation, which is why we were given the unique communicative abilities we possess.

Personal ministry must begin with a humble recognition of the inescapable nature of our need. If there had been no Fall, if we had never sinned, we would still need help because we are human. A proper understanding of yourself and the work God has called you to starts here.

PEOPLE THINK

The second thing that distinguished Adam and Eve from the rest of creation was that they were created to be *interpreters*. People are meaning-makers; we have been created with the marvelous ability to think. We are always organizing, interpreting, and explaining what is going on inside us and around us. We all think, though some of us do it better than others. We do not live life based on the bare facts of our existence; we live our lives according to our *interpretation* of those facts. God gave Adam and Eve the unique ability to think, but only his words could accurately interpret their world.

When I was a young pastor in Scranton, Pennsylvania, our family lived in an old Victorian home with a long, steep staircase. One afternoon I was sitting in the living room when I heard someone falling down the steps. I ran to the bottom of the staircase to see my three-year-old son, Ethan, fall three or four more steps and stop. I asked him if he was okay, and he assured me that he was.

As I was turning to go back to my newspaper, Ethan said, "Thank

you." I said, "Ethan, you don't need to thank me. I didn't do anything." "Not you, Daddy. I'm thanking the angels," Ethan responded,
looking at me as if I should have known exactly what he meant. *That's
sweet*, I thought, as I turned to walk away again. But before I could
take a step Ethan said, "I know how they do it!" I said, "Who?" "The
angels, Daddy, I know how the angels do it. Everybody has two angels
that you can't see. One stands on this side [his right] and one stands
on this side [his left] and they carry a big beach ball that you can't see
over your head. [We had just returned from a vacation at the shore.]
When you start to fall, they stick the beach ball in front of you, you
bounce off it and you are okay!" And off he walked, quite satisfied
with his explanation.

Perhaps your response is, "How cute!" But something remarkable
is happening here as well: Immediately after escaping a fall down the
steps, this little boy was trying to make sense of what happened. Three
years old and he was already thinking, organizing, interpreting, and
explaining! Ethan combined a Sunday school fact and a family vacation fact, out of which he formed a (seemingly) plausible explanation
of his experience.

That little boy is now twenty-three years old. Think of the thousands of times he has interpreted his world, and how those interpretations have set the direction for his life.

A situation with another of our sons illumines how our interpretations shape the way we respond to what goes on around us.
Our youngest son, Darnay, was also three years old when he was
wandering in our back yard, oblivious to the fact that his older
brother was playing baseball by hitting stones with a rake handle.
Before long, Ethan accidentally hit Darnay square in the forehead.
Darnay fell to the ground, bleeding profusely. While his sister
functioned as an ambulance siren, his brother anxiously pled his
innocence, and I mopped away the blood to determine the extent
of his injury, Darnay lay quietly, utterly at peace. I noticed his lips
were moving, so I bent down, put my ear near his mouth, and
heard him say to himself over and over again, "I'm just so glad my
daddy is a doctor!"

Darnay knew that his daddy had a "Dr." in front of his name, and that he occasionally had appointments with people. To him, that meant Daddy must be a medical doctor. But when I heard him whisper those words, my thought was, *You're in deep trouble because that is not the kind of doctor I am!*

This little family crisis demonstrates the significance of our interpretations. We not only interpret situations and relationships, we interpret ourselves. We assign ourselves an identity and we live it out. Darnay did not respond to his situation based on his sister's screams, his brother's panic, or the amount of blood that flowed. He responded according to the identity he had assigned himself—one that was, unfortunately, terribly mistaken. Because he thought his daddy was a medical doctor, he was at peace when he would otherwise have been afraid. But it was a false peace, and he would soon find out that he was not who he thought he was.

Notice how Darnay's interpretation shaped his responses to the situation. First, it conditioned his *emotions*. His lack of fear was based on a particular assumption about how much danger he was in. Second, his interpretation of life defined his *identity*. He was (he thought) the son of a competent medical professional. This interpretation defined, third, how he thought about *others*. He had infinite confidence in me and he didn't need to be upset with Ethan when help was so nearby. Fourth, his thinking shaped his view of the *solution*. Very simply, Daddy would take care of it! Fifth and finally, his assumptions about reality shaped the way he would receive *counsel*. In his ignorance, Darnay would have had implicit faith in whatever instructions and assessments I offered!

When we say that God designed human beings to be interpreters, we are getting to the heart of why human beings do what they do. Our thinking conditions our emotions, our sense of identity, our view of others, our agenda for the solution of our problems, and our willingness to receive counsel from others. That is why we need a framework for generating valid interpretations that help us respond to life appropriately. Only the words of the Creator can give us that framework.

YOU GOTTA SERVE SOMEBODY

Those words from one of my favorite theologians, Bob Dylan, capture the third thing that separates us from the rest of creation. Human beings by their very nature are *worshipers*. Worship is not just something we do; it defines who we are. You cannot divide human beings into those who worship and those who don't. Everybody worships; it's just a matter of what, or whom, we serve.

God intended worship to be the motivational core of our lives. Adam and Eve were created to live so that everything in their lives drew its meaning and purpose from the person, presence, and purpose of God. This is called a God-ward referent. Because of this design, everything a human being does expresses worship. What you do and the way you do it express your desire to serve *something*. Some central love commands our allegiance and directs our behavior.

We begin to worship from our earliest years. Have you ever been a parent taking a young child to a toy store? You can steer your cart down the center of the aisles and keep your child's hands from touching everything in sight. All is well until you reach the checkout line. There Johnny spies the Captain Bonco X-Rider Poseable Space Figure. "Mommy, I want this! Can't I have it, Mommy?" Johnny pleads. "No, not today. Remember, Mommy said she was only going to get you one thing today," you respond. "I want it! I want it!" Johnny wails. "Billy has all of the X-Riders, and he even has the tabletop play station! It's not fair. I never get anything!" "That's not true," you respond, as your patience slips away. "I bought you a puzzle, and it is all you are going to get today."

At this point Johnny stiffens his body, throws back his head and begins to scream. You feel every eye in the store on you. You wish you could fall through a trap door that would lead to your car. You begin contemplating a catalog of disciplines, looking for the one most appropriate for this crime.

This incident is not merely a horizontal problem between a mother and her son. Their problem stems from the fact that even as a child, Johnny is a worshiper, and his responses express worship.

What's wrong with Johnny is not just that he wants a toy and throws a fit when his parent says "no." On a deeper level, Johnny is displaying the natural human instinct to live for oneself and one's own pleasure, oblivious to the presence of God. This relatively minor mother-child struggle reflects our built-in desire to serve something, and our sinful assumption that the "something" should be us! Johnny wants to be the sovereign ruler of his little universe, and he is demanding that his mother go along. If you stand in his way, you will pay dearly. Little Johnny is a worship thief.

Stolen worship is at the core of what is wrong with fallen human beings. Sadly, we are all guilty of the crime. Because we are worshipers by nature, we are always (1) giving proper worship to God, (2) serving something else, or (3) worshiping ourselves, demanding to be the center of our own universe. Isn't this what fantasy is about? In a person's disappointment with the real world, he creates worlds of his own where everyone does his bidding. Who has ever fantasized about someone saying "no"? Fantasy is an attempt to be God.

Adam and Eve were created as worshipers. They needed God to come to them and say, "I am your Creator, and you belong to me. You were created to love, serve, worship, and obey me. These things should underlie everything you do." They needed lives with a God-ward referent, and for that they needed God's revelation.

PUTTING IT ALL TOGETHER

You cannot understand the world of personal ministry without Genesis 1. It explains that our need for help is part of our design. It is not a result of the Fall. Human beings need truth from outside themselves to make sense out of life. We need God's perspective to interpret the facts of our existence. We were created to be worshipers.

These facts lead to a radical observation. If it is true that all human beings are constantly trying to make sense out of life, then *all* of life is counseling or personal ministry. Counseling is the stuff of human life! We are always interpreting and always sharing our interpretations with one another. This "sharing" ultimately amounts to advice or counsel about how to respond to life.

The bottom line is that you cannot have a relationship without being a person of influence. You give and receive counsel every day. It is not a task confined to paid professionals; it is woven into the fabric of human relationships. The problem is that we don't often recognize the powerful impact of those everyday encounters.

Proverbs captures this dynamic well. From the wise words of a father to his son, to the life-complicating advice of the fool, Proverbs depicts life as one huge counseling forum. Within that forum are two sectors, the counsel of the wise and the counsel of the fool. You and I receive wise and foolish counsel every day. The different voices compete for your attention. They influence your thoughts, desires, choices, and actions. The counsel comes to you in the words of a friend, the content of a TV show, and the Sunday sermon. There is counsel in the rebuke of a parent and the opinion of your spouse. People counsel people. It is inescapable.

We should be concerned about the thousands of hours of formal counseling that are not based on God's Word. But we should also be concerned about the far greater amount of counseling that goes on every day between people who do not know what they are doing and people who do not know how much they are being influenced. If you are alive on this planet, you are a counselor! You are interpreting life, and sharing those interpretations with others. You are a person of influence, and you are also *being* influenced. There are people in your life who have your ear. Perhaps without even knowing it, they will shape your thinking, direct your desires, and influence your plan of action. The issue is not *who* is counseling. All of us are. The core issue is whether that counseling is rooted in the revelation of the Creator.

THE ENTRANCE OF ANOTHER COUNSELOR

We've seen our need for help from the perspective of Creation. We need to view it from the vantage point of the Fall as well. Genesis 3 has thunderous implications for the world of personal ministry.

Now the serpent was more crafty than any of the wild animals the LORD God had made. He said to the woman, "Did God really say, 'You must not eat from any tree in the garden'?"

The woman said to the serpent, "We may eat fruit from the trees in the garden, but God did say, 'You must not eat fruit from the tree that is in the middle of the garden, and you must not touch it, or you will die.' "

"You will not surely die," the serpent said to the woman. "For God knows that when you eat of it your eyes will be opened, and you will be like God, knowing good and evil."

When the woman saw that the fruit of the tree was good for food and pleasing to the eye, and also desirable for gaining wisdom, she took some and ate it. She also gave some to her husband, who was with her, and he ate it. Then the eyes of both of them were opened, and they realized they were naked; so they sewed fig leaves together and made coverings for themselves. (Gen. 3:1–7)

For the first time in history we witness the entrance of another voice, another counselor. Notice the content of his counsel, his advice to Eve. He takes the very same set of facts (the things God said to Adam and Eve) and gives them a different interpretation. The Serpent puts a particular spin on the words of God because he is anything but objective.

Eve stands in one of the most important moments of history. You can almost imagine the deathly silence of creation as it waits to see what she will do. Will she follow the counsel of the Creator or the counsel of the Serpent? Where will she find her meaning and purpose? To whom will she entrust herself? What, finally, will she believe about God, his character, and his plan? These are the underlying questions of the moment.

The moral drama here gets to the core of human existence. Notice that the passage says that Eve saw the fruit as "desirable for gaining wisdom." Satan was not just selling Eve the best fruit in the garden, but something more fundamentally appealing. He was telling

Eve that if she ate the fruit, she would be independently wise. The promise was autonomous personal wisdom, without any need for God or his revelation! This was the attraction that led to the Fall.

Satan was offering a different path to wisdom, holding out the promise that people can discern life on their own. His words suggest that however beautiful God's revelation, it is not really necessary. Satan's wisdom places peoples' lives in their own hands, so that they rely on their own ability to think, interpret, understand, and apply. The Serpent is selling Eve the most attractive and cruelest of lies, the lie of autonomy and self-sufficiency. He offers her wisdom that does not need to bow the knee to God.

If Adam and Eve choose to follow the counsel of the Serpent, they will have to do two things. First, they will have to deny God and his revelation of himself as their Creator and Counselor, the one who defines their identity and purpose. The apostle Paul says of Christ, "in [him] are hidden all the treasures of wisdom and knowledge." He says that what is wrong with the "hollow and deceptive philosophy" of the world is that it "depends on human tradition and the basic principles of this world rather than on Christ" (Col. 2:3, 8). The Bible declares that wisdom is a person, and his name is Christ! This has been true from the beginning. Thus in a real way Adam and Eve are rejecting not just God the Father, but Christ, believing they can find elsewhere what only he can offer.

Psalm 14 says that this is the core of all foolishness. Foolishness is more than being stupid, that deadly combination of arrogance and ignorance. The core presupposition of fools is that there is no God, and we don't need his revelation in order to live. Genesis 3 is a counseling passage, a wisdom passage. Whose voice will I listen to? What will be the source of my wisdom? Adam and Eve must listen to one voice or the other, and their decision, like ours, has lasting implications.

To listen to this new counselor (Satan), they must not only deny God, but their own nature. What the serpent offers as a credible option is no option at all. Adam and Eve were created for a certain kind of existence. They cannot live successfully outside their design. Yet this is what Adam and Eve are about to do, and what millions of people attempt every day.

WHY OBEY GOD?

This alternate system of wisdom, with its new counselor, is not neutral. It carries a clear moral agenda. If Adam and Eve decide to believe the interpretation of this new speaker, they would be stupid to continue to obey God. God would be unmasked as a liar and a cheat, a manipulative, insecure deity who is afraid that they will become like him.

This is how it is with all advice, counsel, and personal ministry. The interpretations we share with one another always define right and wrong, good and bad, true and false, wise and foolish. They always tell us what to desire, think, and do. My interpretations all rest on some view of God, myself, and others. And they always tell me what to do with both my heart and my hands.

If Adam and Eve reject the words of God and follow the Serpent, they will think and act in very different ways. Sadly, they followed the Serpent, and life has never been the same. Now we live in a world with thousands of voices that interpret life and compete for the allegiance of our hearts. No wonder we are confused! No wonder we can't think straight! These voices tempt us because they appeal to one sinful, deluded desire first felt in the Garden: to be out on our own, to have it our way, to answer only to ourselves, and to find life somewhere other than at the feet of the Creator.

This is what sin does to us. It reduces us to fools who live in ways that deny both God and our own nature. We may not profess to be atheists, but in practice we live purely horizontal, godless lives. The things of this world capture and enslave us. We may go to church and possess a high level of biblical and theological knowledge, but these pursuits can exist on the fringes of our lives. They are the icing on an all too self-absorbed, self-directed, and self-sufficient cake. Another system of counsel commands the thoughts and motives of our hearts.

PEOPLE, THE SERPENT, AND PERSONAL MINISTRY

What principles can we draw from Genesis 3 to develop our biblical understanding of personal ministry?

1. Thoughts, opinions, advice, and relationships are always agenda setting. Though we may be unaware of it, we daily advise each other what to desire, think, and do.
2. Advice is always moral, defining right and wrong, true and false, good and bad, wise and foolish.
3. We should hunger for the simple dependence of Genesis 1, where everything people thought, said, and did was based solely on the words of God.
4. The voices of the world appeal to a core delusion in sinful hearts, the desire to *be* God, able to understand and live life on our own. We need people in our lives who love us enough to call us back to a life with God at the center.
5. We need the words of God (Scripture) to make sense out of life. We need to listen for the one reliable voice of the Creator. His Word alone can cut through the confusion of the world's philosophy and our own foolishness to make us truly wise. Real knowledge begins with knowing him. Wisdom is the fruit of worship, and received on bended knee. It is the product of a life lived in submission to the One who is wisdom, Christ.

SAVED, BUT STILL NEEDY

Are Christians still people who need help? Is personal ministry a necessity for those who have been forgiven by God's grace, adopted in his family, and indwelt by the Holy Spirit? Isn't the public ministry of the Word enough? In emphasizing personal ministry, aren't we simply following the lead of a therapeutic culture?

A woman once approached me during a seminar on this material and asked, "If I have the Bible in my hands and the Holy Spirit in my heart, why do I need to be counseled by others?" How would you answer her? Indeed, the Holy Spirit is the Wonderful Counselor of the church. He enables us to understand God's Word, convicts us of sin, works in us a willingness to obey, and enables us to do what we have been called by God to do. But does this mean that I no longer need one-on-one ministry? You could use the same logic to argue that you don't need public worship and the public ministry of the Word. This woman was missing something significant, which is captured by a few short verses in Hebrews: "See to it, brothers, that none of you has a sinful, unbelieving heart that turns away from the living God. But encourage one another daily, as long as it is called Today, so that none of you may be hardened by sin's deceitfulness" (Heb. 3:12–13).

There is a lot packed into these two short verses. First, notice that the passage is written to "brothers," that is, believers. The writer is addressing issues that are part of the normal life of every Christian. He is not talking to those outside the faith or to some special class of believers. The writer is saying that there is something in each of us that places us in danger, and because of that, we need the daily ministry of others.

Next, look at the content of the warning: "See to it that none of you has a sinful, unbelieving [i.e., turning away, ultimately hardened] heart." The fact that there is a need for this kind of warning should get our attention. What is being described here is a process, one I have seen many times in people I have counseled.

It all starts with the person giving in to the sinful desires of his or her heart. A married man becomes interested in a woman at work. He thinks about what it would be like to get to know her better. He begins to spend way too much time studying the way she dresses, the look of her face, the way she keeps her hair, and the shape of her body. As he does this, his desires grow. He has not considered a physical relationship, and he is not thinking of leaving his wife at this point. He decides to talk with the woman. What harm could it do? After all, she is colleague, so he ought to have a good relationship with her.

It isn't long before they are having long lunches together and talking often during the day. One day he offers to take her home and spends forty-five minutes sitting close to her on the couch. He touches her hand and tells her how much he appreciates their friendship. On the way home, for the first time he wishes he wasn't married. When he arrives home he is careful about how he reports on his day. That night he lies in bed next to his wife, thinking about the woman at work. He is progressively giving in to subtle patterns of sin, but he doesn't see them for what they are.

Yet there is something else going on inside him, the conviction of the Holy Spirit. He is uneasy. He feels a bit guilty. He doesn't experience the joy he once did at seeing his wife at the end of a long day. He knows he is all too excited to go to work in the morning. He knows he has begun to be more critical of his wife and that he feels a unique kinship with this other woman. So he argues with himself, trying to quiet his conscience. He doesn't see it, but he is responding to subtle patterns of sin with subtle patterns of unbelief. He tells himself that he hasn't done anything wrong, that the Bible does not forbid a man's friendship with a woman, that he is a faithful husband, and that he hasn't done anything adulterous. He convinces himself that this relationship is a good thing, that he needs more of these kinds of relationships at work, that he has existed too long in the comfortable Christian ghetto, and that God is actually pleased that he has reached out to someone.

Not only is he acting upon the sinful desires of his heart, he is subtly backing away from the interpretive authority of Scripture. Giving in to patterns of sin has been followed by unbelief, and all the while the man and his wife are still actively involved with their church. But underneath, he has begun to lose his spiritual moorings. A childlike trust in and obedience to the Word had been his moral anchor. He had been sensitive to the ministry of the Holy Spirit. But now he has cut the anchor chain and is adrift. And he doesn't even know it.

Because he has lost his spiritual moorings, he drifts away further. Before long he and his coworker are leaving at lunch and not returning. He begins to volunteer for business trips when he knows she is going. The relationship is increasingly physical. His relationship with his wife is disintegrating, but he doesn't care. In fact, he wonders why in the world he married her. He is spending more time at work in the evenings and on weekends, and so he is less involved with activities at his church. He has quit reading his Bible and praying; he feels quite trapped by the whole "Christian thing." His wife pleads with him to go with her for counseling, but he is not interested.

There are more evenings when he doesn't even come home. Lies fill his conversations with his wife. His pastor pursues and pleads with him, but he is unmoved, no longer attentive to the Word or sensitive to the ministry of the Holy Spirit. His heart has become hard. He is not sure he believes "that stuff" any more, and before long he is making plans to leave his wife.

Sinful → unbelieving → turning away → hardened hearts. What a terrifying progression! Perhaps you are wondering, "How could this ever happen to a believer?" This passage answers the question with its detailed description of how things went wrong. Notice the words in Hebrews 3:13: "so that none of you may be hardened by sin's deceitfulness." This explains why we need the daily ministry of fellow believers.

The writer of Hebrews directs us to the doctrine of indwelling sin. On the cross and in the resurrection, Christ broke the *power* of sin over us (Rom. 6:1–14), but the *presence* of sin remains. Sin is being eradicated within us, and this process will continue until we are sin-free. But while sin remains, we must remember that sin is deceitful. Sin blinds—and guess who gets blinded first? Me! I have no trouble seeing the sins of my family, but I can be astonished when mine are pointed out! Christ captures this truth with his word picture in Matthew 7. He says we can see a speck of dust in our neighbor's eye, but we are oblivious to a huge piece of lumber sticking out of our own!

Since each of us still has sin remaining in us, we will have pockets of spiritual blindness. This problem has a great impact on personal ministry.[1] Our most important vision system is not our physical eyes. We can be physically blind and live quite well. But when we are spiritually blind, we cannot live as God intended. That is why so many Old Testament prophecies say that the Messiah would come to open blind eyes. That is why he is called the Light. Physically blind people are always aware of their deficit and spend much of their lives learning to live with its limitations. But the Bible says that we can be spiritually blind and yet think that we see quite well. We even get offended when people act as if they see us better than we see ourselves!

The reality of spiritual blindness has important implications for the Christian community. The Hebrews passage clearly teaches that personal insight is the product of community. I need you in order to really see and know myself. Otherwise, I will listen to my own arguments, believe my own lies, and buy into my own delusions. My self-perception is as accurate as a carnival mirror. If I am going to see myself clearly, I need you to hold the mirror of God's Word in front of me.

Notice also that this is a universal need. There are no "haves" and "have nots" here. There is no group that has arrived spiritually and therefore can provide all the ministry to a group of strugglers. This passage teaches that everybody ministers and everybody needs ministry. It warns us to admit our need for help and to become God's helpers. I need to wake up in the morning and say, "God, I am a person in desperate need of help. Please send helpers my way and give me the humility to receive the help you have provided." And I need to pray further, "Lord, make me willing to help someone see himself as you see him today."

As Christians who still have pockets of spiritual blindness, we need two character qualities. First, we need the *loving courage of honesty*. We need to love others more than we love ourselves, and so, with humble, patient love, help them to see what they need to see. Second, we need the *thankful humility of approachability*. We need to forsake defensiveness, be thankful that God has surrounded us with help, and be ready to receive it—every day!

BRINGING IT ALL TOGETHER

The world of personal ministry is rooted in three principles: First, we were created with the need for truth outside ourselves to live life properly. Second, many interpretive voices compete with God's Word for our hearts' attention. Third, the power of sin has been broken, but the blinding presence of sin remains. Therefore, we need to live in humble, honest community with one another, where personal ministry is part of the daily culture.

Do people really need help? The answer from the perspective of Creation, Fall, and Redemption is a resounding "yes." Each of us needs help, and each of us is called to offer it. In the next chapter, we will explore what that means for our individual lives and for the life and ministry of the church.

4 | THE HEART IS THE TARGET

I grew up in Toledo, Ohio, and our family usually went east for our vacations. But when I was sixteen years old, my dad decided to take our family on the Great Trip West. That year, Dad loaded my mother, my brother Mark, and me into a Ford Falcon and we headed out. Although we were to see many things (Yellowstone, the Rockies, etc.), the highlight of the trip for my father was seeing the Grand Canyon. For Dad, everything else we did was but a prelude to this experience.

As background, I should note that Dad approached vacations as a contract between the family and himself. His part of the bargain was to plan and finance the trip. Our part was to have a good time. Thus whenever he would ask us if we were having fun, the prudent answer was a hearty "yes." Otherwise, he would launch into a well-rehearsed speech about how much money he was spending and how much time he had invested in planning our trip. He would conclude by saying that if he had known we were not going to have fun, we would have stayed home where we could do it for free!

Finally, the "Day of the Grand Canyon" came. Dad had never been more excited—an emotion that was obviously not shared by my mother. He awakened us early and we soon were on our way. When we reached the Grand Canyon, Dad refused to see it at a location that was "all fences and tourist traps." He began to explore, and we ended up driving down a dirt road and then over open ground until we parked 200 feet from the rim.

Mark and I immediately ran for the edge. We pretended to push each other over the rim and sat dangling our feet over the mile-high wall of rock. We threw stone after stone over the edge, oblivious to anyone who might have been hiking and camping below us. It was amazing to witness stones silently disappearing without ever hearing or seeing them hit. We were having a blast, totally unencumbered by fear.

Meanwhile, Mom hadn't even gotten out of the car. She had one foot on the ground, tapping to make sure that the turf was solid. She had visions that the rim would crumble and we would all fall to the bottom of the Canyon with the car on top of us.

My dad knew she was struggling so he had placed himself near the car. But then Mom would say, "Bob, the boys, the boys!" and Dad would run toward us to make sure we were okay. At that point, Mom would get queasy and call him back. In short, I don't think my dad saw much of the canyon that day; he was too busy running back and forth, ensuring that everyone was having fun according to the plan. All of us were in the very same place at the very same moment, inter-acting with the very same natural phenomenon, but each was of us having a very different experience.

I tell this story because it gets to the heart of what personal min-istry is about. Effective personal ministry takes the Kingdom promise of lasting change to the place where it is needed—the heart. In my vacation story, the heart of each member of our family was revealed in our behavior that day. Why did each of us experience such a dif-ferent day when we were in the same location at the same time? Why did each of us act so differently? The answer goes back to our hearts.

My dad's heart was filled with a desire for his family to have a great time. Everything he said and did was controlled by that desire. Mom's heart was gripped by a powerful fear of heights and her con-cern for her sons, and this was reflected in her words and actions. Mark and I approached the scene with the fearlessness, invincibility, and immaturity of teenage boys. We just wanted to have fun. Each of us brought a different heart to the situation and so our experiences and actions differed. Our hearts directed our behavior.

WHY DO PEOPLE DO THE THINGS THEY DO?

If you want to be part of what God is doing in the lives of others, you need to understand how God designed human beings to function. Why *do* people do the things they do?

Why can your toddler be so contrary? Why did your friend get upset in the middle of the conversation? Why is your teenager so angry? Why is Amy swallowed up by depression and despair? Why would a man risk his family for twenty minutes of sexual pleasure? Why do you get angry in traffic? Why is that once-romantic couple now engaged in guerilla warfare? Why is Bill driven in his career? Why is Sue so critical and controlling? Why does George speak so bluntly and unkindly? Why is your daughter afraid of what her friends will think? Why does Pete refuse to talk? Why do people do the things they do? The simplest, most biblical answer is the heart.

Even though the heart is one of the Bible's most dominant themes, there is much confusion about the term. In western culture the term is relegated to the fields of romance (Valentine's Day) and sports ("he plays with a lot of heart"). In the Bible, however, the heart is an essential category. You cannot understand the human being without understanding the heart. So, what does this term describe?

The Bible uses "heart" to describe the inner person. Scripture divides the human being into two parts, the inner and outer being. The outer person is your physical self; the inner person is your spiritual self (Eph. 3:16). The synonym the Bible most often uses for the inner being is the heart. It encompasses all the other terms and functions used to describe the inner person (spirit, soul, mind, emotions, will, etc.). These other terms do not describe something different from the heart. Rather, they are aspects of it, parts or functions of the inner person.

The heart is the "real" you. It is the essential core of who you are. Though we put a tremendous amount of emphasis on the outer person, we all recognize that the true person is the person within. For example, when you say that you are getting to know someone, you are not saying that you have a deeper knowledge of his ears or nose! You are talking about the inner person, the heart. You know how the person thinks, what he wants, what makes him happy or sad. You can predict what he is feeling at any given moment. Because the Bible says your heart is the essential you, any ministry of change must target the heart. This perspective is explained in several Scripture passages.

FRUIT, ROOTS, AND THE HEART

One of the most important word pictures in the New Testament reveals Christ's perspective on how people function. It is Christ's answer to the age-old question, "Why do people do the things they do?"

> No good tree bears bad fruit, nor does a bad tree bear good fruit. Each tree is recognized by its own fruit. People do not pick figs from thornbushes, or grapes from briers. The good man brings good things out of the good stored up in his heart, and the evil man brings evil things out of the evil stored up in his heart. For out of the overflow of his heart his mouth speaks. (Luke 6:43–45)

Christ used ordinary physical things to explain unfamiliar truths. Here he likens the way people function to a tree. If you plant apple seeds and they take root, you don't expect to see peaches or oranges growing. You expect apple seeds to become apple trees that produce apples. There is an organic relationship between the roots of the plant and the fruit it produces. Christ is saying that the same is true with people.

In Christ's metaphor, fruit equals behavior. The particular fruit (behavior) this passage discusses is our words. Christ says that our words are literally our heart overflowing. People and situations don't make us say what we say, though we tend to blame them. ("He made me so angry!" "If you had been there, you would have said the same thing!" "These kids simply make me insane!") Rather, this passage says that our words are controlled by our hearts. A tree produces fruit, and our hearts produce behavior. We recognize a tree by the fruit it produces, and, in the same way, the Bible says people are known by their fruit.

In my early pastoral days we lived in a twin home, with our elderly landlady living in the other side of the house. In exchange for reduced rent, I agreed to do all of the yard work. In the busyness of ministry and family life, it was sometimes hard to find time to mow, rake, or shovel, but I tried to be prompt and faithful. However, no matter how disciplined I tried to be, my work never seemed timely enough for our landlady. To get me to work on her schedule, she would go out and start shoveling or raking, knowing full well that I would rush out and complete the job. I was unaware of how irritated I had become over her manipulation until one afternoon when I heard the leaves rustling outside. I looked out the window to see my landlady, in her housedress and slippers, raking the leaves. In my anger, with my hands on my hips, I said aloud, "If she thinks I'm going to rush out there and rake for her, she's nuts! I'm going to rake on my time or not at all!"

What I didn't realize was that one of my sons had been standing beside me. In a split second, to my horror, I saw him in the front yard, hands on *his* hips, yelling at my landlady, "My dad says if you think he is going to rush out here and rake for you, you're nuts!" I couldn't believe it. I was mortified. I wanted to back away from my words and rush out to tell my landlady that I had said no such thing—or at least that my son had misunderstood what I'd said. But I had to face the fact that the words *had* come out of me, that I *had* said what I'd meant, and that the words were the fruit of anger I had carried for quite a while. There was an organic connection between my words and my heart. You would not solve my heart problem by removing my son or teaching me to be more judicious with my words (though you would save me a lot of embarrassment!). The problem with my words was directly tied to the problem with my heart, which is where a comprehensive solution needed to be applied. This leads us to the second half of Christ's illustration.

In Christ's example, the roots of the tree equal the heart. They are underground and therefore not as easily seen or understood. But Jesus' point is that a tree has the kind of fruit it does because of the kind of roots it has: we speak and act the way we do because of what is in our hearts.

There may be no more important thing to say about how people function, yet this seems to be hard for us to accept. In many ways we deny this connection and blame people and circumstances for our actions and words. Here Christ calls us to humbly accept responsibility for our behavior. He calls us to humbly admit that relationships and circumstances are only the occasions in which our hearts reveal themselves.

If my heart is the source of my sin problem, then lasting change must always travel through the pathway of my heart. It is not enough to alter my behavior or to change my circumstances. Christ transforms people by radically changing their hearts. If the heart doesn't change, the person's words and behavior may change temporarily because of an external pressure or incentive. But when the pressure or incentive is removed, the changes will disappear.

This is the spiritual truth Christ accused the Pharisees of missing in Matthew 23:25–26: "Woe to you, teachers of the law and Pharisees, you hypocrites! You clean the outside of the cup and dish, but inside they are full of greed and self-indulgence. Blind Pharisee! First clean the inside of the cup and dish, and then the outside will also be clean."

Christ looked at the externalism of the Pharisees and said, "You guys just don't get it. You pride yourselves on your right behavior, yet your hearts are a mess! Start with your hearts and right behavior will follow." To make his point, Christ pushes his illustration to the limit. He says, "Clean the inside of the dish and the outside will also be clean." You can't really do this with your dishes at home—washing the inside of a dirty pan will not automatically clean the outside. Yet this is what Christ is advising; that's how powerful the heart is. Do we really believe what Christ is teaching here?

Many of our attempts to change behavior ignore the heart behind the actions. We threaten ("You don't want to even think about what I will do if you do that again!"), we manipulate ("Would you like a car of your own? All you have to do is . . ."), instill guilt ("I do and do for you and this is the thanks I get?"), raise our voices, and do a host of other things to change behavior, but change never lasts. The moment the outside pressure wanes, the behavior reverts to what it was before. The body always goes where the heart leads.

PERSONAL MINISTRY AND FRUIT STAPLING

Christ's word picture helps set the direction for personal ministry, as we can see when we expand and apply it. Let's say I have an apple tree in my backyard.[1] Each year its apples are dry, wrinkled, brown, and pulpy. After several seasons my wife says, "It doesn't make any sense to have this huge tree and never be able to eat any apples. Can't you do something?" One day my wife looks out the window to see me in the yard, carrying branch cutters, an industrial grade staple gun, a ladder, and two bushels of apples.

I climb the ladder, cut off all the pulpy apples, and staple shiny, red apples onto every branch of the tree. From a distance our tree looks like it is full of a beautiful harvest. But if you were my wife, what would you be thinking of me at this moment?

If a tree produces bad apples year after year, there is something drastically wrong with its system, down to its very roots. I won't solve the problem by stapling new apples onto the branches. They also will rot because they are not attached to a life-giving root system. And next spring, I will have the same problem again. I will not see a new crop of healthy apples because my solution has not gone to the heart of the problem. If the tree's roots remain unchanged, it will never produce good apples.

The point is that, in personal ministry, much of what we do to produce growth and change in ourselves and others is little more than "fruit stapling." It attempts to exchange apples for apples without examining the heart, the root behind the behavior. This is the very thing for which Christ criticized the Pharisees. Change that ignores the heart will seldom transform the life. For a while, it may seem like the real thing, but it will prove temporary and cosmetic.

This often happens in personal ministry. From a distance it looks as if the person has really changed. When held accountable, the person does and says different things. The husband seems to be gentle and attentive to his wife. The teenager seems to treat his parents with new respect. The depressed person is up and out of the house. The broken relationship seems to have been restored. But the changes don't last and in six weeks or six months, the person is right back where he started. Why? Because the change did not penetrate the heart, so changes in behavior were doomed to be temporary.

This is what happens to the teenager who goes through the teen years fairly well under the careful love, instruction, and oversight of Christian parents, only to go off to college and completely forsake his faith. I would suggest that in most cases he has not forsaken his faith. In reality, his faith was the faith of his parents; he simply lived within its limits while he was still at home. When he went away to school and those restraints were removed, his true heart was revealed. He had not internalized the faith. He had not entrusted himself to Christ in a life-transforming way. He did the "Christian" things he was required to do at home, but his actions did not flow from a heart of worship. In the college culture, he had nothing to anchor him, and the true thoughts and motives of his heart led him away from God. College was not the cause of his problem. It was simply the place where his true heart was revealed. The real problem was that faith never took root in his heart. As a result, his words, choices, and actions did not reveal a heart for God. Good behavior lasted for a while, but it proved to be temporary because it was not rooted in the heart.

Christ's illustration establishes three principles that guide our efforts to serve as God's instruments of change in the lives of others.

1. There is an undeniable root and fruit connection between our heart and our behavior. People and situations do not determine our behavior; they provide the occasion where our behavior reveals our hearts.
2. Lasting change always takes place through the pathway of the heart. Fruit change is the result of root change. Similarly, in

Matthew 23, Christ says, "Clean the inside of the cup and dish and the outside will become clean." Any agenda for change must focus on the thoughts and desires of the heart.

3. Therefore, the heart is our target in personal growth and ministry. Our prayer is that God will work heart change in us and use us to produce heart change in others that results in new words, choices, and actions.

THE HEART OF THE MATTER

Though the Bible has much to say about the heart, few Christian books on marriage and family, communication, conflict resolution, or even discipleship focus on it. These practical books seldom display an understanding of the centrality of the heart and how it operates. We can't assume that people understand us when we talk about these things. We need to develop the ideas further.

An interesting Old Testament passage can help us do this.

> Some of the elders of Israel came to me and sat down in front of me. Then the word of the LORD came to me: "Son of man, these men have set up idols in their hearts and put wicked stumbling blocks before their faces. Should I let them inquire of me at all? Therefore speak to them and tell them, 'This is what the sovereign LORD says: When any Israelite sets up idols in his heart and puts a wicked stumbling block before his face and then goes to a prophet, I the LORD will answer him myself in keeping with his great idolatry. I will do this to recapture the hearts of the people of Israel, who have all deserted me for their idols.' " (Ezek. 14:1–5)

The elders of Israel have come to the prophet Ezekiel with questions they want to ask God. It would seem like these spiritual leaders are doing the right thing. But God recognizes that there is something wrong with them. What is it?

God points out their idolatry, which is idolatry of a specific kind. They have idols *in their hearts,* a more personal and fundamental form of idolatry than ritual religious or cultural idolatry. An idol of the heart is *anything that rules me other than God.* As worshiping beings, human beings always worship someone or something. This is not a situation where some people worship and some don't. If God isn't ruling my heart, someone or something else will. It is the way we were made.

Romans 1 is helpful here. It is probably Scripture's best analysis of the nature and effects of sin. Paul presents the core of our struggle as a "great exchange."

> For although they knew God, they neither glorified him as God nor gave thanks to him, but their thinking became futile and their foolish hearts were darkened. Although they claimed to be wise, they became fools and *exchanged* the glory of the immortal God for images made to look like mortal man and birds and animals and reptiles.
>
> Therefore God gave them over in the sinful desires of their hearts to sexual impurity for the degrading of their bodies with one another. They *exchanged* the truth of God for a lie, and worshiped and served *created things* rather than the Creator—who is forever praised. Amen. (Rom. 1: 21–25)

Sin is fundamentally idolatrous. I do wrong things because my heart desires something more than the Lord. Sin produces a propensity toward idolatry in us all. We all migrate away from worship and service of the Creator toward worship and service of the created thing. This is the great spiritual war beneath every battle of behavior—the war for control of the heart. This struggle is captured well by the old hymn, *Come Thou Fount of Every Blessing.* The third verse says,

> O to grace how great a debtor daily I'm constrained to be;
> let that grace now, like a fetter, bind my wandering heart to thee.
> Prone to wander—Lord, I feel it—prone to leave the God I love:
> here's my heart, O take and seal it, seal it for thy courts above.

The hymn reflects the fact that a person does not wake up one morning and say, "You know, I'm tired of being a theist. I think I'll become an atheist." No, the hymn depicts the great exchange that takes place within our hearts in the routine moments of life. Sin leads us to believe that life can be found away from the Creator, and so we, in subtle and obvious ways, forget the Creator and deify the creation. Our behavior is ruled, not by worship and service of the Lord, but by a ravenous desire for something in the creation. As John Calvin said, our hearts are "idol factories," and our words and actions are shaped by our pursuit of the things our hearts crave.

To make matters worse, this idolatry is hidden. It is deceptive; it exists underground. We can make this great exchange without forsaking our confessional theology or even our observance of the external duties of the faith. So we hold onto our beliefs, tithe, remain faithful in church attendance, and occasionally participate in ministry activity. Yet at the level of what we are really living for, we have forsaken God for something else. This is the silent cancer that weakens the church, robs individuals of their spiritual vitality, and leads to all kinds of difficulty in relationships and situations.

At its core, sin is moral thievery. It steals the worship that rightly belongs to God and gives it to someone or something else. It robs the Trinity to purchase the creation. Every sinner is in some way a worship thief.

At its center, sin is also spiritual adultery. It takes the love that belongs to God alone and gives it to someone or something else. It is a life shaped by the satisfaction of cravings, rather than by heartfelt commitment and faithfulness. Every sinner is in some way a spiritual adulterer.

The deepest issues of life are issues of worship. Worship is more fundamental to our essential nature than the pain, pressures, or pleasures of our experiences. What we worship determines our responses to all our experiences. Sin is much more than doing the wrong thing. It begins with loving, worshiping, and serving the wrong thing. Sin in some way always involves the great exchange.

GOD'S RESPONSE

The Ezekiel passage then gives God's response to the elders. Because these men have idols in their hearts, God says he is going to answer them "in keeping with their great idolatry." What does this mean? God is saying, "Because you have idols in your hearts, the only thing I want to talk about is your idolatry." Why? Maybe these men had important things to ask God. Maybe they had pressing decisions to make. Why would God refuse to talk to them about anything but the idols?

A crucial phrase explains God's response and reveals much about how the heart functions: "These men have set up idols in their hearts and *put wicked stumbling blocks before their faces*" (Ezek. 14:3).

Imagine that someone places his hand up to his face so that he is looking through his fingers. What will happen to his vision? It will be seriously obstructed, and the only way to clear it is to remove his hand. In a similar way, an idol in the heart creates a stumbling block before the face. Until the idol is removed, it will distort and obscure everything else in the person's life. This is the principle of *inescapable influence: Whatever rules the heart will exercise inescapable influence over the person's life and behavior*. This principle has obvious implications for personal growth and ministry.

I once counseled a successful executive from New York City. He was the most controlling man I have ever met. He had been married for thirty years and handled all of the financial, parenting, and decorating decisions of the family. He was so obsessed with control that he would rearrange his wife's clothes closet according to his prescribed plan (blouses, skirts, pants, and dresses, in graduated shades of color)! Now, imagine that I did not know all this as I spoke to his wife. His controlling tendencies would not be in my mind as I listened to her complain that she and her husband never talk and that many conflicts are left unsolved. What would happen if I rolled up my counselor's sleeves and gave the husband good biblical instruction on communication and conflict resolution? Would this lead to basic changes in his marriage? The answer is no, because he would use his new understanding and skills to get what his heart worshiped. Because my counsel would not have addressed this man's idols of the heart, it would only produce a more successful controller. As long as the desire for dominance ruled his heart, he would use whatever principles and skills he learned to establish even greater control over his family.

If we fail to examine the heart and the areas where it needs to change, our ministry efforts will only result in people who are more committed and successful idolaters. This is why God will only answer the elders of Israel in keeping with their heart idolatry. If they do not change there, whatever God tells them will only be used to serve the idols that rule their hearts. We will even use the principles of the Word to serve our idols!

Because idolatry operates in the subtle shadows of the thoughts and motives of our hearts, most committed idolaters have no idea that this is their problem. But the influence is powerful just the same.

COVERT AND OVERT IDOLATRY

I have traveled to northern India several times. Spiritually, this is one of the darkest places on earth. Idolatry permeates every aspect of individual and cultural life. Stand almost anywhere in northern India and you can see an altar to one of Hinduism's many gods. One day I stood in a temple and watched a young priest feed, bathe, and clothe an idol. I watched his colleague lie prostrate on the floor before an image of wood and gold. I was overcome by their sincerity and devotion. These inanimate images controlled every waking moment of the priests' young lives, even though they had no ability to see, speak, or act in any way beneficial to their worshipers. I witnessed hordes of poverty-stricken pilgrims bathing in the Ganges River after long, arduous journeys, so that their souls would be cleansed and their prayers answered.

One day I entered a temple and watched person after person do homage to a fifteen-foot, black stone phallus. I thought to myself, *How blind and deceived these people must be! How utterly disgusting this must be in the eyes of the true and living God!* I literally ran out of the temple, overcome with the darkness, saying to myself, *I am glad I'm not like these people!* But as I looked back at the temple, I was humbled by the thought that I am like them. My idols are not the overt idols of Hindu polytheism; they are the covert idols of my heart. But either way, they are god-replacements. From God's vantage point, my idols are just as disgusting as anything I had seen that day. They command my daily devotion, shape my daily routine, and guide the way I interact with life, though they have no power whatsoever to deliver. There are times when I am just as deceived and blind as the young priests I observed. Overt idolatry has much to tell us about how covert idolatry controls our lives.

Nowhere but in Scripture will you get this perspective on human motivation. The Bible alone declares that human beings are worshipers by their very nature and that everything we say and do is shaped by worship. God's Word alone insists that we are always serving God or some aspect of the creation, and *whatever rules our hearts will exercise inescapable influence over our lives and behavior.*

Heart idolatry can subvert even our most worshipful moments. For example, prayer is our most God-directed act, yet it too can be warped by an idolatrous heart. Have you ever rehearsed a prayer before publicly praying it? (You know, "Our dear Heavenly Father . . . No, no . . . Our sovereign, gracious Heavenly Father . . . no . . . Father in heaven, we are. . . ."). Why do we do this? Are we trying to get it right for the Lord? That doesn't work because he hears the rehearsal! Isn't it really an attempt to use public prayer to gain the respect of the people around us? Because our hearts are captured by a desire for human approval, we use an act of worship to get glory for ourselves!

This is why the principle of the Ezekiel passage is so important, and why the focus of God's transforming grace is heart change. Our spiritual battle is a war for the heart. When that war is won, people behave in ways that please their Creator. God will never be satisfied with the crumbs of externalism. He rails against this in Isaiah: "These people come near to me with their mouth and honor me with their lips, but their hearts are far from me" (Isa. 29:13a).

APPLYING THE PRINCIPLE

My daily behavior is my attempt to get what is important to me in various situations and relationships. My choices and actions always reveal the desires that rule my heart. I never come empty. This is the deepest issue of human experience and a major answer to the question, "Why do people do the things they do?" As James says, we are led away by our own desires (James 1:14).

This principle has several applications for personal growth and ministry.

1. Our hearts are always being ruled by someone or something.
2. The most important question to ask when examining the heart is, "What is functionally ruling this person's heart in this situation?"
3. Whatever controls my heart will control my responses to people and situations.
4. God changes us not just by teaching us to do different things, but by recapturing our hearts to serve him alone.
5. The deepest issues of the human struggle are not issues of pain and suffering, but the issue of worship, because what rules our hearts will control the way we respond to both suffering and blessing.

IT'S A MATTER OF TREASURE

Christ also talked about what rules the heart using the metaphor of treasure, as we see in Matthew 6:19–24:

> Do not store up for yourselves treasures on earth, where moth and rust destroy, and where thieves break in and steal. But store up for yourselves treasures in heaven, where moth and rust do not destroy, and where thieves do not break in and steal. For where your treasure is, there your heart will be also.

The eye is the lamp of the body. If your eyes are good, your whole body will be full of light. But if your eyes are bad, your whole body will be full of darkness. If then the light within you is darkness, how great is that darkness!

No one can serve two masters. Either he will hate the one and love the other, or he will be devoted to the one and despise the other. You cannot serve both God and Money.

Three principles in this passage speak to what we have been considering.

1. Everyone seeks some kind of treasure. (This is Christ's operating assumption.)
2. Your treasure will control your heart. ("For where your treasure is, there your heart will be also.")
3. What controls your heart will control your behavior. ("No one can serve two masters.")

There are only two kinds of treasures, earthly and heavenly, and whatever treasures we choose will become our rulers. They exercise control over us, for if something is your treasure, you will live to gain, maintain, and enjoy it. Sadly, we often fail to see this in ourselves, though we can see it in others. One of the most tragic things that could happen to a human being is to invest his life in pursuit of the wrong treasure.

Luella has always been the fire marshal in our family. Whenever we moved into a new house, she explored all the possible exit routes and came up with exit plans in case of fire in various parts of the house. She would then gather the family, explain the plans, and quiz us until she was sure we all knew what to do in an emergency.

This usually worked well, except for the time when I had recently acquired the guitar of my dreams. I had been in a music store buying new strings when I saw a handmade nine-string guitar. Its sound was more beautiful than any guitar I had ever heard. When I told my mother about it on the phone, in a miracle moment she said that she and my dad would buy it for me. This was more than I had ever hoped for, but in a week, I was the owner of my beloved instrument. Every evening after supper, I would retire to the living room and play, scarcely believing that this guitar belonged to me.

Shortly thereafter, Luella held her fire safety talk around the dinner table. She turned to me and asked, "Paul, if a major fire broke out on the main floor of our house, what would you do?" Without a moment's thought, I responded, "I would run into the living room, grab my guitar, and get it out of the house!" I will never forget the look on the faces of my family, or the silence that seemed to last about a year. Finally, one of my children asked, "What about us, Dad?" My embarrassment and shame were deepened by the look on Luella's face that asked the same question.

The guitar in the music store had become a dream, the dream had become a purchase, and the purchase had become a major treasure capable of rearranging my priorities in a fundamental way. So it often is. We rarely say, "I am going to set my heart on this thing and let it completely control my life," but that is exactly what happens.

The person you met and mildly enjoyed becomes the person whose approval you cannot live without. The work you undertook to support your family becomes the source of identity and achievement you can't give up. The house you built for the shelter and comfort of your family becomes a temple for the worship of possessions. A rightful attention to your own needs morphs into a self-absorbed existence. Ministry has become more of an opportunity to seek power and approval than a life in the service of God. The things we set our hearts on never remain under our control. Instead, they capture, control, and enslave us. This is the danger of earth-bound treasure.

Every human being is a worshiper, in active pursuit of the thing that rules his heart. This worship shapes everything we do and say, who we are, and how we live. This is why the heart is always our target in personal ministry.

5 | UNDERSTANDING YOUR HEART STRUGGLE

They were at it again, the twenty-seventh verbal gunfight of the year. It started over nothing and would accomplish little except to make them ready for the next skirmish. I waited and listened, increasingly angry that I would have to play referee for the thousandth time. One underhanded comment followed another. They fought with commitment and skill, using words to inflict pain. Finally I had enough. I threw down my book and stomped upstairs. I told them what I thought of their petty little self-centered wars. They said I didn't understand. I told them I had forgotten more than they would ever understand. They started blaming each other and even blaming me for not doing something sooner! Suddenly I began to hear what I was saying. I was not the peacemaker I had intended to be. I had become another gunslinger. The conflict did not cease with my presence—it widened. I asked them to be silent for a moment, asked for their forgiveness, and then said I was going to pray. Afterwards, we sat down and talked about living in a house full of gunslingers.

Do you have any conflict in your life? Do you experience moments of extreme irritation toward someone you otherwise love? Are there people who simply push your buttons more than others? Do certain things drive you crazy on a daily basis? Did you have a lot of conflict last year? How about last month? Last week? So far today? If you could watch the video of a typical week in your life, you would recognize an astonishing amount of conflict going on around you. Conflict is one of the principal effects of the Fall, and it doesn't take much to incite it.

It could be the bathroom in the morning. You are rushing to get ready for work. You walk down the hallway and the bathroom door is closed. You have probably never once thought, "How nice that *some-one* in the family is going to be ready on time!" No, you bellow at the door, "Who's in the bathroom?" What happens next is interesting. No one ever gives a name! They simply say, "Someone's in here." You respond, "Well, if you know who it is, please tell him I need to get in there right away!"

Perhaps the conflict is more serious. Maybe your marriage has deteriorated into a cycle of irritations followed by unkind comments that escalate into mini-wars. You are living a "don't trouble trouble 'til trouble troubles you" life with the one who was once your best friend. Or maybe there is severe brokenness in your extended family. There are blood relatives you have no desire to see or talk to again. When you think of them, your heart floods with anger and bitterness.

Maybe it's the guy in your department at work. He critiques every suggestion you make and obstructs everything you try to do. You walk long distances to avoid his desk. You dread the team meetings you used to enjoy. You are convinced he is out to get you, and you are determined not to let him do it.

Conflict is all around us, from petty quarrels to all-out war. None of us is immune, and conflict is actually a very illuminating window into our hearts. James 4:1–10 uses conflict to give us significant insight into the heart's daily struggle.

> What causes fights and quarrels among you? Don't they come from your desires that battle within you? You want something but don't get it. You kill and covet, but you cannot have what you want. You quarrel and fight. You do not have, because you do not ask God. When you ask, you do not receive, because you ask with wrong motives, that you may spend what you get on your pleasures.
>
> You adulterous people, don't you know that friendship with the world is hatred toward God? Anyone who chooses to be a friend of the world becomes an enemy of God. Or do you

think Scripture says without reason that the spirit he caused to live in us envies intensely? But he gives us more grace. That is why Scripture says:

"God opposes the proud,
but gives grace to the humble."

Submit yourselves, then, to God. Resist the devil, and he will flee from you. Come near to God and he will come near to you. Wash your hands, you sinners, and purify your hearts, you double-minded. Grieve, mourn and wail. Change your laughter to mourning and your joy to gloom. Humble yourselves before the Lord, and he will lift you up.

LOOKING FOR CONFLICT IN ALL THE WRONG PLACES

James gets our attention, not only because he addresses an issue in all of our lives but because he explains *why* it is there. Wouldn't you like to understand why some people irritate you more than others? Why relationships turn sour, and your own anger can flare so quickly? Why it's hard not to replay those hurtful words over and over in your head? Shouldn't we consider why we, as sinners, are better at making war than making peace?

James answers his first question with a series of questions that challenge us to something radically different from our usual reactions to conflict. When angry, most people explain their anger by blaming something or someone outside themselves. ("She makes me so angry!" "This traffic drives me crazy!" "He has an uncanny ability to push my buttons!" "The noise in our house would drive anyone insane!") James says we will never understand our anger that way. Instead, he counsels us to do the exact opposite—to look within. This is a fundamental biblical principle. The only way to understand your anger is to examine your own heart. According to Christ, angry words and actions are the heart overflowing (see Luke 6:45). Our feelings of anger and the words and actions that follow reveal very important things about our hearts.

If you really pay attention, you will realize that people and situations do not force us to be angry. For one thing, the same relationships and situations do not make *every* person angry. Recently I was sitting in traffic, stewing over the important things I was about to miss, when I glanced out the window toward the car next to me. The driver was a woman who seemed quite relaxed, even relieved, to be stuck. She was using the unexpected free time to put on her makeup! People don't affect us all the same way either. The talkative person who drives you crazy may be quite interesting to the person next to you. Though there are situations and relationships that we all dread, there is enough variety in the how, when, and where of our anger to suggest that something else is going on. That something is the heart. We do not respond to people and situations in the same way because we do not bring the same heart to them. This is why any attempt to examine the causes of conflict must begin with the heart.

Notice, further, that James's focus is not just on the heart, but on the *desires* of the heart. James makes a strong connection between our desires and our conflict, between what we want and what makes us angry. Understanding this connection can pave the way to lasting change in your life. The desire-conflict connection is the foundation on which James builds all the practical insights of this passage. What does James's second question reveal about our desires?

AN ARMY OF DESIRES IN A WORLD AT WAR

You and I are always desiring. Desires precede, determine, and characterize everything you do. Desires get you up in the morning and put you to bed at night. Desire makes you work with discipline to get one thing done, and run as hard as you can to avoid another. Desires sculpt every relationship in your life. They are the lenses through which you examine every situation. At the foundation of all worship, whether true or false, is a heart full of desire.

James encourages us to examine our desires because it is the only way to understand our anger. Desire lies at the base of every angry feeling, word, and action. But we need to add some qualifications in order to properly understand James's counsel. First, he does not say it is wrong to desire. God is a God of purpose and desire, and desire is one way our design mirrors God. Here we are much closer to him than we are to the rest of creation, which either functions by instinct or by biochemical processes. To stop desiring is impossible, because when you quit desiring, you are dead!

Notice also that James does not place the word "evil" before the word "desire." Although evil desires for wrong things can be a source of conflict, James is addressing something more fundamental. He says, "Don't your conflicts come from your desires that *battle within you?*" Beneath the wars between people is another, more fundamental war that rages every day but never makes a headline. It is a "within you" war, a direct attack on God's "within you" kingdom.

We don't typically think about our desires waging war. We think of surprising, powerful, or wrong desires. But we must understand the war metaphor James is using. If a war is being fought between nations, it is fought for geographical and political control. Control is the purpose of war. So it is with our desires, which fight for control of our hearts. What controls our hearts will exercise inescapable influence over our lives and behavior.

In that little phrase, "desires that battle within you," James gives us a window into how the heart operates. The heart of every person is a fount of competing desires. We rarely do anything with one simple motive. Most of the time there is a battle within. For example, let's say that you are driving home after a long day at work. You can't wait to see your family, but you would also like to relax. You want to be a good parent, but you would also love to take a run, or study for that Sunday school class. The desire that wins will shape your behavior when you get home that night.

Yet there is a deeper battle beneath that one: the battle between our desire for anything in the creation and our desire for God. Every day creation battles with the Creator for the control of our hearts. The stakes are high, because whatever rules our hearts will control our behavior. James is saying that our horizontal desires (for people, possessions, recognition, control, acceptance, attention, vengeance, etc.) compete with the Lord for the rule of our hearts.

Our desire to set up our own kingdom is in direct conflict with the King who has come to rule in our hearts. This is the war beneath all others. Who will rule that tense situation at work—your desire for a raise, or God's glory? Will God rule that conversation with your child, or your desire for peace and quiet? Will God rule your relationship with your father, or your desire for vengeance for years of mistreatment? These skirmishes within your heart are battles in the most important war.

DUELING KINGDOMS AND RELATIONAL CHAOS

What does all of this have to do with conflict? It points us to the cause. James connects our horizontal conflicts to the internal war between the kingdom of creation and the kingdom of God. Think about it this way. If my heart is ruled by a certain desire, there are only two ways I can respond to you. If you are helping me get what I want, I will be happy with you. But if you stand in my way, I will be angry, frustrated, and discouraged when I am with you. There will be times when I will wish you weren't in my life.

My problem is not you or the situation we are in together. My problem is that a legitimate desire has taken over my heart and is now in control. This desire has so much power that it is no longer legitimate. It has become an inordinate, sinful desire, because it has grown to a position of authority over my heart. This authority belongs to God alone, who sent his Son to set up his kingdom there. The focus of James's discussion is not evil desires (desires for the wrong thing), but inordinate desires (desires that may be right in and of themselves, but must never rule my heart). It is not wrong to desire relaxation at the end of a long day. It is wrong to be *ruled* by relaxation in such a way that I am irritated with anyone who gets in the way. It is not wrong to desire the tender attention of your husband. It is wrong to be so ruled by it that your days are filled with bitterness because of its absence and your nights are filled with manipulative attempts to get it.

A humbling example from my own life took place on a Wednesday night. I was driving home particularly exhausted. I love to cook and find it relaxing, so I stopped and bought the ingredients for a traditional Cuban meal. I could hear the meat searing in the pan, and I could smell that wonderful combination of tomato, garlic, cumin, and lemon. I left the grocery store tired but happy, thinking about how much my wife would appreciate the meal, since she was born and raised in Cuba. I was thinking about how our children love black beans and rice, and how they would appreciate me as well ("We are so blessed! We have a dad who cooks!"). The vision of a happy family and a relaxed dad made me smile as I drove into the garage.

But I was not even out of the car when my daughter greeted me and said she needed a ride downtown (nearly an hour round trip) right away. I couldn't believe it! I could already feel my emotional temperature rising. I was not yelling, but I drove her downtown in silent irritation. On the way back I gave myself the "this always happens to me" speech. A few blocks from home, Luella called on my cell phone to tell me that she had to see someone on her way home from work. She suggested that I not wait for her for supper. She also asked me to run to the store because Darnay, our high school son, didn't have a thing for his lunch the next day. With my wonderful Cuban meal decaying in the trunk, I drove past our house to another grocery store. This time I was not a happy man! I flung the lunch items in the basket and when I got to the checkout line, I was quite irritated at the elderly lady in front of me who couldn't find a pen to write her check.

I finally arrived home an hour and a half later to find Darnay standing in the door with a paper in his hands. On the paper were the exact specifications for a scientific calculator he needed for math the next day. Before he could get another word out of his mouth, I exploded. "What am I, the delivery boy for the world? Do you have a clue what my day has been like? Whatever happened to really learning math, instead of learning how to use a calculator that does it for you? Is this what I am paying for at that school of yours?" I walked to the car, and he followed—at a great distance behind me.

Waiting outside the store, I examined my shattered hopes, wishing someone would pay a little attention to me, and angry with the people who had gotten in my way. I suggested we pick up a couple pizzas for supper, drove home in silence, stored the ingredients for my Cuban meal, and went into the living room to sulk.

Don't miss the point of this story. *My anger was not caused by the people and situations I encountered.* My anger was caused by completely legitimate desires that came, wrongly, to rule me. By the time I finished shopping for the Cuban meal, I was holding the desire for a relaxing evening with a closed fist. But God had another plan. He had arranged to give me an evening where I could serve him by serving my family. He gave me the blessing of giving, the joy of laying down my life for others. Yet I did not see it because I was ruled by my own desires. Beneath my war with people, the war for my heart was raging.

SPIRITUAL ADULTERY AND ANGER WITH PEOPLE

James calls the people he is addressing "adulterous" (James 4:4). Is he changing the subject? No, what he is talking about *is* spiritual adultery. If adultery is the sin of giving someone the love I have promised another, then I am a spiritual adulterer whenever I give the rule of my heart to someone or something other than God. Verse 4 gives us the core principle of this passage: *Human conflict is rooted in spiritual adultery.* My problem is not sinful people and difficult situations. My problem is that I give the love that belongs to God to someone or something else.

It is my own spiritual adultery that causes me to be angry with you. You stand in the way of what I crave, so I lash out against you. This battle goes on in us all the time. We all tend to worship and serve created things rather than the Creator (see Rom. 1:25). If you want to understand what causes you to be angry, you must look at your own heart.

James points out that what is true of our horizontal relationships is also true of our relationship with God. If my heart is ruled by the desire for a certain thing, it will affect my relationship with God in two principal ways. First, it will shape my attitude when I pray. Rather than prayer being a worshipful act of submission to God, I will pray self-centered and demanding prayers—if I pray at all. I may be so intent on getting what I want that I forget God. Not only will my attitude in prayer be affected, but the kind of god I want will change as well. Let me explain.

If a certain set of desires rules my heart, I will not want God to be a wise, loving, sovereign Father who gives me what he knows is best. Instead, I will want a divine waiter who delivers what I have set my heart on. Imagine going to a restaurant and ordering a sixteen-ounce, medium-rare prime rib with a huge baked potato slathered in butter and sour cream. The waiter takes down your order and disappears into the kitchen, only to emerge twenty minutes later with a dry salad. You say to the waiter, "This is not what I ordered!" and he responds, "Well, I took down your order, but I began thinking about your age and your health, and I decided that what you ordered was the worst thing you could possibly have. So I had the chef prepare this salad." Would you thank the waiter and dive into your lettuce? Of course not, because the desire for steak is ruling your heart.

When a certain set of desires rules our hearts, we reduce prayer to the menu of human desire. Worse, we shrink God from his position of all-wise, all-loving, all-powerful Father to a divine waiter we expect to deliver everything we ask. But God will not shrink to this size. He will only be our Father and King, who "satisfies your desires with good things so that your youth is renewed like the eagle's" (Ps. 103:5). He knows what is best, and he will not let there be peace until he alone controls our hearts. He is a Warrior King, who will not rest when we are captive to other kings. He fights *for* us, for the thoughts and desires of our hearts.

A JEALOUS GRACE

Does the thought of this constant inner war discourage you? Then you need to hear the encouragement James includes in this passage.

We are not battling by ourselves—God battles for us! James is saying, "Don't you know that the Spirit who lives inside you envies intensely? In the middle of the battle you can't forget that God is a jealous God. He loves you too much to make room for other lovers. He will oppose your proud and self-absorbed living, not because he is against you, but because he loves you." Praise God that he will settle for nothing short of the final victory in our hearts. Our hope to be who we were meant to be is directly tied to his jealous desire for our hearts.

We should be encouraged by God's jealousy. Wives, how would you react if your husband plopped down on the couch, pulled you close and said, "Dear, of all the women I love, tonight I think I love you the most"? You would *not* be encouraged. You would be outraged! True love is always jealous.

James says more. This jealous God is a giver of grace, the most powerful weapon in the war for the heart. God's grace gives us power to say no to powerful desires. It enables us to turn from the creation toward the Creator. It makes us willing to forsake our kingdoms for his. God's grace forgives, but it also constrains and draws and wins. It is jealous, God-focused grace, fitted for the moments we are tempted to follow our desires. This is the grace Paul talked about when he wrote to Titus:

> For the grace of God that brings salvation has appeared to all men. It teaches us to say "No" to ungodliness and worldly passions, and to live self-controlled, upright and godly lives in this present age, while we wait for the blessed hope—the glorious appearing of our great God and Savior, Jesus Christ, who gave himself for us to redeem us from all wickedness and to purify for himself a people that are his very own, eager to do what is good.
>
> These, then, are the things you should teach.
>
> (Titus 2:11–15)

Paul is saying, "Titus, keep reminding people what the great story of redemption is all about. It is not simply about God helping flawed people to be a little better. It is not simply about his willingness, through the sacrifice of Christ, to forgive sinful people. The goal of God's grace is his own glory, as he calls out and purifies a people that belong to him alone. When he owns their hearts unchallenged, these people will be eager to do what is good in his eyes." Paul wants Titus to teach the theology of jealous grace, so that people place their personal stories in the larger story of God's kingdom, for his glory.

Jealous grace doesn't simply focus on the forgiveness of the past and the hope of eternity. It gives us immediate hope for the struggles at the end of the day, after years of marriage, in the life of a church, or in the journey of a family. It reminds us that we can win the one war that *must* be won, the war for the heart. His jealousy for our hearts is not a threat, but our one true hope. Our God is eternally unwilling to share our hearts. Thank him for that!

THE CAPTURE OF THE HEART

If you have understood everything up to this point, perhaps you wonder how our hearts get captured by our desires. How do we wander away from serving the Lord to serving other things? How do desires that were okay in themselves become our functional masters? These questions lead us to examine the stages of the war for the heart.

The objects of most of our desires are not evil. The problem is the way they tend to *grow*, and the control they come to exercise over our hearts. Desires are a part of human existence, but they must be held with an open hand. All human desire must be held in submission to a greater purpose, the desires of God for his kingdom. This is what Christ expressed in the Garden of Gethsemane when he cried, "Not my will, but yours be done" (Luke 22:42).

When I was engaged to Luella, I prayed every morning with my hands open and outstretched before the Lord. My posture was a metaphor. I was holding Luella with open hands. I was not ashamed that I wanted her as my wife, but I was concerned that my desire for her would overwhelm my desire for the Lord and his will. So each morning, with open hands, I would say, "Lord, I love Luella. I think you have brought her into my life. My prayer is that you would give us a life together, but today I say again, 'Not my will but yours.' "

The problem with desire is that in sinners it very quickly morphs into *demand* ("I must"). Demand is the closing of my fists over a desire. Even though I may be unaware that I have done it, I have left my proper position of submission to God. I have decided that I must have what I have set my heart on and nothing can stand in the way. I am no longer comforted by God's desire for me; I am threatened by it, because God's will potentially stands in the way of my demand. I can no longer conceive of a good life (moment, day, week, situation, location, relationship) without this thing. The morphing of my desire changes my relationship to others. Now I enter the room loaded with a silent demand: *You must help me get what I want.* If you are an obstacle, I will immediately be angry and impatient with you. But you don't know the rules of the game. I haven't announced my demand to you because I am unaware that my heart is increasingly controlled by it.

The expansion of desire doesn't end there. Demand quickly morphs into *need* ("I will"). I now view the thing I want as essential to life. This is a devastating step in the eventual slavery of desire. To give a rather silly example, cake is nice after a meal, but it is not essential. Respiration, on the other hand, is a basic human need. Without oxygenated blood, I will die. To "christen" desire as need is equivalent to viewing cake as I do respiration. Cake no longer has a simple "nice if you can get it" quality. Now I must have it at the end of every meal. If I do not get it, I will be angry.

If you are a parent, you know how quickly and frequently desire morphs into need. I have never had a child come to me and say, "Dad, I sort of desire a new pair of shoes, but I am holding this desire with an open hand. You know what is best for me and what you can afford." No, my children come to me and say, "Dad, I neeeeeeeeed a pair of shoes, really bad!" I look down at the ends of their legs and see leather-encased feet. Their shoes aren't lost or falling apart. The sight of a cool pair of shoes had simply sparked desire, and in an instant the shoes were viewed as something they could not live without.

How often do we live with a sense of need for things we do not need at all? How does this change the way we view ourselves, our lives, others, and God? How much envy, discouragement, bitterness, and doubt of God comes from being convinced that we are being denied the things we need to live life as it was meant to be lived? This silent (and often unseen) war for the heart is taking place all the time.

Perhaps no word is used more poorly and improperly than the word *need*. As James reminds us, it quickly surfaces in our relationships. When my heart is ruled by the desire for a certain thing, it cannot help but affect my relationship to you. Need inevitably produces *expectation* ("You should"). If I am convinced I need something and you have said that you love me, it seems right to expect that you will help me get it. The dynamic of (improper) need-driven expectation is the source of untold conflict in relationships.

Eventually I will come to accept the logic of my neediness. I will find it painful to live without the thing I desire. I will think it is appropriate to do everything in my power to get it. It becomes my right. This powerful expectation will not only shape my relationships with people, but with God as well. This is an "I love you and I have a wonderful plan for your life" view of relationships. My plan for our relationship is that it would meet my needs.

But it doesn't stop there. You do not know that I have christened these desires as needs, and you do not meet my expectations. Expectation very quickly leads to *disappointment* ("You didn't!"). The direct relationship between expectation and disappointment is clear to anyone who has looked at resort brochures before a family vacation. When our children were young, we decided to go to Disney World. We sat with them and pored over the gloriously multi-colored brochures that only Disney can produce. We approached the park with thoughts of amusement park bliss. No one told us that we would actually experience a fifty-five-minute wait to get into rides that lasted thirty-three seconds, while we endured a temperature of ninety-seven degrees accompanied by 100 percent humidity! There is a direct relationship between expectation and disappointment, and much of our disappointment in relationships is not because people have actually wronged us, but because they have failed to meet our expectations.

Disappointment then leads to some form of *punishment* ("Because you didn't, I will . . ."). We are hurt and angry because people who say they love us seem insensitive to our needs. So we strike back in a variety of ways to punish them for their wrongs against us. We include everything from the silent treatment (a form of bloodless murder where I don't kill you but act as if you do not exist) to horrific acts of violence and abuse. I am angry because you have broken the laws of *my* kingdom. God's kingdom has been supplanted. I am no longer motivated by a love for God and people so that I use the things in my life to express that love. Instead I love things, and use people—and even the Lord—to get them. My heart has been captured. I am in active service of the creation, and the result can only be chaos and conflict in my relationships.

THE HUMBLE CLEANSING OF THE HEART

What is James's solution? The turnaround in this passage is very interesting. You would think that his first counsel would be to go the people we have sinned against and confess it. But James's turnaround is first *vertical* (with respect to God) and then *horizontal* (with respect to people). James's first call is for us to "humble ourselves before God." This is a direct plea to deal with the idolatry (spiritual adultery) of our hearts. If human conflict is rooted in spiritual adultery, change must begin by bowing before God in humble repentance for the idols that have replaced him in our hearts.

James also calls us to "cleanse our hearts" (4:8). Reconciliation and restoration in our relationships begin with the purification of the heart. The unrighteous anger we experienced and the conflict that took place are direct results of our heart idolatry. The biblical logic is clear. You can't keep the second Great Commandment unless you are first keeping the first. Only in bowing before God and submitting to his desires can we really turn to one another in peace and love. Any agenda for change that forgets this vertical causality will prove temporary and cosmetic. But grace and blessing are promised to those who humble themselves before him. This is God's way of change. All of our relationships have a worship base, driven by active worship and service of the Creator or the creation. Problems in relationships are rooted in problems of worship, so James's advice is clear: "Start with God."

James provides a helpful window into the struggles of the heart. Galatians 5:13–26 literally takes us onto the scene and shows us how the struggle takes place.

> You, my brothers, were called to be free. But do not use your freedom to indulge the sinful nature; rather, serve one another in love. The entire law is summed up in a single command: "Love your neighbor as yourself." If you keep on biting and devouring each other, watch out or you will be destroyed by each other.
>
> So I say, live by the Spirit, and you will not gratify the desires of the sinful nature. For the sinful nature desires what is contrary to the Spirit, and the Spirit what is contrary to the sinful nature. They are in conflict with each other, so that you do not do what you want. But if you are led by the Spirit, you are not under law.
>
> The acts of the sinful nature are obvious: sexual immorality, impurity and debauchery; idolatry and witchcraft; hatred, discord, jealousy, fits of rage, selfish ambition, dissensions, factions and envy; drunkenness, orgies, and the like. I warn you, as I did before, that those who live like this will not inherit the kingdom of God.
>
> But the fruit of the Spirit is love, joy, peace, patience, kindness, goodness, faithfulness, gentleness and self-control. Against such things there is no law. Those who belong to Christ Jesus have crucified the sinful nature with its passions and desires. Since we live by the Spirit, let us keep in step with the Spirit. Let us not become conceited, provoking and envying each other.

POWERFUL PASSIONS AND POWERFUL DESIRES

This passage adds a dimension to our understanding of the struggles of the heart. Like James, Paul's logic is simple. He reduces our living to two foundational lifestyles. Our lives are either shaped by indulging the sinful nature or by self-sacrificing love. Loving your neighbor as yourself summarizes God's will for us. This is true because only those who love God first will love their neighbors as themselves. In verse 15 Paul follows his command with a stern warning that what we do and say *does* make a difference. Your words and actions can lead a person into temptation. You can crush a person's hope. You can do and say things that weaken someone's faith. If God intends us to be instruments of change, then we are people of influence, for good or for evil.

Take note especially of the phrase, "indulge the sinful nature [flesh]" (v. 16). This little phrase dynamically captures the war that rages within. The rest of the passage exposes its true nature (see vv. 16–18). Paul is addressing the same war that James does, the war between the flesh and the Spirit for control of the heart.

What does it mean to "gratify the desires of the sinful nature"? When you indulge something, you feed it. You go where it takes you. What does this look like in daily life? Verse 24 says, "Those who belong to Christ Jesus have crucified the sinful nature with its passions and desires." The inclusion of the words "passions and desires" is very helpful. When you are in a situation with someone, you will be greeted with motivating emotions (passions) and desires. You and I experience the powerful draw of our emotions and desires every day.

Let me give you a common example of this phenomenon, since we spend most of our time in insignificant moments that teach us things about the more significant struggles of life.

I am not known to my family as a handyman. In fact, I have an extensively documented reputation as a home-repair incompetent! Early in my marriage our kitchen sink was clogged, so I removed that U-shaped pipe that is under every sink in the universe. As I did, I discovered it was full of water. As I lay under the sink, holding the pipe,

I got a brilliant idea. *I have a sink above me. I'll reach up and pour it in there.* So I reached up and dumped out the pipe, only to have the water come splashing down on my face, since the pipe meant to catch that water was in my hand! As I lay there with head drenched, I could hear my wife laughing hysterically.

With that level of ability, it should come as no surprise that I dread home repairs. But on one occasion, the closing mechanism on our front storm door was not operating properly. We were living in an old house where simple jobs often proved to be anything but. Still, the door could not be ignored and I promised Luella that I would fix it.

Early Saturday morning, with tools in hand and delusions of expertise, I approached that broken door. What should have taken me a few minutes occupied my entire day, but I did it. I completed the task and the door was operating perfectly! I walked through the rest of the day with a spirit of self-satisfied celebration. On Monday, Luella had forgotten that the door was fixed, and one of our children had propped the door open. When she saw the door hanging open, she yanked it shut as she had done every day for months. With one swift yank, she re-broke the thing I had spent all Saturday repairing.

As I drove home, I had been looking forward to saying to Luella, "Isn't it nice not to come home to that door flapping in the wind?" But when I hopped on the porch, I saw the door, broken again, swinging back and forth as always. In an instant my self-satisfaction became intense anger. I could not believe it! After all my hard work! I wanted to find the perpetrator, stick my tools in his hands, and say, "I don't care if it takes you a millennium. You will stay on this porch until this door is in perfect working order!"

Galatians 5 is about what we do next. In the face of powerful emotions and desires, what will we do? As sons and daughters of the King, will we live in self-imposed bondage to our emotions? Will we submit to the mastery of our sinful desires? Or will we grab hold of the promises of the gospel and turn in a completely different direction?

That Monday evening on the porch, a war was raging. Would my heart be ruled by the Lord and the servant love to which he has called me, or would it be ruled by the powerfully motivating passions and desires of my flesh? By God's grace, I had just come from teaching this material. I was acutely aware of the temptation to storm into the house with guns blazing. I am so thankful for the privilege of working with this material day in and day out! I stood on that porch, looked at that door, and prayed that, as I entered the house, I would not forget who I am in Christ.

Not only does this passage capture the nature of the struggle for the heart, it takes the gospel out of the realm of abstract theology to where we live every day. The fact is that although I experience powerful emotions and desires, I *can* say "no" and go in another direction because of the resources that are mine in Christ. I am indwelt by the Warrior Spirit (vv. 16–18) who battles with my flesh. He lives with power and glory in my heart. I can choose to go where he leads rather than where the passions and desires of the flesh would lead me. I have also been crucified with Christ (v. 24). When Christ died, I died. When Christ rose, I rose to a new life. Because I am united with Christ in his death and resurrection, the mastery of sin over me has been broken. I no longer have to submit the members of my body to its rule. In the face of difficulty, I can do and say what is right.

TWO REALITIES

Galatians 5 calls us to hold onto two realities. The first is the everyday reality of the war for the heart, the war between God's "within you" kingdom and the kingdom of creation. I must face the reality of indwelling sin and my propensity to run after god-replacements. I am called to face my duplicity and my idolatry, and the fact that this war is the most significant inner dynamic of human experience. It rages in every moment of suffering and blessing. What rules my heart will shape the way I deal with life's saddest and sweetest moments. Though I am powerfully influenced by my experiences and my biology, what rules my heart will determine how I respond to life.

The second reality must be held tightly at the same time. It is the reality of my identity as a child of God and the resources that are therefore mine in Christ. The apostle Paul tends to reduce these resources to two foundational themes. The first is the reality of the person and work of the *indwelling Holy Spirit*. Our condition is so desperate it was not enough for God to forgive us. He had to unzip us and get inside us, or we would not be able to do what he has called us to do. We no longer live under the control of the flesh, but by the power of the Spirit, who daily battles the flesh on our behalf.

The second theme is the reality of our *union with Christ*. On the cross, Christ did not purchase potential save-ability. No, he took our names to the cross! His death and resurrection is efficacious; that is, it will accomplish his purposes in the lives of each of his children. Our union with him in his death and resurrection means that we do not have to obey sinful desires any longer. We can say no and go in another direction.

There is a war going on beneath the human skirmishes of everyday life. On one side is a jealous God, the giver of a jealous grace. He will not rest until our hearts are completely his. He will not deny the covenant he has made. On the other side is a devious enemy, who allures us with the attractions of the creation. He knows our weaknesses all too well. He knows that we are prone to wander, prone to replace God. He whispers in our ears the lie of lies, that life can be found apart from God. When we begin to believe that created things give life, he's got us. We will seek and serve the creation, often unaware of our idolatry. We will blame people and situations for the resulting chaos and conflict, when they are really the fruit of our idolatry.

We must humbly admit we are sinners while we lay hold of the hope of our union with Christ. We don't simply suffer; we suffer as sinners with a deep propensity to run after god-replacements. And, as believers, we don't just suffer as sinners, but as those who have been united with Christ and therefore no longer live under the mastery of sin. We bring these two realities to times of blessing as well. Holding onto both truths is the only way to do battle with our own hearts, and the only way to be part of what God is doing in our lives and others'.

This is a perspective on life that only those who believe God's Word will ever embrace. It is the heart of biblical personal ministry. It is more than a topical list of problem-solving principles, more than a collection of morals on how to live life, more than an empathetic relationship or a dynamic therapeutic encounter. Biblical personal ministry is rooted in the story of a war and a Savior King. As we place our stories within this great story of the compassion and love of Christ, we will understand who we are and live as we were meant to live.

6 | FOLLOWING THE WONDERFUL COUNSELOR

I was a young pastor and I loved to preach. I worked hard on my sermons and planned my preaching series a year at a time. I prepared weeks in advance for every message and developed creative outlines to support my key points. I carried my sermon files around with me so that I could add or delete illustrations when inspiration struck. I would preach each sermon to myself until it was almost completely memorized so that I would only need a brief outline in the pulpit. I tried to preach with a passion that matched the content of my message. I was sure that our congregation was being well fed on the spiritual food I was serving them each week.

One day a member of the congregation asked to meet with me privately. I was so excited! I was convinced that my preaching had convicted "Pete" to talk about things God had exposed in his heart. But when we sat down, Pete said, "I know you probably think I am here to talk about me, but I'm here to talk about your preaching. You're killing us. At first I thought it was just me, but I know that many others feel the same way. You're driving us crazy, so I am here to give it to you straight." I asked, "Is it the content or the delivery that upsets you?" He said, "It's the whole package, but I have a solution." He handed me a set of tapes by a well-known preacher. "Just listen to these and do what he does until you understand how to preach a decent sermon." I went home devastated.

I knew that the conversation had affected me, but I didn't realize how much until I got up to preach the next Sunday. Everyone looked normal to me except Pete. His head seemed like the size of a blimp!

Everywhere I looked, I seemed to see his disapproving face. I stumbled and stammered my way through the sermon, relieved when it was finally over.

The next Sunday was the same. I felt as if only Pete and I were in the room. By the third week, I was determined to get Pete to approve of my preaching. Although I didn't fully realize it, I tried to craft sermons to his liking. But they were not me and they did not fly.

This went on for about two months until, finally, the oldest lady in our congregation approached me after the service. She said she wanted to talk to me about my preaching. *Oh no, not you too!* I thought. She pointed her finger at me and said, "Paul, I don't know what has happened to you or who has gotten to you, but you have lost your freedom in preaching. You may be preaching out of fear or the need to please, but something is wrong. You need to get up tomorrow and prepare what God has given you to preach. Then preach it with courage or we're all in trouble!" With that, she walked out.

I stood there, knowing that she was exactly right. I had quit serving God and had begun preaching to please Pete. I had been evaluating the success of each effort by the reaction of one man and I was becoming enslaved and embittered.

SO YOU WANT TO BE AN INSTRUMENT OF CHANGE?

We all have Petes in our lives, people who attack the borders of our comfortable lives. We have all had attempts at ministry blow up in our faces. We have all been torn between God's calling and the fear of man, between compassion and anger, between love and bitterness. Given the messiness of sinners helping sinners, we need a model. And as God's people, we do not have to stumble around. We have the example of the Wonderful Counselor. This chapter will consider his example and its implications for us as we seek to be part of his work.

Being an instrument of heart change means following Christ's example and focusing on the heart—starting with your own. Pete's attacks and criticisms had filled me with the fear of man and caused me to forget my primary allegiance to God. These heart issues subverted my knowledge and skill, rendering them ineffective. This was a vivid demonstration of the way my heart shapes my response to the ministry opportunities God sends me. Paul said it to Timothy this way: "Watch your life and doctrine closely. Persevere in them, because if you do, you will save both yourself and your hearers" (1Tim. 4:16).

Starting with your heart means understanding and submitting to God's calling, which will shape your life and relationships. God has called us to nothing less than *incarnating Christ* to others. I am to be rooted in the Word, and zealous to bring the living Word—Christ— to lost, blind, and struggling people. You and I are called to put flesh and blood on who Christ is and what he came to do.

TO UNDERSTAND YOUR CALLING, YOU NEED TO UNDERSTAND THE INCARNATION

Most of us think of the incarnation as an *event*—that moment when Christ came to earth, took on human flesh, and lived as a man. Yet, as central as the incarnation is to everything we believe, I don't think we fully understand it. We do not grasp that the *event* of the incarnation is also an *agenda* and a *calling*. Understanding the elements of agenda and calling will help us understand the nature of personal ministry and the importance of starting with our own hearts.

No one captures better than John the amazing historical moment when Christ came as a baby to this fallen world. Two of John's summary statements are very helpful. "The Word became flesh and made his dwelling among us. We have seen his glory, the glory of the One and Only, who came from the Father, full of grace and truth. . . . No one has ever seen God, but God the One and Only, who is at the Father's side, has made him known" (John 1:14, 18).

John's summary includes an observation with powerful implications. The power of the incarnation is that it makes the presence and glory of God visible. By taking on flesh and blood, Christ made known the unseen God. Why does the Light need to shine on earth?

Because people are groping around in darkness. Why does God need to be revealed? Because people do not see him. In coming to earth, Christ died for his own, but he also gave sight to eyes that had been blind for far too long.

The incarnation addresses a problem that is so comprehensive, so deep, so essentially human that it is almost impossible for us to recognize. The problem is that *we can't see God*. Part of the problem is that God is a Spirit, so we can't physically see him. Another part of the problem is that our sin makes us morally unfit to look on God. But in our spiritual blindness as sinners, we also do not see God in the sense that we do not recognize the glory of his grace and power operating in, around, and through us all the time.

Yet the Light bursts into our darkness. God addresses our blindness by sending his one and only Son to earth. In seeing him, you see the Father. If you know him, you know the Father. The Old Testament records times when God made himself visible to human eyes, but Christ's appearance is the culminating event.

The bottom line is this: The problem is not that God is not here or that he is inactive; the problem is that we don't see him. Our perspective on life is often tragically godless. We miss the one thing worth seeing, the glory of the ever-present God. When this happens, our lives are not built on the foundation of God's glory, which was intended to give our lives a starting point and a destination, a reason to get up and the strength to go on. Every aspect of my existence was meant to be filled with the glory of God. Everything I think, every decision I make, every word I speak was meant to be shaped by a humble acknowledgement of his claim on my life. I was created to live for his glory.

As we've seen, every human life pursues some kind of glory. If it is not the glory of God, it will be some kind of earthbound pseudo-glory. It may be money and possessions or acceptance and respect. It could be achievement and success or intellectual prowess and philosophical acumen. Perhaps it is the power to control people, the affection of a certain person, or a certain standard of living. At the root of many difficulties and disasters is the pursuit of the wrong glory.

The incarnation gets right to the heart of this struggle because it confronts people with the one thing that can make a lasting difference, the glory of God. The revelation of God in his awesome glory is the only thing that exposes the utter emptiness of all the other glories we crave. If you understand the incarnation this way, you have already learned much about your calling. Personal ministry is not just about confronting people with principles, theology, or solutions. It confronts people with the God who is active and glorious in his grace and truth, and who has a rightful claim to our lives. Only as our hearts are transformed by this glory will the principles of Scripture make any sense to us.

GRACE AND TRUTH

John doesn't simply explain the goal of the incarnation, but its character as well. He says that the glory revealed on earth was full of "grace and truth." Jesus incarnated the ultimate marriage of grace and truth. In his life, death, and resurrection, we come to understand the grace of God. God sends his own Son, as the second Adam, to face the full range of temptations in a fallen world. He does so to keep the Law on our behalf, thereby satisfying God's requirement for life. He willingly offers up himself as the perfect sacrificial Lamb, so that the penalty of sin is fully paid. He rises from the tomb, purchasing new life for all who trust in him.

Since the central character of the great story of Scripture is Christ, a central theme of the story is grace. It must be a central theme of our personal ministry, biblical counseling, and discipleship as well. We point people to a God who not only sets the goal for their lives, but who enables them to do what they have never done before. His grace results in reconciliation, restoration, and peace. The impossibility of sinners becoming godly becomes possible through his grace.

By his grace parents can pursue rebellious teenagers with patient, persevering love. By his grace a wife can put away bitter memories and fully forgive her husband. By his grace people can exit the pris-

ons of depression, anxiety, and compulsion to live in hope-filled freedom. By his grace those bound by lust, greed, fear, or vengeance can
live in the purity and courage of faith.

Biblical personal ministry must not be reduced to a set of principles to live by. Its central focus is the Redeemer who rescues people
from the power of sin and progressively eradicates its presence from
their lives. We are simply agents of this grace. Our goal is to help people understand it and follow where it leads while they wait for their
Redeemer's return.

The glory revealed in Christ's incarnation was full of truth as
well. This is the second great theme of the story of Scripture. Sin
not only makes us helpless rebels and idolaters, it also reduces us to
fools. We tend to love lies, to be self-deluded, to be the strongest believers of our own empty arguments. We are susceptible to the Enemy's tricks and temptations. We live for what is already in a state of
decay and ignore what will remain forever. We tend to hide, ignore,
or be blind to our own sin, while we are obsessively focused on the
sins of others. To paraphrase Proverbs 14:12, the way that seems
right to us is the way of death. If grace addresses the moral results of
the Fall (our rebellion and inability) then truth addresses the *noetic*
effects of the Fall, sin's impact on how we think about life and interpret it.

In Christ, the truth of God takes on flesh. Jesus is the ultimate ex-
position of how God intends people to think and live. In his life and
teaching, he confronts our foolishness with true wisdom. He calls us
to a way of life that is the opposite of where our sinful instincts lead
us. Who would naturally choose to live for what cannot be seen, to do
good to someone who has mistreated you, or to believe that there is
greater blessing in giving than receiving? The fact that these things
seem radical and paradoxical demonstrates how far we have drifted
from the truth. Personal ministry must offer people truth that destroys
their old ways of thinking about themselves, relationships, circumstances, suffering, and God. The foolish things people do are rooted
in a worldview riddled with foolishness. Our problem is not just
wrong behavior and its results, but the thoughts that produced it.

We offer people a whole new way of making sense out of life—a worldview in which God is central, where unseen things are of the highest value, and where eternity is what makes sense of the present moment. In confronting people with truth, we confront them with Christ. This is quite radical, for it says that truth, in its most basic form, is not a system, a theology, or a philosophy. It is a *person* whose name is Jesus. Living a godly life means trusting him, following him, and living like him. Personal ministry weaves the threads of grace and truth through every part of a person's life. In that it is truly incarnational, because grace and truth will always lead people to Christ.

A NEW AGENDA

The incarnation is not just an event; it also establishes an *agenda*, a set of plans to accomplish a goal. God's agenda is for the church to be an incarnational community on earth, so that our very presence would reveal his grace and truth-laden glory.

Just before his arrest, Christ prayed for his disciples and those who would believe as a result of their ministry (all of us). In the middle of the prayer, Jesus says,

> My prayer is not for them alone. I pray also for those who will believe in me through their message, that all of them may be one, Father, just as you are in me and I am in you. May they also be in us so that the world may believe that you have sent me. I have given them the glory that you gave me, that they may be one as we are one: I in them and you in me. May they be brought to complete unity to let the world know that you sent me and have loved them even as you have loved me.
> (John 17:20–23)

This is a remarkable prayer for a unity comparable only to the Trinity. Jesus prays that his followers would be characterized by such deep love that the community of faith would be as unified as he is with the Father. His prayer also reveals the purpose of this unity. Relationships within the community of faith are meant to reveal the person and work of Christ to a watching world. This unity has a greater goal than enjoyable friendships. The goal is for the world to see and know Christ.

Christ sets the bar so high! We are called to achieve a quality of unity that can only be compared to his relationship with the Father. Before you get discouraged, think of Christ and his disciples. On one side of the room is Matthew, the tax collector, a Jew who collected Roman taxes from his own people. Tax collectors were despised as turncoats and Roman sympathizers.

Across the room sat Simon the Zealot. The Zealots were the conservative extremists of their day, much like the radical militia and terrorists of our world. The Zealots were convinced that the Roman government would only be overthrown by violence, and they were ready to provide it. There was no one a Zealot hated more than a tax collector.

Christ's purpose for Matthew and Simon was that their relationship display such an amazing unity and love that the surrounding world would take notice—and in so doing, see Christ. Does this seem completely unrealistic? Isn't it enough that Simon and Matthew sit in the same room without coming to blows? For Christ this is not enough. Christ's prayer tells us that he has provided what is necessary for his people to be truly one. In his prayer he makes a statement of redemptive fact. He says, "Father, I have given them the glory that you gave me, that they may be one as we are one" (v. 22). Do you hear the echo of John 1 in these words? Jesus is saying, "Father, do you remember the glory I revealed on earth as I took on flesh and blood? I have placed that same glory on your children so that they can continue to reveal that glory on earth."

God's agenda is glory received and glory given so that glory would continue to be incarnated on earth. Maybe the best way to think of the incarnation is as an ongoing event: God made known, no longer in the physical presence of Christ, but in the glory of his work through his people as we live incarnationally.

Incarnation helps us understand the purpose and character of personal ministry. People are changed by seeing Christ in new ways, ways that reveal the bankruptcy of their own agendas and the emptiness of the glories they seek. Their most important encounter is not with the counselor, but with Christ. We are there to set up that encounter. As they see him and the emptiness of their own ways, they begin to hope that things can be different. God has placed his glory on us so that our lives and ministry would reveal him on earth. In this way, incarnation for us is a life agenda.

A FOCUSED CALLING

The incarnation is also a *call*. Paul defines this call for us in 2 Corinthians 5:14–6:2.

> For Christ's love compels us, because we are convinced that one died for all, and therefore all died. And he died for all, that those who live should no longer live for themselves but for him who died for them and was raised again.
>
> So from now on we regard no one from a worldly point of view. Though we once regarded Christ in this way, we do so no longer. Therefore, if anyone is in Christ, he is a new creation; the old has gone, the new has come! All this is from God, who reconciled us to himself through Christ and gave us the ministry of reconciliation: that God was reconciling the world to himself in Christ, not counting men's sins against them. And he has committed to us the message of reconciliation. We are therefore Christ's ambassadors, as though God were making his appeal through us. We implore you on Christ's behalf: Be reconciled to God. God made him who had no sin to be sin for us, so that in him we might become the righteousness of God.
>
> As God's fellow workers we urge you not to receive God's grace in vain. For he says,

"In the time of my favor I heard you,
and in the day of salvation I helped you."

I tell you, now is the time of God's favor, now is the day of salvation.

What should we do to be part of God's work in the lives of others? Paul uses the word *ambassadors* to define what it means to live incarnationally.

The job of an ambassador is to represent someone or something. Everything he does and says must intentionally represent a leader who is not physically present. His calling is not limited to forty hours a week, to certain state events, or to times of international crisis. He is always the king's representative. He stands in the place of the king (or the government of his country) wherever he is, whatever he is doing. His relationships are not primarily driven by his own happiness. He decides to go places and do things because they will help him to faithfully represent the king. Thus the work of an ambassador is incarnational. His actions, character, and words embody the king who is not present.

Paul says that God has called us all to function as his ambassadors. Our lives do not belong to us for our own fulfillment. The primary issue is, "How can I best represent the King in this place, with this particular person?" This is not a part-time calling; it is a lifestyle. When an ambassador assumes his responsibilities, his life ceases to be his own. Everything he says and does has import because of the king he represents. Anything less is an affront to the king and a denial of the ambassadorial calling.

What is God calling you to in your marriage? To be an ambassador. What is God calling you to as a parent? To be an ambassador. What is God calling you to regarding your friends and neighbors? To be an ambassador. What is God calling you to at work and in leisure? To be an ambassador. We represent God's purposes to the people he places in our lives. This is much broader than a commitment to formal ministry occupying a portion of our schedule. It acknowledges that our lives belong to the King.

But this is where we get ourselves into trouble. We don't really want to live as ambassadors. We would rather live as mini-kings. We know what we like and the people we want to be with. We know the kind of house we'd like to own and the car we want to drive. Without even recognizing it, we quickly fall into a "my desire, my will, and my way" lifestyle, where the things we say and do are driven by the cravings of our own hearts. If we were honest, we would have to confess that the central prayer of our hearts is "my kingdom come."

Imagine what a marriage becomes when two mini-kings are required to share time and space. Underneath the vows, both persons are driven by their own cravings and expectations. What they really want is for the other to make them happy, and as long as he or she does so, they remain committed to the marriage. Now imagine how these mini-kings approach parenting. What they really long for is pre-sanctified, self-parenting children. They find the daily service and sacrifice of godly parenting to be a huge imposition. This is why Christ said that to be his disciples we must die to ourselves. No one can serve two masters. Ambassadors must die to their own kingship to properly represent the one true King.

It is so easy to slip back into the "my will be done" kingdom. I travel between forty and forty-five weekends a year. I usually fly out on Friday morning and return early Saturday evening. Because of this, I look forward to the weekends when I actually wake up in my own bed. During one of those rare weekends, no one was around on a Saturday afternoon. My mind went to something I am rarely able to do: watch college football. I poured myself a big, cold Diet Coke, collected my favorite munchies, and went downstairs to the family room. I found the remote control and was about to sit down when out of the bathroom came my then sixteen-year-old son—with bright green hair!

He had used a dye on his hair called "Manic Panic," which made his hair look like shredded green plastic wrap. It had the look of one of those cheap, plastic, tabletop Christmas trees. He came out of the bathroom, saw me standing there and said, "Well, what do you think?" What do I think? What do I think!! What I thought was, *Get the ornaments, Christmas tree boy!* In a second, my emotional temperature changed.

My mind was racing as he stood before me with his head cocked. "Well, don't you have anything to say?" he asked. I simply could not stop looking at his hair, and the more I looked, the more personal it felt.

You see, I was home that weekend to speak in a local church. They were concluding a biblical study on the family and they had asked me to come *and bring my whole family*. I was imagining the scene. They would march us down to the first row—Luella, me, our three other children, and Christmas tree boy! *Who's going to listen to anything I say?* I thought. I wanted to say to him, "Don't you have a clue what I do? Do you have no idea whatsoever why I am here this weekend? Do you just sit around and think of ways to drive me crazy?" A huge war was going on in my heart. What I did and said next would be determined by which king I chose to follow.

As it turned out, what my son had done was *not* personal. He had not said to himself, *Dad's home this weekend. I know what I'll do. I'll dye my hair an outrageous green color, hide in the bathroom, and jump out just when he sits down to relax. It'll be great!* It only felt that way because his appearance disrupted my plan. But it was not an accident that we were both in the room. Our meeting had been planned by the King. He wanted me to represent him to my son that afternoon. With a struggle going on within me, I asked my son to sit down, and we talked. As I sought to understand the motivation behind the green head, I soon realized that it was not directed at me, nor was it an act of teenage rebellion. It was just the result of teenage brain cramp! It seemed like the cool thing to do at the time. In fact, he got up the next morning, looked in the mirror, and had an "Oh no, what have I done?" moment. He immediately shaved his head, only to discover that his scalp was green, too!

Why are we so good at turning moments of ministry into moments of anger? Why are we so adept at personalizing what is not personal? Why does it seem that people, things, and situations are in our way? Why do we seldom go through a day without some experience of conflict? The answer to all of these questions is that we think of our lives as our own, and we are more committed to the purposes of our own kingdom than we are to God's. We need to recognize that the people in our way have been sent to us by a wise and sovereign King. He never gets a wrong address and always chooses just the right moment to expose our hearts and realign them to his.

THE WORK OF AN AMBASSADOR

Living a representative lifestyle can be summarized by three points of focus. As an ambassador, I will represent:

1. The *message* of the King. An ambassador is always asking, "What does my Lord want to communicate to this person in this situation? What truths should shape my response? What goals should motivate me?"
2. The *methods* of the King. Here I will ask, "How does the Lord bring change in me and in others? How did he respond to people here on earth? What responses are consistent with the goals and resources of the gospel?"
3. The *character* of the King. Here I ask, "Why does the Lord do what he does? How can I faithfully represent the character that motivates his redemptive work? What motives in my own heart could hinder what the Lord wants to do in this situation?"

How could this tri-fold focus change the way you respond to your friends, your family, or your coworkers? We have been sent by the King. We must turn our backs on the claustrophobic confines of our own mini-kingdoms and open ourselves up to the grandeur of the Kingdom of God and the glory of representing him.

The message, methods, and character of the King permeate the pages of Scripture. As we read the Bible, we hear his message over and over again. (See Matt. 5–7 or Luke 15–18.) We are repeatedly confronted with his methods. (See John 3:1–21; 4:1–26; Luke 9:18–27; 10:25–37.) And Scripture is filled with the beauty of his character. (See Phil. 2:1–12; Eph. 4:29–5:2; 1 Peter 2:23.) Being an ambassador means following the example of the Wonderful Counselor in our words and responses, wherever and with whomever we are.

AN APPEAL FOR THE HEART

Second Corinthians 5 brings our ambassadorial calling into sharper focus. In verse 20 Paul says, "We are therefore Christ's ambassadors, as though God were making his appeal through us." An appeal is an argument or a plea. God is using you to appeal for something in the life of another. Certainly, this has an evangelistic application, yet Paul is writing to Christians and saying, "Be reconciled to God." Something more than evangelism is also in view here.

Look back at verse 15: "And he died for all, that those who live should no longer live for themselves but for him who died for them and was raised again." What is the purpose of the cross? Paul would say that it is not just an eternity in heaven, but also the recapturing of people's hearts to serve God alone. Our sin causes us to be incredibly self-absorbed, reducing us to idolatrous worshipers of self. Christ died to break the back of our self-absorbed idolatry.

The focus of Christ's work is to deliver us from our bondage to ourselves! This is our most subtle, yet most foundational form of idolatry. And when Paul says, "Be reconciled to God," he is echoing James's call to "draw near to God." Why do believers need to be reconciled to God? Because as long as sin indwells us, we will tend to wander away from the worship of the Lord to serve ourselves.

Here, once more, God is intent on owning our hearts unchallenged. He is not content with theological knowledge or participation in church programs. He will settle for nothing less than the core of your being, the real you. His goal is that our lives would be shaped by our worship of him and nothing else. He has sent us as his ambassadors to make his appeal for peoples' hearts.

LOVE, KNOW, SPEAK, DO

How to live as an ambassador is the focus of the rest of this book. We will examine four ways to function as God's instruments of change in another person's life.

Suppose God opens your eyes to a harvest of bad fruit in a friend's life. Perhaps it is a conflict in her marriage, a broken relationship, fears that are dominating her life, or a paralyzing discouragement. This struggling person reveals these things and asks for your help. Whatever the circumstances, your goal should be that God would use you to produce a harvest of good fruit in your friend, even though she may remain in the exact same situation with the exact same people.

However, one of the things you will quickly discover is that when most people seek change, they seldom have the heart in view. They want change in their circumstances, change in the other person, or change in their emotions. They think that if "things" would change, they would be better off. But when the focus is put only on the outward circumstances, the solutions are seldom more than temporary and superficial. Certainly, it is true that elements in a situation often need to change, but you cannot stop there. Your goal must be to lead your friend to a deeper, fuller view of change. Your goal is to help her to examine her heart and to see the importance of change at that level.

So, as you seek to help your friend, there are two things to hold onto. First, whatever you do must have the goal of heart change. Second, whatever you do must follow the example of the Wonderful Counselor. I want to introduce a model of personal ministry that takes both things seriously. It gets its shape from the way Christ brings about change in our lives, and it gets its direction from the biblical call to heart change. Four words represent four aspects of a personal ministry relationship, four ways to serve as an ambassador in someone's life. The words are **Love, Know, Speak** and **Do**. (See Figure 6.1.)

These words do not represent a four-step process. They are not phases of a personal ministry relationship, as if you start at the first (**Love**) and push people through until the last (**Do**). They are simply four important elements of biblical ministry. Although there is some logic to the order, you will be doing all of these things simultaneously as you seek to be the Lord's ambassador. Let's look at each element separately.

Fig. 6.1

Serving as an Instrument of Change.

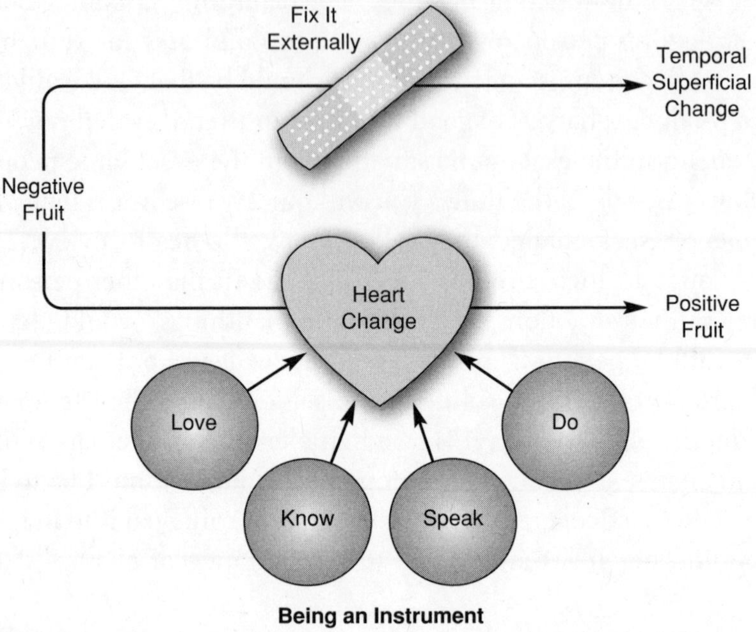

Being an Instrument

LOVE

Love highlights the importance of relationships in the process of change. Theologians call this a covenantal model of change. God comes and makes a covenant with us. He commits himself to be our God and he takes us as his people. In the context of this relationship, he accomplishes his work of making us like him. As we understand the way God works in our own lives, we realize that relationship to him is not a luxury, but a necessity. It is the only context in which the lifelong process of change can take place. In the same way, we are called to build strong relationships with others. God's purpose is that these relationships would be workrooms in which his work of change can thrive.

KNOW

Know has to do with really getting acquainted with the people God sends our way. When you assume that you know someone, you won't ask the critical questions you need to ask to get below the surface. We tend to think we know people because we know facts about them (who their spouse is, where they work, some likes and dislikes, their children, etc.), but we really don't know *them*.

Knowing a person means knowing the heart. When you say you are getting to know someone better, it's not that you are gaining a more intimate understanding of her kneecap! You mean that you know more about her beliefs and goals, her hopes and dreams, her values and desires. If you know your friend, you will be able to predict what she will think and how she will feel in a given situation. Friendship is the connection of hearts.

Hebrews 4:14–16 teaches us that Christ entered our world and lived here for thirty-three years. He faced everything we face so that we could know that he understands our struggle. So the **Know** function is very important, whether it involves asking good questions within a friendship or gathering data in a more formal counseling setting. The goal is to get below the surface. As you do, you can help your friend know herself more accurately and desire the deeper heart change that is God's goal.

SPEAK

Speak involves bringing God's truth to bear on this person in this situation. To do this you need to ask, "What does God want this person to see that she doesn't see? How can I help her see it?" The Gospels are full of brilliant examples of the way Christ helped people to see the truth. Through stories and questions, he broke through their spiritual blindness and helped them see who they were and the glory of what he could do for them.

Speaking the truth in love does not mean making grand pronouncements. It means helping your friend to see her life clearly. For lasting change to take place, your friend must see herself in the mirror of God's Word. She also needs to see God and the resources for change that he has provided in Christ.

DO

Finally, you must help your friend **Do** something with what she learns—to apply the insights God has given to her daily life and relationships. Insight alone is not change; it's only the beginning. Insights about who we are, who God is, and what he has given us in Christ must be applied to the practical, specific realities of life. God calls your friend not just to be a hearer of his Word, but to be an active doer of it as well. As Christ's ambassador, you are called to help your friend respond in personal ways to this call.

One more thing needs to be said about the **Love-Know-Speak-Do** model of personal ministry. This is not just an aspect of the formal ministry of the local church, but a lifestyle to which God has called each of us. This lifestyle will work in the formal counseling office as well as in informal conversations with a struggling Christian friend. This ministry model can be easily adapted to whatever opportunities God gives you to function as one of his ambassadors of change.

▶ LOVE
KNOW
SPEAK
DO

7 | BUILDING RELATIONSHIPS BY ENTERING THEIR WORLD

It was one of those moments that a teacher couldn't buy for a million dollars. I was teaching a counseling course required of all third year seminary students in the pastoral track. The class tended to be populated by guys who thought that if they preached well-honed theological sermons, their congregations wouldn't need any personal ministry. They saw my course as a pointless addition to an overcrowded schedule. This didn't make for a lively learning environment.

The first year I taught the course, I jumped right into the material without trying to demonstrate its importance. It was a long, hard semester. The next year, I decided to begin each class with true pastoral horror stories until the class cried "uncle." I told story after story of late night emergencies and relational catastrophes that were scattered throughout my ministry as pastor. I kept it up until it was clear that the students were convinced that they needed what I was about to teach.

In the middle of one of my graphic anecdotes, something happened that I will never forget. An exasperated future pastor threw up his hand and blurted out, "All right, we know we are going to have these *projects* in our churches. Just tell us what to do with them so we can get back to the work of the ministry!" A hush covered the room. In his frustration, this man had verbalized the attitude of many pastors toward the world of biblical counseling, discipleship, and personal ministry. I knew this was a golden teaching moment and I wanted to be a good steward. I asked him to repeat the word he had used for people in difficulty. In hesitating embarrassment, he mumbled, "Projects," as the other seminarians snickered in their seats.

There were many things wrong with this young man's perspective on pastoral ministry, but the most serious is this: it was devoid of love. There was no zeal to incarnate the self-sacrificing love of Christ. He saw lost and struggling people as impediments to what he was called to do, and the need to respond to them as a huge interference. His view of ministry centered on well-delivered sermons and well-attended programs that would produce a thriving and growing church. He saw the church as a well-designed, well-led, successful organization. But when I look at the church, I see a hospital full of people in various stages of dealing with the disease of sin.

Imagine a doctor coming out of an examining room to say to his receptionist, "Sick people, sick people, sick people! All I ever see is sick people! Why don't healthy people ever come and visit me?" The church is full of people dealing with the effects of sin, people who are not fully formed into the image of Jesus Christ. The church is full of people who have lost their way and don't even know it, who haven't made a connection between their daily problems and the transforming grace of Christ. Everywhere you look, you will find couples who are struggling to love, parents who are struggling to be patient, children who are attracted to temptation, and friends who battle the disappointments of imperfect relationships. This is 100 percent of the church's membership!

The church is not a theological classroom. It is a conversion, confession, repentance, reconciliation, forgiveness, and sanctification center, where flawed people place their trust in Christ, gather to know and love him better, and learn to love others as he has designed. The church is messy and inefficient, but it is God's wonderful mess—the place where he radically transforms hearts and lives.

In class that afternoon, I wondered how this student could have gotten it so wrong. But as I drove home that night, the closer I got, the more uptight I became. I was thinking, *Wouldn't it be nice to come home just once to a house that wasn't full of problems I needed to solve?* As I voiced that frustration to myself, it hit me. I was just like my student! I wanted children who had never suffered the effects of the Fall and who possessed the innate ability to make all the right choices. I wanted family devotions and a few lectures to produce children who would do quite well on their own. I, too, lacked the self-sacrificing love essential in a family full of sinners. Like my student, I saw my children as being in the way of the plan, rather than the focus of it.

FOUNDATIONAL LOVE

I am deeply persuaded that the foundation for people-transforming ministry is not sound theology; it is love. Without love, our theology is a boat without oars. Love is what drove God to send and sacrifice his Son. Love led Christ to subject himself to a sinful world and the horrors of the cross. Love is what causes him to seek and save the lost, and to persevere until each of his children is transformed into his image. His love will not rest until all of his children are at his side in glory. The hope of every sinner does not rest in theological answers but in the love of Christ for his own. Without it, we have no hope personally, relationally, or eternally.

This love is not a band-aid attempting to cope with a cancerous world. It is effective and persevering. It is jealous, intent on owning us without competition. It faces the facts of who we are and how we need to change and simply goes to work. Any hope for the problems we face—with our own hearts and with a dark and corrupt world—is found in the love of the Lord Jesus Christ for us. Hear the words of Paul:

> What, then, shall we say in response to this? If God is for us, who can be against us? He who did not spare his own Son, but gave him up for us all—how will he not also, along with him, graciously give us all things? Who will bring any charge against those whom God has chosen? It is God who justifies. Who is he that condemns? Christ Jesus, who died—more than that, who was raised to life—is at the right hand of God and is also interceding for us. Who shall separate us from the love of Christ? Shall trouble or hardship or persecution or famine or nakedness or danger or sword? As it is written:

"For your sake we face death all day long;
we are considered as sheep to be slaughtered."

No, in all these things we are more than conquerors
through him who loved us. For I am convinced that neither
death nor life, neither angels nor demons, neither the present
nor the future, nor any powers, neither height nor depth, nor
anything else in all creation, will be able to separate us from the
love of God that is in Christ Jesus our Lord. (Rom. 8:31–39)

Paul says, "You are the recipients of Christ's love and nothing can
separate you from it." This love offers hope to anyone willing to confess sin and cry out for transformation.

Yet this is where we often get stuck. We want ministry that doesn't
demand love that is, well, so demanding! We don't want to serve others in a way that requires so much personal sacrifice. We would prefer to lob grenades of truth into people's lives rather than lay down our
lives for them. But this is exactly what Christ did for us. Can we expect to be called to do anything less? Hear again the words of Paul in
1 Corinthians 13:

If I speak in the tongues of men and of angels, but have
not love, I am only a resounding gong or a clanging cymbal.
If I have the gift of prophecy and can fathom all mysteries and
all knowledge, and if I have a faith that can move mountains,
but have not love, I am nothing. If I give all I possess to the
poor and surrender my body to the flames, but have not love,
I gain nothing.

Love is patient, love is kind. It does not envy, it does not
boast, it is not proud. It is not rude, it is not self-seeking, it is
not easily angered, it keeps no record of wrongs. Love does
not delight in evil but rejoices with the truth. It always protects, always trusts, always hopes, always perseveres.

Love never fails. But where there are prophecies, they will
cease; where there are tongues, they will be stilled; where

there is knowledge, it will pass away. For we know in part and we prophesy in part, but when perfection comes, the imperfect disappears. When I was a child, I talked like a child, I thought like a child, I reasoned like a child. When I became a man, I put childish ways behind me. Now we see but a poor reflection as in a mirror; then we shall see face to face. Now I know in part; then I shall know fully, even as I am fully known.

And now these three remain: faith, hope, and love. But the greatest of these is love.

The love of Christ is not only the foundation for our personal hope, but our incarnation of that love is our only hope for being effective for Christ with others. Sadly, many of us have forgotten this, and we are resounding-gong people in cymbal-clanging relationships. There is a whole lot of noise but not much real change! As I drove home from class that day, I knew I was going to be called to love my family more than myself. I knew I would need to incarnate the love of Christ. But what I wanted was a good meal, a relaxed encounter with my newspaper, a nice conversation with my wife, and a few moments reading in bed before the lights went out. And I knew that the people in the house would surely step all over my plan!

We cannot be part of Christ's life-giving work without being willing to lay down our own. That is why Jesus said, "If anyone comes to me and does not hate his father and mother, his wife and children, his brothers and sisters—yes, even his own life—he cannot be my disciple. And anyone who does not carry his cross and follow me cannot be my disciple" (Luke 14:26–27). Christ is not calling us to hateful relationships. As verse 27 makes clear, the call is to die daily to our own selfish agenda, so that we may be part of his. Otherwise, we will hinder what the Lord is doing rather than help it.

How much are the people in your life a source of personal frustration? How often do you give in to stress and do things that do not honor Christ or incarnate his character? How often do you see people as obstacles to ministry rather than the objects of it? Whom have you given up on? We have been loved by Christ and called to incarnate that self-sacrificing love wherever he places us. Do people sense that love in you?

REDEMPTIVE RELATIONSHIPS

When we forget the call to incarnate the love of Christ, we take our relationships as our own. Soon they are governed by our pleasure, comfort, and ease. We get irritated at people who interfere with these things, and much of our anger is due to the fact that we are relationship thieves. People do not belong to us; they belong to God! Relationships are not primarily for our fulfillment. On the contrary, relationships between sinners are messy, difficult, labor-intensive, and demanding, but in that, they are designed to result in God's glory and our good as he is worshiped and our hearts are changed. Effective personal ministry begins when we confess that we have taken relationships that belong to God and used them for our own selfish purposes.

When we have confessed and repented, we are ready to ask what role our relationships can play in the work Christ wants to do. If the relationships God gives us are not mere luxuries for our own happiness, what is God's plan for them? This brings us to the **Love** function in personal ministry. God's relationship to us is loving and redemptive, and he wants our relationships to mirror those qualities. This means at least three things:

1. He has a higher goal for our relationships than our personal happiness.
2. He wants our relationships to be the context for the change he works in and through us.
3. We need to build relationships that encourage this work of change.

We can understand this by considering the way Christ works in our own lives. Scripture uses three words to describe his work: *justification, adoption,* and *sanctification.* (See Figure 7.1.)

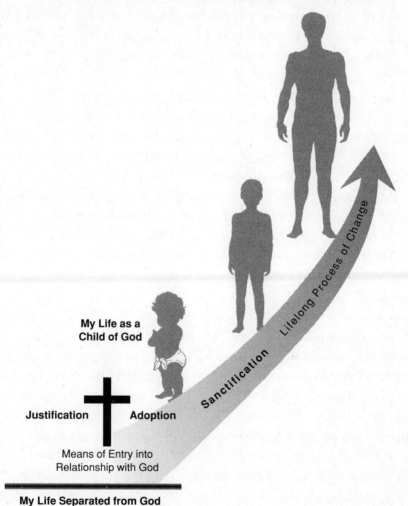

FIG. 7.1

The Relational Foundation for Ministry: Salvation as Our Model.

My Life as a
Child of God

Lifelong Process of Change

Sanctification

Justification   Adoption

Means of Entry into
Relationship with God

My Life Separated from God

Justification and adoption explain how we enter into relationship with God. In justification by faith, God declares me to be righteous based on the perfect life, death, and resurrection of Christ. In *justification* Christ's righteousness is legally credited to my account. Justification removes the sin that separates me from God and gives me

Christ's righteousness, making me acceptable to God and enabling me to have a relationship with him.

Adoption also involves my relationship with God. God not only justifies me, he adopts me; he welcomes me into his family with all the rights and privileges of a son. Justification and adoption give me a full and complete relationship with God.

As a result of justification and adoption, am I okay? This is a bit of a trick question. If you are talking about my *standing* or relationship with God, the answer is "yes." Nothing needs to be added to Jesus' work. I don't need to do anything else to secure God's acceptance. It is a gift of his grace.

But if you are talking about my *condition* as a person, the answer is "no." I still struggle with sin daily, and radical change still needs to take place in me so that I can be and do what God has planned. Unlike justification and adoption, which are events, this work of personal transformation is a process—a process called *sanctification*. Sanctification is the process by which God actually makes me what he legally declared me to be in justification—holy.

This framework sheds light on the ministry God has given each one of us. God doesn't justify and adopt me because I am okay, but precisely because I am *not* okay. He knows that lasting change will take place in me only when I am living in a personal relationship with him. In his magnificent love, he makes that relationship a reality. Only those who have a relationship with God through justification and adoption will undergo the radical change process of progressive sanctification. Without the relationship, there is no personal change. Our relationship with God is the beginning of our salvation, not the end; a necessity, not a luxury.

As Christ's ambassadors, we, too, must begin by building relationships of love, grace, and trust with others. This is the covenantal view of change we considered earlier. Like the relationship God establishes with us through Christ, the relationships we build provide the context for his continuing work of change.

When we see God's work *in* us as the model for our work *for* him, three practical principles emerge:

1. God's redemptive activity always takes place within relationships.
2. God's first step in changing us is to draw us into relationship with him.
3. Our relationships are essential to the work God is completing in us and in others.

This is why our relationships do not belong to us; they belong to the Lord and are holy. God uses them to prepare a people for himself. These everyday relationships are essential to the plan of personal transformation ordained before the world began. God daily gives us opportunities to serve the troubled, angry, discouraged, defeated, confused, and blind. This is the way he works and he calls each of his children to be part of it.

This view of our relationships must transform the way we respond to one another. A tense discussion about disappointments in marriage is more than a time of searing honesty between a husband and a wife. God is at work, revealing both their hearts. He is using the relationship to transform them both. If the couple remembers this, they will respond to each other in ways remarkably different from their normal pattern. But if their only goal is their own personal happiness, each spouse will say, "I want my partner to see how unhappy I am and to try harder to make me happy." If they both have this goal, the conversation will be nothing more than a self-centered war for personal happiness. They may claim to love each other, but at the level of their hearts' desires, both wife and husband are committed only to getting what they want out of the other person.

If this conversation takes place between two people who want to be part of God's work of transformation (sanctification), things dramatically change. It begins with their *attitudes*. When they think of each other only from a horizontal perspective, they are discouraged, hopeless, and cynical. After all, they have done everything they can think of to get the other person to shape up, but nothing has worked. But when they are aware that God is present with his own redemptive purpose, they have every reason for hope. Yes, they are at the end of themselves, but the Redeemer is active in all of his power and glory. He has been changing them and will continue to do so. There is every reason to believe that he is up to something good in this marital difficulty.

Viewing this moment redemptively will also change their *posture*. In the horizontal model, they stand opposed to each other as enemies with competing agendas. They battle to ensure that *their* will prevails. From a redemptive standpoint, husband and wife stand on the same side. They ultimately want God's will to be done in their marriage. They are not threatened by the presence of an enemy (each other); on the contrary, they know that they are members of the same family. Their Father has their highest good in mind. He will not forsake one in order to lovingly transform the other. So they do not have to compete and they do not have to win. They can be gently and peacefully honest about their relationship because they have forsaken their own agenda for the Lord's.

Does this sound unrealistic? Have we slipped so far from God's purposes for relationships that we can't conceive of doing this? When you study what the New Testament says about relationships, this is the model that emerges. For example, what is God's goal for your parenting? It goes way beyond clean rooms, good manners, proper dress, the right college, a good career, and marrying well. In all these things God calls parents to work toward something deeper and more lasting. Paul captures it in Ephesians 6 when he calls parents to bring their children up in the "training and instruction of the Lord." This radically changes the parental agenda. Gone is the horizontal focus. The call is to be part of God's work of heart transformation—to help the child change from a self-absorbed sinner to one who loves God above all else. Paul's model of parenting is distinctly redemptive, but when parents forget that moments of difficulty are moments of redemption, they stand in the way of what the Lord is doing.

Or take this model to a more formal counseling context. A person asks to talk with you about a complicated situation. You can see that she is very discouraged—almost paralyzed. What should your goal be? It is wonderful to offer wisdom that clarifies confusion and makes the situation bearable. It is grace to offer her understanding, comfort, and hope. It is good to function as her advocate where appropriate. But a deeper focus must shape this counseling moment.

God is continuing his work of transformation in this woman's heart and life. He has brought her to the end of herself, revealing the fruit of her choices and behavior. He is in the process of revealing her heart. His goal is that she would be conformed to the image of his Son, one step freer from her bondage to the creation, and one step closer to the freedom of worshiping the Creator. His goal is that he would consistently rule her thoughts and motives; that increasingly, her identity would be rooted in him rather than in the arid soil of personal achievement or the acceptance of others. Timidity and cynicism would give way to courage and hope rooted in his presence, power, love, and grace. God's goal is deeper than emotional and situational change. It is nothing less than personal transformation.

WHAT DOES A REDEMPTIVE RELATIONSHIP LOOK LIKE?

What practical things can help the quarreling husband and wife to function redemptively? How can the counselor build a relationship that promotes God's work in the discouraged, struggling woman? How can parents establish such relationships with their children? How can pastors build them into their ministry? What do relationships that promote personal change look like? Scripture highlights four things when it calls us to love someone in a way that promotes God's work of heart change. Each aspect of **Love** promotes relationships where God's goals are central. (See Figure 7.2.)

1. *Enter* the person's world.
2. *Incarnate* the love of Christ.
3. *Identify* with suffering.
4. *Accept* with agenda.

Fig. 7.2

The Four Elements of a Loving Ministry Relationship.

A Loving Ministry Relationship

1	Enter	the person's world,
2	Incarnate	the love of Christ.
3	Identify	with suffering.
4	Accept	with agenda.

In this chapter and the next, we will consider these elements of love in a redemptive relationship.

▶ **ELEMENT OF LOVE 1:**
ENTER THE PERSON'S WORLD

There is no shortage of need in this world. Our problem is that we miss the opportunities God places in our path. How can we pursue them effectively? We begin by recognizing the *entry gates* God gives us, the means of entry from a casual relationship to a life-changing one. How can you recognize them?

It helps to understand what an entry gate is not. First, it is not the *problem* the person wants to talk about. We can focus on the problem and miss the person in the middle of it. Biblical personal ministry certainly includes problem solving, but it must be person-focused. God's work of change certainly involves changes in situation and relationship, but it has radical personal transformation as its core goal.

Second, the entry gate is not a particular *situation or circumstance* in the person's life. Beneath these are deeper heart struggles that are God's focus. Nor is the entry gate another *person* or a *problem in relationship*. We should resist the tendency to be entirely problem-focused in ministry. When we have a problem focus as we listen to people, we will be like someone at the shooting gallery at the county fair. We will be hunting for problems like they are plastic ducks floating by, and when we hear them, our goal will be to shoot them down. We will listen for a problem word (adultery, doubt, fear, lust, stealing, greed, envy, conflict) and then fire away until we have said everything we know about the Bible's views on the topic. Not only does this do violence to the way God wants his Word to be used, it completely misses the heart struggles of the person with the problem.

This is why it is so important to recognize God-given entry gate opportunities. An entry gate is a particular person's *experience* of the situation, problem, or relationship. To recognize an entry gate you do not ask, "What are the problems in this person's life?" Instead you ask, "What is this person struggling with *in the midst of* the situation?" Or, "What has this person in its grip right now?" The entry gate is not what *you* think the person is struggling with; it is the struggle the person confesses. People will tell you how they are struggling, and their struggle will give you common ground with them and a door of opportunity into a deeper level of ministry.

Is the entry gate strategy still fuzzy in your thinking? Here is an example. Imagine that a woman from your church calls you. She has been married for fifteen years and has three children. She awakens one morning to find that her husband is gone. She rolls over to turn on the bedside lamp and notices a note leaning against it. In it, her husband announces that he has left the marriage. He has fallen in love with someone else, taken his clothes, emptied the bank account, and hired a lawyer. Immediately after reading the note, your friend calls you. Ask yourself: what has this woman in its grip at that moment? What is she struggling with right then? In her heart, what is she experiencing? What has the power to paralyze her and rob her of hope?

The obvious answer is fear. She is flooded with terrifying questions: "What will happen to my house? How will I provide for us? Will he want the children? What will my family think? What will I tell the kids? How much is left in our bank account? Who has my husband talked to and what has he said? How can I face people? What does this other woman have that I do not?" Perhaps the scariest question of all is, "Why would God let this happen to me?" Fear is the most significant heart issue at this moment. It is where the war is taking place and where your ministry begins. This woman would not be helped by a recap of all the Bible has to say about marriage and divorce. If that's all you offer, you will likely lose future opportunity to help her.

On the other hand, helping her face her fears gives you a wonderful opportunity to show love and build a ministry relationship. When we speak to people's real struggles, they respond, *This person has heard me. This person understands me. I want more of this kind of help.* This is the power of a loving relationship. So an entry gate is not the objective problem a person has encountered, but his particular

experience of that problem (fear, anger, guilt, anxiety, hopelessness, aloneness, envy, discouragement, desires for vengeance, etc.).

RECOGNIZING ENTRY GATES

How can you recognize the entry gates God sends your way? Listen with purpose. Focus on the *person* in the middle of the problem. As she tells her story, it will come out as a chaotic mix of the present, the past, emotions, and personal interpretations. Train yourself to listen for four things that will show you where the person is struggling.

1. Listen for *emotional* words. ("I'm angry." "I'm afraid." "I can't stop crying.")
2. Listen for *interpretive* words. ("This shouldn't happen." "I guess I'm getting what I deserve." "I wonder if it's even worth getting up in the morning.")
3. Listen for *self talk*. ("I am such a failure." "This always happens to me." "I don't have what it takes to face this.")
4. Listen for *God talk*. ("I thought I was doing what God wanted." "He simply doesn't hear my prayers." "How could God let this happen to me?")

Remember, your focus should be on the person and what she is struggling with at that moment. As you listen for the four things listed above, look for a theme (anger, fear, guilt, hopelessness) to emerge. Then grab hold of that theme, meet the person in the midst of that struggle, and incarnate the loving Lord she may be unable to see. We know that God has not given up on the person, gone home, or gotten busy helping others. But the dark clouds of circumstances can blind a person to the God who is there and active. God is her only source of hope as she faces a situation that is out of her control. As she is flooded with questions (many of which no one can answer), what she really needs is the rest that can only be found in the Lord who is "an ever present help in trouble," who will never leave her or forsake her. In these first moments of ministry, I have a wonderful opportunity to reveal God to someone who is having trouble seeing him. He is here! He understands! He is able to help! He is up to something good!

Have you ever had a frustrating experience you wanted to share with someone? Perhaps you had an important appointment that you missed because you were held up in traffic. How would you feel if you told your friend, only to have him respond with a lecture on the fact that you took the wrong way and that he learned years ago that there was a much more efficient route you could have taken? How would you feel if he interrupted your story to share a tale of his own that had no connection to what was troubling you?

Your friend was not listening for *you* in the middle of your story. His responses may have had some logical connection to the facts you shared, but they weren't helpful because they didn't connect with the impact of the situation on your heart and life. In your friend's mind's eye, he saw traffic, but he didn't see you. He didn't see you nervously looking at your watch. He didn't see you desperately trying to make a call. He didn't see you pounding on the steering wheel. He only saw traffic and when he responded, he spoke to traffic and not to you. In many little ways we have all faced this frustration. But imagine the pain of facing a huge struggle, only to feel as if no one is really hearing you; no one is speaking to what you are battling in the midst of your crisis.

This is not God's way. We can offer love that is personal and specific, not aimless and platitudinous. We can follow the model of the Wonderful Counselor, the Good Shepherd who goes right to where his lost sheep is, wraps him in his arms, and carries him to a place of safety. Following the Lord's example means that we communicate several things to a struggling person:

Let the person know that you have heard her struggle. As you see the theme emerging, you need to restate it for her, ideally in her own words. In so doing you are saying, "God has sent you someone who hears you, who has begun to understand what you are going through." Let her know that your focus is on her as a person, not just the issues she is facing.

Let the person know that God is there and that he understands the struggle. Don't do this by referring the person to a theological outline. Turn to passages of Scripture that speak to the exact thing that has her in its grip. In so doing, you accomplish two things. You help her (1) to recognize that Scripture speaks to the deepest issues of human experience and (2) to see that God meets his people most powerfully in experiences where they fear he is absent.

The Psalms are particularly helpful here. I think the Psalms are in the Bible to keep us honest. They remind us that living by faith is not easy. The life of the believer is a daily war fought in our hearts, and the battles are dramatically depicted in the Psalms. Again and again, the Psalms put words to the struggles of the people God sends my way. But the Psalms do more. They are not only dyed with human struggle, they are dyed with the presence of the Lord. Again and again they remind us that we have hope, not because we are able and wise, or because circumstances are easy, but because God is our Father.

Let the person know you will stand with her. Returning to the example of the friend counseling you after a traffic jam, the friend's words gave the impression that all you needed to do was recognize your mistake and acknowledge that you paid the price for your error. He believed he did his job properly and moved on. The problem is he didn't counsel *you*, he counseled the problem. He didn't recognize what you were struggling with as a result of the traffic jam. Little wonder that he felt free to throw a quick correction at you that in no way addressed the thoughts and desires of your heart. He thought he had been helpful, but he wasn't. He was right that you went the wrong way, but he forgot that in doing so, *You missed your appointment!* And the implications of *that* fact would still trouble you. I fear that many of us offer care that doesn't cure because, from the outset, our eyes are so focused on the problem that we miss the person and the struggles within.

One of the most common struggles in crisis is the feeling that you are all alone. Because of this, it's very discouraging when people throw quick answers at you and walk away. It feels as if they have quickly let go of your life and gone back to their own. This is why it is so important to incarnate God's "I will be with you" promises from the outset. In so doing we address a theological lie, the lie that God is absent in trouble. We offer people a living, loving presence that puts real flesh and blood on the presence of the Lord. We also do battle with the Enemy, who whispers in the ear of the believer, "Where is your God now?" Let the person know that you not only will help her address the problems she is facing, but you care for *her* and are with *her*.

THE BEGINNING OF CHANGE

When you seek to minister to people in this way, their hearts will respond in three ways that set the stage for more ministry—and more change—in the days ahead.

1. *Horizontal trust.* Often, people in difficulty do not open up easily. They are afraid of further hurt and find it difficult to entrust themselves to others. But when I can connect with the person's real experience in the midst of a trial, I have an opportunity to engender trust. The person says to herself, *He really heard me. He understands what I am going through. He appears to be a person I can trust.* This willingness to trust is crucial to a relationship in which God's work can thrive. As you seek to serve this person, you are asking her to place the "fine china" of her life in your hands. You are going to ask her to talk about the most important and sensitive issues of her life. She will only do this when she trusts you. Most of our conversations are impersonal and self-protective. We talk a lot, but without much substance. We reserve moments of personal self-disclosure for people we trust. Trust is vital in a heart-changing relationship.

2. *Vertical hope*. God not only surprises struggling people with his grace, he calls them to do things that are difficult and unexpected, things that contradict the person's normal instincts. God is going to say, "Hear me. Trust me. Follow me." If the person is going to follow the Lord, he needs to look in his face and see hope. But often a person under great trial looks at the Lord and sees anything but hope. So, in those early moments we are helping the person to see the Lord, to recognize that he understands the secret struggles, that he is present with him or her, and that he offers help that really helps. We want to help the person move toward the Lord rather than away from him. We want to help a person who is hiding, avoiding, denying, accusing, doubting, running, or giving up to become a seeker—and not just a seeker after help, but a seeker after God. This is important because a counselee is not a counselee until he is a seeker.

3. *Commitment to the process*. A person will rarely come to you and say, "I know that God wants to work wonderful change in my heart. I wondered if you would be willing to help." The person may not be seeking help at all, just a place to vent and tell his story. He may be searching for an ally or someone to validate his actions and interpretations. Even when people make a formal appointment to talk with me, not all of them are committed to seek help or to change.

But when you have identified with a person's struggle and offered the hope of God in the midst of it, he will want more. I always tell my students to aim low at first. They shouldn't try to solve a world of difficulty in a few moments. The main thing they should try to accomplish in their first talk with a person is to help him to be willing to talk again. The first talk may be nothing but venting, but the second talk signifies some kind of commitment to God's process of change. That is my goal—to encourage the person to entrust himself to him.

ENTRY GATE QUESTIONS

Recognizing entry gate opportunities involves learning to ask the right questions. Here are some entry gate questions you might ask the woman whose husband left her. (However, it is unlikely that you would ask all these questions at once, especially when she first calls.)

- "What came into your mind as you read the note?"
- "What are you struggling with most right now?"
- "What are you facing now that you thought you would never face?"
- "What are you feeling?"
- "What are you afraid of right now?"
- "Are you feeling angry? Where is that a real struggle?"
- "Describe how you see God right now. What do you think he is doing?"
- "Do you feel hopeless? Do you feel like God is asking you to do the impossible?"
- "What questions do you wish you could ask your husband?"
- "What questions do you wish you could ask God?"
- "When you can't sleep, what thoughts keep you awake?"
- "What part of the situation is getting to you most?"
- "What regrets do you struggle with?"

As you ask questions like these, listen for themes that show you where the war is raging within this woman. The goal is that the resulting horizontal trust, vertical hope, and commitment to the process would provide a platform for God's work of change. But this is just the first way I seek to love the person. Let's now consider the second.

▶ ELEMENT OF LOVE 2:
INCARNATE THE LOVE OF CHRIST

If someone asked you how God uses us to change people, what would you answer? Is it just through the things we say? Do we simply confront people with the truth and call them to obey? Is personal ministry just a biblical form of talk therapy? Or does God use us in other ways to change people?

Think of the people God has used in your own life. Was it just because of what they said? No doubt God used their words power-fully at key moments. No doubt you benefited from their advice, in-sights, honesty, and confrontation. But in what other ways did God use the relationship to encourage change in you? Perhaps their will-ingness to forgive you taught you more about the true nature of for-giveness than any conversation. Perhaps you learned about the resources of Christ by watching them endure great difficulty. Maybe you began to grasp the power of biblical love by watching them love someone who was quite unlovable. Perhaps they stood as evidence that the promises of God were true as you saw them fulfilled in their lives. Maybe it was their willingness to stand with you for the long haul that gave you strength to continue. If you stop to reflect on these people, you will quickly recognize that their ministry was made up of more than words.

As Christ's ambassadors, it's not just what we say that God uses to encourage change in people; it's also who we are and what we do. During his ministry on earth, Jesus said, "If you have trouble believ-ing what I say, then look at the things I have done. They are all the evidence that you need" (paraphrase of passages like John 14:11). As ambassadors, we are not only called to speak the truth but to be real, living, flesh-and-blood illustrations of it. We are not just God's spokespersons; we are examples. We are not simply God's mouth-pieces; we are his evidence. Our lives testify to the power of his grace to transform hearts. It is seen in the way we display the love God has shown to us.

THE RIGHT CLOTHES FOR THE JOB

Colossians 3:12–17 captures what it means to incarnate the love of Christ in ministry.

> Therefore, as God's chosen people, holy and dearly loved, clothe yourselves with compassion, kindness, humility, gen-tleness and patience. Bear with each other and forgive what-ever grievances you may have against one another. Forgive as

the Lord forgave you. And over all these virtues put on love, which binds them all together in perfect unity.

Let the peace of Christ rule in your hearts, since as members of one body you were called to peace. And be thankful. Let the word of Christ dwell in you richly as you teach and admonish one another with all wisdom, and as you sing psalms, hymns, and spiritual songs with gratitude in your hearts to God. And whatever you do, whether in word or deed, do it all in the name of the Lord Jesus, giving thanks to God the Father through him.

Verses 15–17 contain one of the New Testament's clearest calls to personal ministry. In this remarkable passage, Paul calls us to activities we would normally assume are restricted to formal ministry. We are called to have Scripture so deeply engrained in our lives that we are wise and thankful, and thus always ready to teach and admonish (confront) one another. Paul is calling us to a state of biblical readiness for the ministry opportunities he will bring as he changes us through the ministry of others. The passage summarizes what this book is about. But to really understand it, you must start with verse 12.

Here Paul uses the metaphor of clothing—the thing that covers us, identifies us, and describes our function. Paul is reminding us that what we "wear" (that is, the character qualities we put on) to moments of ministry is as important as what we say. The list of character traits Paul gives is a summary of the character of Christ. Paul is saying, "If you are going to be involved in what God is doing in others, come dressed for the job!"

Paul's view of change involves process as well as content, the manner as well as the message. It involves teaching with my life as well as with my words. As I incarnate the character of the Lord I am calling people to trust and obey. In effect, Paul is saying, "If you are going to teach and admonish one another, you must first put on Christ." God changes people not simply because you have spoken the truth to them, but because those words were said with compassion, kindness, humility, gentleness, patience, and love. When we do this, we become the physical evidence of the truths we present. We are not only incarnating truth, but Christ himself.

From all physical appearances, they were a lovely young couple. She had called me and asked to get together. As we sat down, the emotions in the room changed. She began to cry before I had prayed or asked my first question. The more she cried, the more he squirmed in his chair in embarrassment and anger. She was beginning to tell her story when he jumped up with a red face and said, "I can't do this! I can't talk about my private life to some shrink [which I am not] who may not have a clue and who definitely doesn't know me!" Looking at his wife, he said, "If you are stupid enough to subject yourself to this, then have fun, but I'm out of here!" And he stormed out of the room. I quickly prayed aloud for both of them and told the wife that I was going out to talk to him. I found him in the parking lot, ready to get into his car. He glared at me and said, "Would you please leave me alone?" I told him that I understood that he was angry and afraid and that it was hard to share private struggles with other people. I told him that I was willing to be patient, and that I would do whatever I could to help him get through the discomfort of these early moments. I said a few more things and told him I was going back to rejoin his wife.

As I walked down the hallway, I realized that he was behind me. He said, "I can't run away . . . I just can't," and this time we began to really talk. Months later, we recalled that first day and he told me that he did not remember what I had said to him in the parking lot, but the fact that I came after him was what God used to soften him. It was not what I said but what I did that God used to rescue a man on the verge of destroying his life.

There are four main reasons to incarnate Christ in the relationships God gives us.

1. *It is a protection for you.* In personal ministry, the sin of the person you are helping will eventually be revealed in your relationship. If you are ministering to an angry person, at some point that anger will be directed at you. If you are helping a person who struggles with trust, at some point she will distrust you. A manipulative person will seek to manipulate you. A depressed person will tell you he tried everything you've suggested and it didn't work. You can't stand next to a puddle without eventually being splashed by its mud!

Galatians 6:1 says, "Brothers, if someone is caught in a sin, you who are spiritual should restore him gently. But watch yourself, or you also may be tempted." In ministry relationships, not only is the heart of the person I am helping being revealed, but my own as well. I am capable of being angry, proud, self-righteous, argumentative and harsh, impatient and unforgiving. When I do, I get in the way of what the Lord is doing. I need the very Christ I am holding out to the other person. The comforting reality is that he is working on us both!

We need to be aware of our reactions to the people we serve. They will sin against us in the same way they have sinned against others. One of the most loving things we can do is to be committed to humble self-examination: How do we respond when sinned against? As the person's sins become part of our experience, are we demonstrating the power of Christ's grace? Are we incarnating Christ as we deal with sin? Sometimes we will live up to our calling as Christ's ambassadors; at other times we will fail. Even then, we can minister effectively if we apply the gospel to our own lives by confessing our sin, asking forgiveness from God (and the other person when appropriate), and claiming God's strength to go on and serve him faithfully.

2. It offers a living example. We do not have to struggle to come up with creative definitions of the character qualities God desires his children to display; instead, we have an opportunity to model them. If we follow the example of Christ, the person we are seeking to help should experience in us what real love, compassion, gentleness, forgiveness, forbearance, kindness, and humility are like, even though we are fallen human beings. In this way, moments of personal ministry are not just the lecture part of a class; they are the lab as well! Life isn't just discussed; it is lived! The things God calls us to do and be should be evident in the person who is ministering—as that person depends on Christ.

3. *It gives evidence of what the Lord can do.* The goals we lay out for people can seem unrealistic. They will have trouble imagining how they could ever do these things in their present circumstances. They may be so aware of their failures that they will see God's new way as completely impossible. Personal ministry provides a sweet opportunity to speak to this doubt and fear, not only in words, but with your life as well.

If I am following the example of Christ and functioning as an ambassador, I will live as evidence that what the Lord says is true. He has given us everything we need to do what he calls us to do. He is with us in trouble. He will supply everything we need, when we need it. His grace is sufficient when we are weak. He gives wisdom as it is needed. When I love an unloving person, when I am gentle in the face of angry arguments, when I am patient in the face of failure, when I speak kindly to one who is unkind, and when I ask forgiveness when I have sinned, I demonstrate that God's calling is possible. It is possible not because we are wise and strong or because our circumstances are easy, but because *he is with us* in the power of his glory, goodness, and grace.

4. *It keeps Christ central.* The hope we offer people is more than a set of strategies. Our hope is Christ! In him alone do lost, confused, angry, hurt, and discouraged people find what they need to be and do what God intends. We are not gurus. We are nothing more than instruments in the hands of a powerful Redeemer. The hope and help we offer is always focused on him. The most important encounter in ministry is not the person's encounter with us, but his encounter with Christ. Our job is simply to set up that encounter, so that God would help people seek his forgiveness, comfort, restoration, strength, and wisdom.

It is foolish to embark on personal ministry without counting the costs. An ambassador not only delivers the message of the King, he incarnates it as well. He stands in the King's place. Just as Christ's ministry to sinners meant sacrifice and suffering, so it will for us (though on a different level). Because suffering is inevitable, we must be aware of our response to those trials. Are we representing the King well? Are we willing to die to ourselves to see life in this other person? Are we willing to be mistreated for the sake of the gospel? Are we willing to involve ourselves in things we would normally avoid so that Christ would change someone through us? Are we willing to be splashed by the mud because we find joy in serving Christ, even when we realize we have gotten dirty?

May Christ strengthen us to love as he has loved and to be part of his work of transformation in people's lives. May this love not only direct our words, but our lives. May we stand as the example, the evidence, and the incarnation of our great Redeemer!

▶ **LOVE**
KNOW
SPEAK
DO

8 | BUILDING RELATIONSHIPS BY IDENTIFYING WITH SUFFERING

She folded up her white cane and I led her to my office. She was not only blind but lame in one leg. I had worked at a school for the blind during seminary and thought it was amazing that God had brought her my way. I was familiar with the lifestyle and struggles of the blind, but I was not prepared for her story.

She was an only child. Her mother had tried for fifteen years to get pregnant, only to endure a string of miscarriages. Finally at forty she got pregnant and didn't miscarry. Her mother felt blessed, as if her life was about to begin. She chose a beautiful name, Grace, and waited in anxious expectation. Early one morning after twenty hours of tortuous labor, Grace was born. But her mother's dream was not to be realized. Grace was fretful, sickly, demanding. There seemed to be few moments when she wasn't crying. She had problems with her breathing and digestion. She seemed to contract every childhood illness. She didn't sleep through the night for her entire infancy. Her mother was seldom able to take her out of the house.

Grace's mother thought she was the victim of a cruel fate. After all the years of waiting, she was left with a child who could barely live. Increasingly the demands, cries, and constant work made her angry. She wondered why she had ever wanted a child. She remembered how easy life had been before. In subtle ways at first, her anger began to spill over toward Grace: a yank here, a little slap there. But the irritation eventually grew into full-blown rage. When she looked at her little girl, she saw someone who had robbed her of life. Grace began to listen for her mother's footsteps so she could hide under the bed or in the closet. Her mother would then have to search for her, making her even angrier. In one of those angry encounters Grace's leg was permanently injured.

By the time Grace was eight years old, her eyes had begun to fail as a result of repeated blows to her head. She could no longer see to read, yet she was afraid to let anyone know how bad her eyesight actually was. She thought she was fooling everyone, but she wasn't. Just after her ninth birthday, Grace went to school for what she thought was a normal day. She was asked to leave her classroom and go to the office, where a lady she didn't know stood with a suitcase full of Grace's clothes. Without saying goodbye to her mother or her friends, she was transferred to a residential school for the blind where she would remain until she graduated from high school. Grace never lived at home again.

She now sat before me, telling her story with angry tears. Grace was still alone. In her fearful, judgmental anger, she had trashed every relationship she had ever had. Yet she was deeply persuaded that people were abusing her as her mother once did. Her willingness to talk to me was itself an act of angry desperation. During her time in the school for the blind, Grace had taken a religion class where she met a wonderful teacher who shared the gospel with her. She had sought me out because she wanted to talk to a Christian; she was convinced it was the only way she would hear the truth. At the same time, she didn't want anyone to feed her a bunch of biblical platitudes.

I listened to her in tears, praying as she talked, quite aware that I was called to incarnate the Lord in this suffering woman's life.

What would you say to Grace? What do you think she needs to hear? What does the Bible say to the Graces of the world? How would you like Grace to look at her past, her present, and her future? How would you build a relationship with her in which God's kingdom work would thrive?

IN A WORLD WHERE SUFFERING IS COMMON

We don't like to think about it, but we live in a world where suffering is common. In a fallen world populated by sinners, we should not be surprised. We should be surprised that we do not suffer more. Our suffering ranges from the temporary wounds of someone's thoughtlessness to horrible experiences of mistreatment and abuse. We are all suffering sinners. It is the thing we share with everyone we meet. As such, it is common ground for personal ministry.

Yet we don't often see it that way. We tend to be shocked when we hear stories like Grace's, and we live with the hope that the really bad things will never happen to us. More importantly, we struggle with how to relate to people who have suffered. Too often we reduce our ministry to biblical platitudes and promises of prayer, establishing a wide buffer zone around people who are in deep pain. Sure, we will send a card, pay a visit, say a prayer, and read a passage, but we are ill at ease and can't wait to be on our way. But sooner or later, we will suffer, too. Our experience differs only in the degree of the pain. No wonder the Bible has so much to say about the reality of personal suffering.

1. *The Bible clearly declares that God is sovereign over all things—even suffering.* Many of us mistakenly think that God has nothing to do with the bad things that happen in our world. Yet Scripture takes us in a completely different direction. It roots our hope in the reality that God is not the author of our suffering, but he is with us in our suffering (Ex. 4:11; 1 Sam. 2:2–7; Dan. 4:34–35; Prov. 16:9; Ps. 60:3; Isa. 45:7; Lam. 3:28; Amos 3:6; Acts 4:27–28; Eph. 1:11).

2. *The Bible clearly says that God is good.* It is faulty thinking to say that a truly good God would never allow a person to suffer, or that if God really loved you, he wouldn't let x happen to you. The Bible declares that an infinitely good God is in the middle of our most painful experiences (Ps. 25:7–8; 34:8–10; 33:5; 100:5; 136; 145:4–9).

3. *The Bible clearly says that God has a purpose for our suffering.* The Bible doesn't present suffering as a hindrance to our redemption, but as a tool God uses to work his redemptive purpose in us (Rom. 8:17; 2 Cor. 1:3–6; Phil. 2:5–9; James 1:2–8; 5:10–11; 1 Peter).

4. *The Bible explains the ultimate reasons why we suffer.*
   - We suffer because we live in a fallen world plagued by disease, natural disasters, dangerous animals, broken machinery, etc.
   - We suffer because of our flesh. Much of our suffering is at our own hands. We make choices that make our own lives painful and difficult.
   - We suffer because others sin against us. From subtle prejudice to personal attacks, we all suffer at the hands of others.
   - We suffer because of the Devil. There really is an enemy in our world, a trickster and a liar who divides, destroys, and devours. He tempts us with things that promise to give life but actually destroy it.
   - We suffer because of God's good purpose. God calls his children to suffer for his glory and for their redemptive good.
5. *The Bible is clear that God's sovereignty over suffering never:*
   - Means the suffering isn't real (2 Cor. 1:3–9; 4:1–16).
   - <u>Excuses the evildoer</u> (Habakkuk; Acts 2:22–24; 3:14–23).

When we enter into other people's experiences of suffering, we want our responses to be shaped by compassionate biblical thinking.[1]

SUFFERING AND PERSONAL MINISTRY

This leads us to the third aspect of the **Love** that promotes God's work in a person's life. Here, too, Christ is our model.

▶ **ELEMENT OF LOVE 3:**
IDENTIFY WITH SUFFERING

Have you ever gone through a hard time and felt completely alone? Have you ever felt as if you were two different people—the private sufferer and the person who is "known" by the people around you? Have you ever wanted to tell your story but were afraid of what others may think? Have you ever wanted to exchange someone's life for your own? Has your suffering ever diminished your desire for personal worship, the teaching of God's Word, or the fellowship of the body of Christ? Have you ever wished you didn't have to get up in the morning because of the difficulty you had to face? Have you ever tried to talk to someone about your suffering only to lose your courage? Have you ever been put off by people's quick suggestions, wrong assumptions, and biblical platitudes? In the midst of life's harsh realities, have you ever cried out (silently or aloud) for help?

If you are alive, you answered yes to at least a few of these questions. You are a sufferer who has been called by God to minister to others in pain. Suffering is not only the common ground of human relationships, but one of God's most useful workrooms. As God's ambassadors, we need to learn how to identify with those who suffer. We do this by learning from the example of the Wonderful Counselor in passages such as Hebrews 2:10–12.

> In bringing many sons to glory, it was fitting that God, for whom and through whom everything exists, should make the author of their salvation perfect through suffering. Both the one who makes men holy and those who are made holy are of the same family. So Jesus is not ashamed to call them brothers. He says,

> "I will declare your name to my brothers;
>> in the presence of the congregation I will sing your praises."

This passage is about how Christ, "the author of our salvation," identifies with us. It tells us that we are in the same family as Christ. This family is more than the family of man. The author of Hebrews is pointing to a very specific shared identity. We are with Christ in the family of those who suffer. We must not forget that we serve a Suffering Savior. We do not seek help from someone who cannot understand our experience. Jesus is compassionate and understanding. He can help us because he is like us. He went through what we are going through now. He knows us and our experiences, because we are in the same family, the family of those who have suffered.

But there is more. The passage says that Christ is not ashamed to call us "brothers." The title *brother* connotes a particular position in the family, a sibling relationship of equals. Christ could not have chosen a more powerful term to identify with us. Three aspects of this identification stand out:

1. We are in the same family.
2. We are in a similar position in the family.
3. We share similar life experiences because of that position.

This captures the humble character of personal ministry. Our service must not have an "I stand above you as one who has arrived" character. It flows out of a humble recognition that we share an identity with those we serve. God has not completed his work in me, either. We are brothers and sisters in the middle of God's lifelong process of change. I am not anyone's guru. Change will not happen simply because someone is exposed to my wisdom and experience. We share identity, we share experience, and we are of the same family.

This posture is essential for God-honoring personal ministry. First, it recognizes that God sends people my way, not only so that they will change, but so that I will too. The Wonderful Counselor is working on everyone in the room. God repeatedly uses the difficulties of a ministry relationship and the revelation of his redemptive glory to challenge, deepen, and strengthen my faith. Because I have a front row seat to the heart-transforming work of God, I minister to others with greater hope, expectancy, and courage. What is more, I live with more courage and hope for my own life. There is no question that the person who has benefited most from my ministry is me!

This shared-identity posture also protects us from the unhealthy dependency that can derail counseling, discipleship, and personal ministry. We are not what people need. Our purpose is to connect them to a living, active, redeeming Christ. *He* gives them what they need so that they can do what they have been called to do amid the difficulties of life. I am nothing more than a brother. I stand alongside you and point you to the Father. I stand next to you and tell you stories of his amazing love and care. I share with you the things I have learned on his lap and at his feet. I take your hand and walk with you to him. As brothers and sisters we put the focus where it must be—on our all-wise, almighty, and ever-present Father. We need more than acceptance or practical strategies for change. We need the forgiveness, deliverance, and empowerment that only God's grace can give.

A humble identity as a brother-in-process also helps my life to be an example. Sometimes people put us on pedestals that rob our stories of their power. They hear our stories but forget that we are sinners just like them. They forget that we live with the pressures of relationships and work. We, too, have to control our thoughts and rein in our desires. As a result, they hear words that are meant to encourage them and think, *Easy for you. Your life bears no resemblance to my impoverished existence. Your advice is nice, but it simply doesn't apply to me.* The more we are honest about who we are, the more we are willing to stand alongside people and not above them, the more our lives will offer hope.

SUFFERING WITH A PURPOSE

Look back at Hebrews 2. The core of our brotherhood with Christ and other people is suffering. But what is the purpose of our common suffering?

Verse 10 says something very interesting (and a bit confusing) about Christ. It says that, like us, he was *made perfect* through suffering. The writer is making a connection between Christ's life and ours. If we understand it, we will gain a better understanding of how he has called us to minister to others.

How did suffering make Christ perfect? Wasn't he already perfect? What did his suffering on earth (the same process we go through daily) add to his perfection?

Scripture teaches that Christ had lived in eternity as the perfect

Son of God, yet something was needed before he, as the Son of Man, could go to the cross as the perfect Lamb for sacrifice. He had to live on earth as the Second Adam, enduring the full range of experiences, tests, and temptations that make up life in the fallen world. The first Adam had failed the test, so Christ had to face sin and suffering throughout his whole life without sinning. So how was Christ made perfect? Not only by being the perfect Son of God, but by proving himself to be the perfect Son of Man. His perfection successfully endured the test of suffering.

The author of Hebrews is suggesting that there is a direct analogy between Christ's life and ours. Just as Christ was declared perfect in eternity, we are declared perfect in Christ (justification). And just as Christ's suffering demonstrated his righteousness on earth, we also become holy through the process of suffering (sanctification). We are being made perfect through the same process that Christ went through! (See Figure 8.1.)

This is also the identity we share with those we seek to love and help. Even with unbelievers, this shared brotherhood (or sisterhood) is our goal. We stand alongside each other. We are equals. We share the same experience of suffering. And our experience has the same goal of holiness. Let's consider the impact of this identity on personal ministry.

It gives us the opportunity to make truth concrete for people. Often the truths we share are robbed of their power because people are unable to see them in action. But because we share identity with those we serve, these truths can be presented as concrete realities in the midst of life. We must incarnate the truths we hold out, carrying them out of the abstract into the familiar locations of everyday life.

It encourages people to depend on Christ rather than on us. We must faithfully present ourselves as people who need Christ every moment of every day. We are never more than his ambassadors, his instruments of change.

It encourages humility and honesty. One of the radical differences between secular therapy and biblical ministry is the importance of

Fig. 8.1

Fellow Sufferers with Christ (Heb. 2:10–11).

sharing our own stories of struggle. Christ wants me to give evidence of what he can do. As I am humbly honest, the Redeemer will use my story to bring hope to another person.

It redeems my story. God has brought me through sin and suffering, not only to change me but to enable me to minister to others. My story is a small chapter in the grand story of redemption, and Christ is on center stage. My story is much more about him than it is about me. In this way even my failures result in his glory. In my own weakness, foolishness, and inability, I have learned the truthfulness of his promises and the reality of his presence. This makes my story a vehicle of change in the lives of others.

It makes my life a window to the glory of Christ. Often people look at us and want to be like us. We may be more mature and we may have greater wisdom, but we are not essentially different from the people we hope to help. But when we emphasize that we are brothers and sisters, we are no longer viewed as idealized models. We become windows people can look through to see the presence, power, love, and grace of Christ. Our lives frame the beauty of what he can do.

It results in worship of Christ. When you have spent fifteen minutes in front of a Monet, you are thankful that he had paintbrushes, but you are not in awe of them. You are in awe of Monet and his ability as a painter. The posture of brotherhood presents Christ as the great redemptive Artist. We are simply brushes in his hands. The glorious changes he paints into the hearts of people are not the result of good brushes, but of the skills of the Painter.

As we point people to Christ, he becomes the focus of our attention and the recipient of our praise. Truly biblical personal ministry always results in increasingly mature worship.

COMFORT, COMPASSION, AND YOUR STORY

What does it mean to comfort those who suffer? How do we come alongside them with compassion? Often we are unsure of what to say. We struggle with how to comfort someone who has lost a loved one, or who faces past experiences that can never be undone. We do not want to communicate truths in ways that are cheap and platitudinous. We want to anchor the person in what is true as he deals with his suffering, but in a way that shows him that we understand the intensity of his trial. We want to show him that the truths we share are robust enough to carry him through. Most of all we want him to know that he is not alone, because Christ is present as his Helper in times of trouble. The question is, "How do we avoid these pitfalls and accomplish these goals?"

A helpful answer is found in Paul's second letter to the church in Corinth.

> Praise be to the God and Father of our Lord Jesus Christ, the Father of compassion and the God of all comfort, who comforts us in all our troubles, so that we can comfort those in any trouble with the comfort we ourselves have received from God. For just as the sufferings of Christ flow over into our lives, so also through Christ our comfort overflows. If we are distressed, it is for your comfort and salvation; if we are comforted, it is for your comfort, which produces in you patient endurance of the same sufferings we suffer. And our hope for you is firm, because we know that just as you share in our sufferings, so also you share in our comfort.

We do not want you to be uninformed, brothers, about the hardships we suffered in the province of Asia. We were under great pressure, far beyond our ability to endure, so that we despaired even of life. Indeed, in our hearts we felt the sentence of death. But this happened that we might not rely on ourselves but on God, who raises the dead. He has delivered us from such a deadly peril, and he will deliver us. On him we have set our hope that he will continue to deliver us, as you help us by your prayers. Then many will give thanks on our behalf for the gracious favor granted us in answer to the prayers of many. (2 Cor. 1:3–11)

This passage summarizes the nature of Christian compassion and the process of communicating it to others. It can be neatly divided into two sections: a model or paradigm (vv. 3–7) and a process or methodology (vv. 8–11).

THE MODEL: VIEWING SUFFERING AND COMFORT REDEMPTIVELY

If you listed everything you know about suffering and comfort, what themes would emerge from your list? Do you struggle to put God's love alongside his call for us to suffer? Do the two appear contradictory? In a culture that canonizes comfort and sees suffering as horrible interference, we need a biblical paradigm of both suffering and comfort. Paul offers that here.

God is the source of true compassion. Real comfort is more than thinking the right things in times of trouble. It involves having my identity rooted in something deeper than my relationships, possessions, achievements, wealth, health, or my ability to figure it all out. Real comfort is found when I understand that I am held in the hollow of the hand of the One who created and rules all things. The most valuable thing in my life is God's love, a love that no one can take away. When my identity is rooted in him, the storms of trouble will not blow me away.

This is the comfort we offer people. We don't comfort them by saying that things will work out. They may not. The people around them may change, but they may not. The Bible tells us again and again that everything around us is in the process of being taken away. God and his love are all that remain as cultures and kingdoms rise and fall. Comfort is found by sinking our roots into the unseen reality of God's ever-faithful love.

But Paul is saying even more here. He says that there would be no such thing as compassion on earth if it were not for God. He is the source of all compassion. This point is important, because if God is the source of compassion, it makes no sense for his children to be uncaring. If we are members of his family and partakers of his divine nature, increasingly conformed to his image, we should be marked by our compassion. We should be more than theological answer machines. Because of our connection to the Father, we can bring comfort to a world where suffering is a constant reality. We should weep with those who weep and mourn with those who mourn, and so incarnate the One who is compassion.

The comfort we have received from the Lord has ministry in view. God has chosen me not only to be the recipient of his grace but to convey his grace to others. I must not hoard the comfort I have received like some spiritual heirloom. I have been called to share what I have received. The comfort we share is not rooted in abstract theology, but in our experience of being comforted by the Lord in our own times of trouble. We want sufferers around us to experience what we have been given by the Lord.

God wants us to share in Christ's suffering. The logic in 2 Corinthians is simple: You have been called to suffer so that you would experience God's comfort. You have experienced God's comfort so that you can comfort others. As they receive God's comfort through you, they can bring that comfort to others. Our suffering is not a gap in God's love, as if the Devil crept in while the Lord's head was turned.

Peter says it this way: "Dear friends, do not be surprised at the painful trial you are suffering, as though something strange were happening to you. But rejoice that you participate in the sufferings of Christ, so that you may be overjoyed when his glory is revealed" (1 Peter 4:12–13). Suffering does not mean that God's plan has failed. It *is* the plan. Suffering is a sign that we are in the family of Christ and the army of the kingdom. We suffer because we carry his name. We suffer so that we may know him more deeply and appreciate his grace more fully. We suffer so that we may be part of the good he does in the lives of others.

Acts 5

Even our suffering does not belong to us, but to the Lord. Perhaps it is easier to recognize that our blessings belong to the Lord than it is to recognize that he owns our suffering. If you watch someone suffer, you will see that we tend to treat suffering as something that belongs to us, something we can respond to as we please. We tend to turn in on ourselves. Our world shrinks to the size of our pain. We want little more than release, and we tend to be irritable and demanding.

It does not take long to learn that suffering gives you power. As you cry in pain, people run to help you. They offer you physical comforts, say nice things, and release you from your duties. I once watched a little boy fall off his bike several houses away from home. He started to cry, but then he quickly stopped. He picked up his bike and walked in silence to his house. When he stepped on his porch, he began to wail in pain. Clearly, he had concluded that crying half a block away from home was a waste of tears. When his mother hit the porch, he tearfully told a story of a mishap that was much more dramatic than anything I had witnessed. He pointed to a minor wound and screamed as if in major pain. I thought to myself, *This little guy is enjoying this moment!*

A whole host of self-absorbed temptations greet us when we treat suffering as something that belongs to us. This passage reminds us that our suffering belongs to the Lord. It is an instrument of his purpose in us and for others. The way we suffer must put Christ on center stage. The Redeemer owns our disappointment and fear. He owns our physical and spiritual pain. He owns those crushing past experiences. He owns our rejection and aloneness. He owns our dashed expectations and broken dreams. It all belongs to him for his purpose. When we feel like dying, he calls us to a greater death. He calls us to die to our suffering so that we may live for him.

This is not a call to some creepy form of Christian stoicism. It is a call to bring the full range of our suffering to him. We are to weep loudly and mourn fully before him, knowing that true comfort can only be found at his feet. We are to place our mourning in his hands, to be used for his purposes in our lives and the lives of others. And it is a promise of comfort from the God who is the source of it all.

The redemptive purpose in all of this is hope in a fallen world. God wants to raise up people filled with hope. True hope is not rooted in my achievements or assets, but in my knowledge that I am the child of the King. He loves me with a love that nothing can take away. He has given me his forgiving and empowering grace. He is daily changing and maturing me. He has promised to give me whatever I need to face what comes my way. And he has promised that I will live with him forever in a place without suffering, sorrow, or sin. This means that in the most difficult moments of my life, nothing truly permanent or valuable is at stake. What I really live for is safe and secure. I don't know what tomorrow will bring, but I know that I am in the family of God, eternally loved and cared for by him. This is real hope.

So this is the paradigm: purposeful suffering, leading to the experience of God's comfort, producing the ability to comfort others, resulting in a community of hope. As we embrace the fact that God is in our suffering, we need to keep Paul's *suffering* → *comfort* → *comfort* → *hope* paradigm in view.

We must also ask ourselves, "Where has God called me to suffer? How has God used people to make his comfort known to me? What have they said and done? How can I use my experience to comfort others? How can I tell my story in a way that gives hope, rooted in the reality of Christ's presence and love?" We can be thankful that Paul not only offers a paradigm but a methodology as well.

TELLING CHRIST-CENTERED STORIES

In 2 Corinthians 1, Paul says that he does not want the Corinthians to be uninformed about his suffering in Asia. He wants his story to result in deeper hope, strengthened faith, and renewed worship among them. Paul's experiences put flesh and blood on the promises of God. In them you see God in action, doing exactly what he promised to do for his children. As people see God in Paul's story, they are given eyes to see God in their own, and they are comforted by this. This is one of the most personal and powerful methodologies of offering comfort. It presents realities that are deeply theological in the context of circumstances familiar to anyone in a fallen world. Our stories take God's truth to the struggles of life and present strong reasons not to give up.

If God wants to use your suffering and his comfort to encourage others, how can you tell your story to accomplish this goal? Paul's example offers some guidelines in verses 8–11.

Tell your story in a way that breaks down the misconception that you are essentially different from the person you are helping. Have you ever been in a Sunday school class where someone raised her hand and said, "This may be a dumb question, but I was wondering . . . ?" When you hear the question, you are thankful because it was precisely the question *you* had but were afraid to ask. This happens in relationships too. People assume that they are the only ones with particular problems; they assume that no one else can understand or help. But God wants us to remember that we are just like the people around us—flawed human beings facing very similar difficulties. Redemptive truth is invigorated when it is shared by those willing to reveal the ways they have faced real life.

Always tell a completed story. Your story needs to include (1) a difficult situation, (2) your struggle in the midst of it, and (3) how God helped you. This is not the "misery loves company" brand of story-telling. This is not disaster one-upmanship. Tell a story that is old enough for you to reflect on how the Lord brought comfort in the middle of it, and how he used people to do it.

As you tell your story, be honest in describing your struggles and failures. Your story must highlight God's grace in your weakness, not your heroic faith. Be willing to expose your sin so that the redemptive glory of the Lord would live in the ears of the listener. Notice the things Paul says about himself, a man of great faith: We were far beyond our ability to endure . . . we despaired even of life . . . in our hearts we felt the sentence of death. Paul, beyond his ability to endure? Giving in to despair? Paul is willing to rip back the curtain of public reputation and take you into the private corridors of his struggles.

Be discerning and purposeful as you tell your story. Limit the amount of "gory" detail. Your focus is not the situation, but the God who met you in the middle of it. Notice that Paul gives almost no detail here, yet we are still able to sense the seriousness and drama of his situation.

Always tell your story in a way that makes God the key actor in the drama. Too often our stories of Christian suffering are incredibly man-centered. We even do this as we tell the great stories of Scripture, focusing on the heroic responses of Moses, David, and Daniel instead of the Lord who sustained them. This turns the great stories of Scripture into moralistic fables with no greater application than "Be like them." But these stories are only chapters of the one great story of Scripture. God is *the* Actor. It is *his* story. Our stories, too, are merely part of the Great Story of redemption. Our stories belong to him and point to him.

Tell your story with humility, admitting your continuing need for grace. Sometimes we have a way of telling our story that has a "good student learning the ultimate lesson" character to it. It communicates spiritual "arrival" rather than continuing need. We must tell our story out of a fresh recognition of our helplessness apart from the resources we find only in Christ. It may even be appropriate to ask for prayer from the person you are serving. Often, when I ask people how I can pray for them, they ask me the same question in return.

Always make it clear that you are not what this person needs—God is. At best, you are one of God's instruments, an ambassador who shares a need for God's daily mercy and grace. Personal storytelling is a natural way to discourage a person's inclination to develop an unhealthy dependency on you. If rightly told, your story will encourage people to trust themselves increasingly to Christ.

The goal of your story should always be worship. All true hope and comfort are rooted in thankfulness for God, his character, and his help. Giving hope is about helping a person see the Lord. Suffering commands our attention and clouds our vision, making it easy to forget what anchors our faith. Because trouble has such power to blind and confuse us, it is a sweet grace to have someone come alongside and point us to the One who is a rock, a fortress, a refuge, a hiding place, and a shield. We all need someone to remind us that life is not defined by our pain but by our union with Christ.

Giving hope is more than convincing people that things will get better, or helping them decide what to do. Giving hope introduces them to a Person. It helps people who are dealing with the unthinkable to view life from the perspective of God's glory and grace and their identity as his children. As you tell your own story, you help people to see that the very suffering that seems to cloud their theology actually expounds it. It is in the darkest night that the glory of the Redeemer's love and grace shines brightest. Hope points people toward the Light.

All of this should not only produce hope but deep thankfulness. Perhaps nothing has as much potential to produce true worship as suffering. Trials reveal critical things about us and wonderful things about God. People discover that there is strength to be found in weakness, love to be found in the midst of rejection, wisdom to be found in the face of foolishness, and that someone is with them even in their most profound loneliness. The result is worship that flows from an experience of the goodness of God. This is the ultimate reason for our personal storytelling.

Since suffering is a common human experience, identifying with suffering is critical to personal ministry. We should not greet these moments with fear, for they are moments of unique opportunity. As we approach suffering people as fellow sufferers and take them to a Suffering Savior, they can walk away with a stronger faith and a more heartfelt appreciation of the Lord. Suffering gives people who have been jolted out of their comfortable lifestyle a reason to stop, look, and listen. It can help them move out of the confines of their self-absorbed world into the grandeur of a world where God is central, where hope is rooted in things that cannot be seen.[2]

Building a relationship in which God's work can thrive means looking for the entry gates of opportunity in the lives of those God brings your way. It means incarnating the love of Christ and being willing to disclose your own stories. And there is one more element in the *Love* function of our personal ministry model.

▶ ELEMENT FOUR: ACCEPT WITH AGENDA

Here again we follow the example of Christ's love for us. The grace that adopts me into Christ's family is not a grace that says I am okay. In fact, the Bible is clear that God extends his grace to me because I am everything *but* okay. As we enter God's family, we are in need of radical personal change. God's acceptance is not a call to relax, but a call to work. Paul says in Titus 2:11–12, "For the grace of God that brings salvation has appeared to all men. It teaches us to say 'No' to ungodliness and worldly passions, and to live self-controlled, upright and godly lives in this present age." The grace God extends to us is always grace leading to change. His acceptance is not the end of his work; it is the beginning! Our justification must never be separated from our sanctification. They are two parts of a seamless work of redemption.

Therefore it is wrong to approach a struggling brother or sister with a condemning, self-righteous spirit. This puts you in the way of what the Lord is doing in their lives. You must grant them the same grace and love that you received from the Lord. At the same time, you do not want that offer of grace to be misunderstood. *God's grace is always grace leading to change.* Since God's purpose is that we would become "partakers of his divine nature" (2 Peter 1:4), change is his agenda. As we offer people a humble, patient, gentle, forbearing, and forgiving love, we must never communicate that it is okay for them to stay as they are. As long as a vestige of indwelling sin remains, change is God's call. It must never be compromised in the relationships he gives us. To do so is to cease to be an ambassador and to stand in the way of the Lord's work in that person's life.

So we sturdily refuse to condemn, but we also refuse to condone. We accept people with a grace that empowers us for God's work of heart change. Anything less cheapens his grace and denies the gravity of our need.

As we seek to minister by entering into people's struggles, we look for ways to incarnate the presence and character of Christ. We come alongside people as brothers and sisters in the same family, going through the same process. As sufferers who are willing to tell our own stories, we become windows to the hope and glory of God. Finally, we offer others the same acceptance we have received from the Lord. It is grace that cannot be earned, but that always calls us to work. This work is our calling until we are fully conformed to the image of God's Son. Relationships built this way become places where God's work can thrive. They become places where people are renewed, restored, rebuilt, and refined; where God is central and given the glory that is his due.

LOVE
▶ KNOW
SPEAK
DO

9 | GETTING TO KNOW PEOPLE

Everyone felt like they knew Betty and Brad. Their presence was so central to the life of our church that no gathering seemed official without them. I had spent many hours in meetings with Brad. I had been impressed by how quietly practical he was. We had picnicked together as families, shared evening meals, and worked together on Christian school projects. We knew their children and their extended family well.

Late one autumn evening, Brad called me to go out for coffee, making it clear that he wanted to do it right then. I heard the urgency in his voice, so I got dressed and we met at a local diner. I arrived first and as I saw Brad enter the diner, I knew that something was seriously wrong.

Brad sat down and said, "I don't know where to start. I guess I should have done this a long time ago, but I kept thinking that we could work things out. Now we're in a mess and I don't know what to do." He seemed both discouraged and angry. "I've put up with her stuff for years," he said. "It has been an everyday thing, constant demands, and when I don't do things just the way she wants, there's hell to pay! There is never a day that I am not in trouble for something. She has called me horrible things in front of our children. Once a month she threatens to leave. For the last week she has been so depressed that she hasn't gotten out of bed, except to eat a cracker or go to the bathroom. The kids keep asking what is wrong with Mommy, and I've made up a thousand stories to cover for her in front of our friends."

But that wasn't the worst of it. Brad went on, "A few years ago Betty was making supper and was very angry that I couldn't help her on a project that night. In the middle of our argument, she threw a saucepan lid at me. I ducked and it flew by me and broke our kitchen window. When I heard that window break, I guess I lost it. I rushed over and slapped her across the face. She responded by kicking me in the groin and we launched into the first of many physical battles. We have been physically fighting ever since. We have broken most of our pottery and lamps and put holes in almost every wall in the house. I have hit Betty so hard that she had to stay out of sight for a week so the bruises could heal. Most of the injuries that you thought were the result of my clumsiness at home repair actually came from Betty."

"It has really affected our children," he continued. "Our three boys swing from whiney and demanding to fearful and timid. They hide whenever they feel like trouble is brewing. They almost always disappear when I am expected home. Recently, when we are in the middle of a fight, our seven-year-old has taken to hitting and kicking whichever of us is closest, while screaming, 'I hate you, I hate you, I hate you.' Betty is constantly telling me that I am destroying the children, yet she regularly points out to them the things that I do wrong. I am here tonight because I don't know where Betty is. We had the most horrible fight we have ever had. Our house looks like a war zone. We fought from room to room. We said the most awful things we could think of and we threw everything we could get our hands on. She is out there now, insanely angry, with all of the debit and credit cards, and a huge bottle of wine."

It was hard for me to pay attention because Brad's story was so disorienting. I had known this man for years, yet I knew *nothing* of what he was telling me now. My mind went to the many hours we had spent with this family. I had assumed I knew them, so I had never asked anything that would give them an opportunity to say anything about the true state of their personal lives. I wondered how this could have gone on for so long without anyone knowing. In that moment I realized that the most personal and important parts of our lives fly under the radar of our typical relationships in the body of Christ. We live frenetically busy lives with activity-based friendships, punctuated only by brief conversations with each other. Now I was sitting across from a friend I did not know.

BREAKING THROUGH THE CASUAL

Have you ever thought you knew someone well, only to discover significant details that you did not know at all? Have you ever started to share a story from your own life and been interrupted by someone who said, "I know exactly what you mean!"—but clearly didn't? Think of someone you believe you know well. Try to identify some of the gaps in your understanding of his or her story. How much do you know of your friend's family of origin? Do you know where he struggles in his relationship with God or in his understanding of Scripture? What do you know about the quality of her marriage or the struggles she experiences with her husband? If he is single, do you know how he spends his hours alone? If she is a mother, does she think she is a failure? Could your friend be fighting disintegrating relationships at work or long-term problems with his extended family? Perhaps his heart is driven by lust or eaten up with bitterness. Might she harbor deep regret over a past decision or jealousy over the successes of a friend? Are there financial woes or physical problems?

We tend to have permanently casual relationships that never grow into real intimacy. There are things we know *about* each other, but they fool us into thinking that we know the human beings who live within the borders of those details. So we fail to pursue them with good questions. This sets the stage for all kinds of misunderstandings. Our effectiveness as ambassadors is blunted because we don't know others well enough to know where change is needed or where God is actively at work.

Think about it. Most of the conversations you had today were mundane and rather self-protective. We spend most of our time talking about things that are of little personal consequence—the weather, politics, sports, and entertainment. There is nothing wrong with this except that it allows us to hide who we really are. A person may be terribly distraught about her marriage, yet when people ask how she is, she will quickly answer, "Fine, how are you?" The person asking doesn't really want to know and the person answering doesn't really want to tell. They are co-conspirators in a casual relationship. Whether it is over the back of a pew, in passing at a school function, or over the phone, we are all skilled at newsy but personally protective conversations.

There are many reasons why our relationships are trapped in the casual. One is that, in our busyness, we despair of squeezing ten dollar conversations into ten cent moments. There are times when we *would* like to tell our story, but there doesn't seem to be an opportunity to do so. We all deal with the disconnect between our public reputation and our private struggles. We wonder what people would think if they really knew us.

Another reason we keep things casual is that we buy the lie that we are unique and struggle in ways that no one else does. We get tricked by people's public personas and forget that behind closed doors they live real lives just like us. We forget that life for everyone is fraught with disappointment and difficulty, suffering and struggle, trials and temptation. No one is from a perfect family, no one has a perfect job, no one has perfect relationships, and no one does the right thing all the time. Yet we are reluctant to admit our weaknesses to ourselves, let alone to others. We don't want to face what our struggles reveal about the true condition of our hearts.

The Bible teaches that people love darkness rather than light because their actions are evil. We all find the searching light of true friendship a bit intimidating. True friendship calls you out of the darkness of personal privacy into the loving candor of mutual concern. It moves you from being a sealed envelope to being an open letter. The best relationships are built on a foundation of mutual trust-giving and truth-speaking.

Another reason we rarely talk beyond a casual level is because we do not see. The Bible has much to say about how blind we are. Sin is deceitful, causing us to see others with a greater clarity than we see ourselves. Because we tend to believe our own arguments and buy into our own excuses, we are often unaware of how great our need for help really is. We can't bare what we don't see. We think we are okay but wonder how the person next to us can be so unaware of his own sin. This not only distorts our perspective on ourselves, but shapes the way we tell our story to others. It may even lead us to question whether we need to tell our story at all.

Perhaps the simplest reason for our lack of self-disclosing candor is that no one asks. The typical rhythms of our lives mitigate against going below the surface. In the busyness of life it seems intrusive to ask questions that cannot be answered without personal self-disclosure. Yet there is a way in which we all hunger for relationships of that quality. These are the relationships in which the Redeemer does his good work.

We must not let ourselves become comfortable with the casual, where ministry is limited to offering general principles that would fit anyone's story. The genius of personal ministry is that it is *personal*. It can take the grand themes of the Great Story and apply them with utter specificity to the particulars of an individual's life. Personal ministry is not preaching to a very small congregation. It is the careful ministry of Christ and his Word to the struggles of heart that have been uncovered by good questions from a committed friend. This means that effective, God-honoring, heart-changing personal ministry is dependent on a rich base of personal information. You cannot minister well to someone you do not know.

CHRIST THE DATA GATHERER

It may seem like a stretch to think of Christ as a model of data gathering, but that's exactly what he did when he walked among us. This is powerfully portrayed for us in Hebrews 4:14–16.

> Therefore, since we have a great high priest who has gone
> through the heavens, Jesus the Son of God, let us hold firmly
> to the faith we profess. For we do not have a high priest who

is unable to sympathize with our weaknesses, but we have one who has been tempted in every way, just as we are—yet was without sin. Let us then approach the throne of grace with confidence, so that we may receive mercy and find grace to help us in our time of need.

This passage encourages us to come to the Wonderful Counselor with the full range of our experiences and the weaknesses they expose. We can come knowing that we will receive mercy and grace appropriate to the need of the moment. This is a promise of personalized help. Christ is able to sympathize with each of our weaknesses. And the Greek word translated "sympathize" here means much more than a flash of compassion or a surge of pity. Our experience of sympathy is usually limited to feeling sorry for someone and being thankful that we're not in the same boat. But sympathy here means to be moved by what has moved someone else. Christ's sympathy is so strong that our problems become his. This is much more than feeling sorry for someone in a tough spot. It is understanding what it is like to live in the middle of someone else's circumstances, coupled with a desire to do whatever is within your power to help him out.

The double negative in the passage ("we do not have . . . who is unable") is a positive assurance that this is exactly how the Wonderful Counselor responds to us as we struggle with life. It is an amazing comfort to realize that the One we run to "gets it." He fully understands what we are going through and is motivated to respond with appropriate help. Isn't this what everyone in trouble wants? You want more than pity, a pat on the back, or some hopeful words. You want someone who is able to grasp what you are talking about and cares enough to help you do something about it. It is a sweet grace to realize that we find all of this in Christ. He is not only our ultimate helper, but our model as well. Only in him do we learn how to interact with people in need.

The Greek word in this passage translated "weaknesses" is also very strong. It is best understood as "the human condition." The writer of Hebrews is saying that Jesus really understands what it means to live in this fallen world. He understands the full catalog of temptations we face. He understands how difficult and complicated our relationships are. He understands betrayal, rejection, physical pain, and aloneness. Jesus knows what it means to be human. He knows *us!*

Perhaps you are thinking, *But Jesus was perfect!* Certainly he was perfect, but this does not mean that he didn't experience the full range of the pressures we face. This is a common misunderstanding. But consider this illustration. Imagine a strong man who performs at a state fair by bending bars of steel. The first bar he picks up is a half inch in diameter. He bends it to a ninety degree angle and it breaks. Then he picks up an inch-thick bar and bends it until the ends of the bar touch, but still it does not break. Which bar endured the most pressure? The obvious answer is the second bar. It absorbed the full force of the man's strength and did not break. On earth, Christ was like that second bar. Because he never gave in, because he did not run away, because he never went where temptation would lead, but stood strong until that moment of temptation was over, he endured the full power of temptation. Christ endured stress, pain, suffering, and sacrifice of an intensity that we will never face because he did not break. He stood strong against sin for us. He endured everything the world could throw at him.

What does all this have to do with data gathering? Look back at Hebrews 4:15: "We have one who has been tempted in every way, just as we are—yet was without sin." Jesus understands us because he entered our world. For thirty-three years, he lived among us, gathering data about the nature of our experience. Not one minute of those years was wasted. Not only was he passing the test that Adam failed, he was also thoroughly acquainting himself with all we would face as we endured life and waited for his return. His years of experience between the stall in Bethlehem and the mound called Golgotha made him a high priest who can fully sympathize with our weaknesses. He entered our world and his understanding is first-hand and complete.

Since Christ is our model for personal ministry, we too want to understand people so that we can serve him in their lives. We too must be committed to entering their worlds. We can begin by taking the time to ask good questions and listen well. Our hope is that others would seek us out and share more of their true struggles, so that they may find, through us, the Lord himself. Entering a person's world enables us to apply the truths of the gospel in a way that is situation- and person-specific.

THE PROBLEM OF ASSUMPTIONS

Why don't we ask better questions and take the time to really listen? Why don't we ask people more often what they meant by what they said, or why they did what they did? Why don't we ask people to define their terms or explain their logic? Why don't we ask people more about what they were thinking and feeling? Why don't we get them to talk more about the purposes and desires that shaped their decisions? There are many answers to these questions, but one in particular seems to get in the way of our call to function as the Lord's ambassadors. It is the problem of assumptions.

When you assume, you do not ask. If you do not ask, you open yourself up to a world of invalid conclusions and misunderstandings. You may try to be God's instrument but miss the mark because you are putting two and two together and getting five—and you don't even know it. Thanks to your assumptions, the person you *think* you are helping may exist only in your mind.

There are two main reasons we assume too much. One is theological and the other is experiential. Let's look at the theological reason first.

When we approach moments of personal ministry, we do not come empty-handed, but with the theology of Scripture. The theology of the Word not only describes God's plan of redemption, it explains people as well. The Bible knows us, even to the deepest thoughts and motives of our hearts. It dramatically depicts our suffering and our joy, untangling the complexities of human relationships. It depicts human feeling, knowing, and communicating. If you read the Bible, you will know and understand people.

This biblical insight is a great gift, but it is also where we get ourselves into trouble. Knowing fundamental things about people in general should not be confused with knowing the particular individuals God has sent your way. Our rich theological base should not make us lethargic data gatherers. However, because we assume we know people, we can easily fail to ask good questions.

We need to remember that God is not only the Creator of every person and the Revealer of who they are in Scripture, but he is also sovereign over every detail of their lives. Because of God's sovereignty, no two people have exactly the same story. People are at once all the same *and* dramatically different. Take human noses, for example. Everybody has one, yet no two are exactly alike. God's creative artistry is endless in its variations. All people are similar, yet the more carefully you look, the more you are impressed with how different we are from one another.

The endless variations of our physical bodies also serve as metaphors of our vast internal differences. Think of the endless variety of personalities or the diverse and unexpected ways different minds work. Some of us are mechanical, while others (like me) have neither the mind to figure out how things work nor the hands to fix them. Some of us are almost coldly rational, while others feel their way through life. Imagine the differences in life experience between a tall man and a short one, between someone who is obese and someone who is very thin. Think of the great difference in life experience between a man and a woman, or a thinker and a doer. The range of God's creativity is vast.

God not only uniquely creates each of us, he also sovereignly authors and directs each of our stories. There are familiar elements in all of them, but each person's story is a labyrinth of details that makes each one dramatically different from another. Because of this, you cannot know me only by knowing what Scripture says about me. You will know wonderfully helpful things about me as a human being, but you will not know how these truths are uniquely manifested in my life *without asking*. We must seek to know one another in a way that recognizes God both as our Creator (universal human truths) and as our sovereign Lord (the unique, individual details). This will not only make us thankful that we come armed with the truths of Scripture, but it will also drive us to know well the particular person God has sent our way.

The second reason we assume too much is our experience. We speak the same language, share many of the same experiences, live in the same community, and often attend the same church, so it is easy to assume that we know more about each other than we really do. More dangerous is the tendency to confuse *similar* experience with *identical* experience. For example, it is safe for me to conclude that you have some kind of family. But when I hear you say the word "family," it is *not* safe for me to fill in the details of what that means from my experience and not yours. When we assume an exact correspondence of thoughts, desires, and experiences, we will not ask the questions we need to ask to be useful in God's hands. We will be left with invalid assumptions about people and we will offer help that does not really fit their needs.

For personal ministry to be effective, the principle is simple: Don't assume—ask. This is true not only for a good counselor, but for a wise teacher, elder, spouse, parent, or friend as well. Assuming that you already know what you need to know almost always leads to misunderstandings that blunt and derail personal ministry. If you think you can take something for granted, ask anyway. Only then can you be sure that the help you offer will fit this person's situation and relationships.

MAKING SURE YOUR CONCLUSIONS ARE CORRECT

In grappling with the reality of shared experience and the temptation to assume, it is important to make a habit of doing three things. They may seem cumbersome at first, but you will soon learn to do them naturally, and you will be thankful that you are able to avoid wrong assumptions.

Always ask people to define their terms (What?). Human language is messy. The more a word is used, the more nuances of meaning it takes on. We will speak with people who use very familiar words, but with very different functional definitions. For example, when a woman says that she and her husband had a huge fight last night, you should not assume that you understand what she means. If you do not ask her to define "huge fight," you have simply reached into your own experience to define it. In doing so, you may have created a subtle but important area of misunderstanding that could affect the counsel you give her. This woman's fight may seem like your normal marital conversation, or it may look like the domestic version of nuclear war. I regularly say to people, "I don't want to put my definition on your words and end up counseling someone who doesn't exist, so I am regularly going to ask you to define your terms."

Always ask people to clarify what they mean with concrete, real life examples of the terms they have used (How?). If point 1 asked for their personal dictionary definition, then point 2 asks people to play us the video. The terms people use are verbal shorthand for significant situations. I want the woman to walk me through, step by step, what happened during the "huge fight" with her husband last night. Listening to her account will make my understanding concrete and personalized, and give me a sense of the drama and emotions of the moment.

Always ask people to explain why they responded as they did in the examples they have given you (Why?). Now you not only have a definition and a concrete situation, but you can begin to get a little bit of the heart behind the person's behavior. Ask the person to share her reasons, values, purposes, and desires. You are asking her to step back and evaluate what was behind the words she said, the choices she made, and the things she did. In so doing, you are taking the camera off the scene and putting it on the person.

When you are careful to ask people to define, clarify, and explain, you will avoid many misunderstandings and false assumptions that rob personal ministry of its effectiveness. Remember, you are not seeking to broadcast the principles of the Word in a general way. Rather, in the privacy of this moment with this person, use the Word with focused specificity. Enter her world, get to know what she is facing, and help her to understand her resources in Christ to face her particular situation. Because you are eager to contextualize the gospel for this person, you won't ask her to define, clarify, and explain just once. You will do it again and again, seeking to avoid subtle misunderstandings and to handle the truth with concrete practicality.

THE IMPORTANCE OF ASKING GOOD QUESTIONS

It is tempting to think that insightful people have all the right answers, and in one sense that is true. But it is also true that you don't get to the right answers without first asking the right questions. The engineer who changes the face of a certain technology is able to do so because he first stepped back and asked questions that no one else was asking. Our thinking always rides on the rails of our questions. Good thinkers like to walk around a topic and look at it from different angles. They like asking new questions and asking old questions in new ways. Good thinkers don't make uncorroborated assumptions, and they don't allow themselves to think they know more than they actually do.

If you want to help people to see brand new truths (and old truths in brand new ways), you need to take on the habits of good thinkers. Asking good questions is one of the most important. I am regularly reminded that people get trapped in the conceptual cul-de-sacs of their own questions. For example, I have often heard people ask, "Why isn't God doing anything in my life?" This is a bad question, based on wrong assumptions that can lead only to theological confusion and the emotional discouragement that follows.

What are the typical answers to our friend's mistaken question? Many people will conclude that God doesn't love them, or that he is not faithful to his promises, or that he plays favorites, or that he is absent in times of trouble, or that God's Word isn't true—or if it is, then it isn't very practical. Remember that people were made by God to be interpreters, and the questions we ask ourselves (sometimes almost unconsciously) are what we use to try and make sense out of life. The answers we give will profoundly affect the direction of our lives. So it is important to understand that when you bring well-constructed, creative, biblically-shaped questions to a person's life, you are doing more than getting to know them and uncovering where change is needed. You are, in fact, ministering to that person.

When I ask you questions you would never ask yourself, I am teaching you to view yourself through biblical lenses. I am doing something God can use to change you in fundamental ways. Perhaps my questions will help you see yourself more accurately. When my questions do this, I am incarnating the Messiah who came to give sight to blind eyes. Perhaps my questions will help you begin to see how Scripture explains your life. When my questions do this, I am incarnating the Messiah who came to teach as people had never been taught before. Maybe my questions will convict your heart and lead you to new levels of repentance. When they do this, I am incarnating the Messiah who sent his Spirit to convict and convince us of our sin. Perhaps my questions will help you to see that the Bible really does speak to the deepest issues of your experience, causing you to hunger to feed on the Word in new ways. In so doing, I am incarnating the Messiah who is the Bread from heaven that feeds his people. In these ways, even in asking questions we can function as the Messiah's ambassadors, incarnating him before others.

Asking good questions *is* doing the work of change. Through them, we give sight to blind eyes and understanding to dull minds, we soften hardened hearts, encourage flagging souls, and stir hunger that can only be filled by the truth. This not only builds a platform for the work the Messiah does through us—it *is* that work!

My brother Tedd, who has always been a mentor to me, was riding home with me after a conference on marriage and family counseling. We were going about sixty-five miles per hour when he said to me, "You know, Paul, we probably should apply the principles that we learned this weekend to our own marriages. Why don't you start?" He then proceeded to ask me a series of questions about my relationship with Luella. I don't remember any of the specific questions, but I do remember the profound impact they had on me. It was as if God was tearing down thick velvet curtains that stood between me and an accurate understanding of my marriage. I saw myself with clarity, and what I saw wasn't pretty! Through those questions I watched myself do and say things I could not believe. Through those questions I finally understood Luella's experience and her frustrations. I saw my defensiveness and self-righteousness, and I saw that I had to change for the sake of the Lord and for the good of my marriage. Those questions were truly life-changing for me.

As Tedd questioned me, I remembered something I had once said to Luella during an argument: "Ninety-five percent of the women in our church would love to be married to a man like me!" (She lovingly informed me that she must be in the five percent minority!) Through Tedd's questions I saw myself repeatedly defend myself by analyzing her words and shifting the focus off me and onto her. I saw that I was much more self-righteous and angry than I had ever realized. With stark clarity I saw how far I had fallen below God's standards for a husband.

That night I got home late and asked Luella if we could talk. She could tell by the tone of my voice that something important was going on. As we sat down, I told her that I had known for a long time that God was trying to show me things about myself through her, and that I had been unwilling to listen. I told her that for perhaps the first time I was really ready to hear. She burst into tears, told me that she loved me, and then proceeded to talk to me for about two hours. That talk continued the work of change that Tedd's questions had begun. Sometimes I wonder what my marriage would be like today if Tedd had not asked me the questions I would never have asked myself.

NOW FOR SOME GOOD QUESTIONS

Since the primary way we get to know people is through the question-and-answer process, it is important to know what is a good question and what is not. Here are four principles to keep in mind.

1. *Always ask open-ended questions that cannot be answered with a "yes" or "no."* Yes and no questions do not give much information. The closed question (leading to a yes or no answer) can lead to misunderstandings because it forces you to fall back on your own assumptions about why the person answered as she did. For example, if you ask someone if she has a good marriage and she answers, "Yes," what have you learned? Not much; you do not know her definition of a good marriage. On the other hand, open-ended questions cannot be answered without the person disclosing what she is thinking, what she wants, and what she is doing. Here are some examples of open-ended marriage questions.

- What things did you see in this person that made you want to marry him?
- What were your goals for your marriage when you were engaged?
- What things in your marriage make you sad?
- What things in your marriage make you happy?
- If you could press a button and change your marriage, how would it change?
- In what ways do you think God is honored by your marriage?
- How would you characterize your communication with your husband?
- Describe how you and your husband arrive at decisions.
- Describe how you as a couple resolve conflicts.
- How would you describe your spiritual life as a couple?
- Are there couples you look up to? What do you respect about their marriages?
- Why do you think you have struggled as a couple?
- What do you see as the strengths of your marriage?
- What do you see as the weaknesses of your marriage?
- What do you think you need to do as a couple to get from where you are to where you need to be?
- Describe the marriage of your dreams.
- What could your spouse do to greatly change your marriage?

- What problems in your marriage do you see as your responsibility?
- What specific things have led you to conclude that your marriage needs help?
- What do you think God is doing in your marriage right now?
- What do you think keeps you as a couple from solving your problems?
- Describe how your marriage has changed over the years.
- When you are hurt or angry with your spouse, what do you do?
- How do you communicate dissatisfaction to your spouse?
- Pick one area of your marriage where you think you have problems. Describe what is wrong and what each of you has done to solve it.
- In what ways have you attempted to communicate love and appreciation to your spouse?
- What are the biggest hot buttons in your marriage?

This list could go on and on. The point is to ask questions that require the person to examine himself or herself and to answer in a self-disclosing manner.

2. *Ask a combination of survey and focused questions.* We need both kinds of questions, because each discloses a different kind of information. We do not want to assume that a problem in one area of a person's life only exists in that area, so we ask *survey* questions. We want to trace problems to their roots in the heart, so we ask *focused* questions. Remember, we want to break through the casual and guard against invalid assumptions so that we can help someone we truly know.

Survey questions scan the various areas of a person's life and look at the person as a whole. Things that seem superficially different may actually be part of a larger theme of thought, motive, or behavior that you want to uncover. For example, Joe was a guy who lived for the respect of other people. The way he sought to get it at home was by establishing a violent autocracy (though what he got was more fear than respect). Outside the home Joe was known as a real servant, a guy who would give you the shirt off his back. People at Joe and Sarah's church found it hard to believe that he could be capable of the things Sarah said he was doing with her and the children. It wasn't until the police were called that Sarah began to get the help she had needed for so long. The point is that the public Joe and the private Joe were not completely different people. His behavior in both arenas was motivated by the same craving for respect.

Survey questions help uncover *themes and patterns* in the person's life. Perhaps the problems in a marriage are part of a larger theme of relational sin in a person's life. A lack of self-control in the area of sex may also be the reason a person is deeply in debt. A problem with tongue control that causes a man to lose his job may also explain his estrangement from his teenage son. Maybe the fear that paralyzes a young girl in one area of her life is more pervasive than it first appears. Take the wide angle view of a person; don't assume that the confessed problem exists in isolation. Ask yourself how things that appear to be different may be different aspects of the same theme.

Focused questions look intensively into one area of a person's life. For Joe, it would mean digging into his constant willingness to serve others, seeking to know the heart behind the behavior. Is this really motivated by a love for God that expresses itself in a love for others? Or is something else ruling Joe's heart? The purpose of the focused question is to uncover *roots and causes*.

To really get to know someone, both kinds of questions should be asked. To illustrate this point, imagine yourself at the end of a motel hallway. The hallway, with doors every several feet, represents a person's life. The rooms behind the doors represent various aspects of the person's life (job, marriage, parenting, family, spiritual life, relationship to the body of Christ, relationship to neighbors, finances, sex, communication, problem solving, goals, motives, desires, etc.). Everything you need to know about this person is in that hallway and in those rooms. As you get to know a person, you will walk down the hallway, taking a peek in each room (*survey questions*). You will begin to notice certain themes (each room has a bed, desk, carpet, chair). Some rooms you will enter (*focused questions*), examining the contents more closely when you see something that seems worthy of special attention. Knowing when to ask which type of question is a matter of wisdom.

3. *Remember that certain kinds of questions reveal certain kinds of information.* To fill the gaps in your knowledge of a person, you must constantly ask yourself what you do not know. For example, I may know what a person did, but not how he did it. Or I may have established how he did it, but not where or when. I may have learned all of these things but still not know why he did what he did. To get the whole picture we need to ask ourselves, "What do I need to know about this person in order to help him? What kind of question will reveal that information?"

There are essentially five classes of questions:

- *What?* questions are the most basic, uncovering general information. ("What did you do?" "I talked to my wife.")
- *How?* questions reveal the way something was done. ("How did you talk to her?" "I yelled at her for fifteen minutes!") Notice how much more we know already, simply by asking a follow-up "how" question.
- *Why?* questions uncover a person's purposes, desires, goals, or motivations. ("Why did you yell so long?" "I wanted her to know how angry I was at what she had done.") Here we have gone beyond the husband's behavior to examine the heart behind it.
- *How often?* and *Where?* questions reveal themes and patterns in a person's life. ("Where did this happen?" "At the supper table. Suppers are hard. We are both tired. We have young children. Meals are not relaxing at all! The evening meal always seems to be tense for us.")
- *When?* questions uncover the order of events. ("Tell me exactly when you began to yell during supper." "In the middle of the chaos my wife said, 'Well, how was *your* day?' She was

obviously annoyed because I hadn't asked about hers. I said, 'Do you really care or are you just being nasty?' She said, 'Well, you're the only one here with an interesting and important life, right?' At that point I blew up.")

Each class of question uncovers different information, so each needs to be followed by the next. This will broaden and deepen your understanding of what took place (the situation), how the person interacted with it (the thoughts and motives of the heart), and what he did in response (behavior). Use these questions whether you are focusing on one area or surveying a person's life.

These questions were very helpful when Jim called me, expressing concern about his relationship to his wife, Bonnie. Frankly, such calls are unusual; typically, the call comes from a frustrated wife. Jim got my attention and I agreed to meet with them. Jim was very successful in his business, where he and Bonnie worked together every day, apparently happily. Outwardly they seemed to be doing well. Their lifestyle had all the hallmarks of success, they were involved in their church, and had a close circle of Christian friends.

Jim was self-consciously theological as he described how he had dedicated many years of his life mastering the doctrines of the Word of God. Bonnie was a new Christian, much more intuitive and private in her faith. As we sat together, Jim shared his grief over the fact that they had never experienced the kind of marriage the Bible describes. He said he had prayed and prayed and sought the counsel of many, to no avail. He said he had done everything he could to encourage intimacy with Bonnie, only to be rejected. He said he didn't care about his business success when he had a cold and lifeless marriage.

It was a convincing story, but I was distracted by the hurt and angry look on Bonnie's face. I knew I needed to ask more, so I asked both Jim and Bonnie the "what" questions, and followed up with the "how," "when," "why" and "where" questions. Then I began to see what was really going on. Yes, Jim was theologically knowledgeable, but it was his business that really drove his life—and therefore Bonnie's. Their daily schedule was completely controlled by work from early in the morning until late at night. Bonnie said that she only felt appreciated as a dedicated (and basically unpaid) employee. By the time she got home, she had nothing to give to the marriage.

I asked Jim to describe how he approached Bonnie with his concerns about the marriage. He repeated conversations, apparently unaware of the name-calling and condemnation he brought to those encounters. Bonnie was tired of being yelled at, tired of being called spiritually immature and romantically inept. She was tired of working hard with no reward, and living with someone who claimed to be close to God but was never thankful. She was at the breaking point, but did not want to tell Jim, since it would only reinforce his negative attitudes. Instead, she was distancing herself from him, hoping to avoid the ugly conversations, the accusations, and the emotional isolation.

What an incredibly different picture the follow-up questions revealed! They got below the surface impression of a godly husband and a cold and critical wife to reveal the driven, condemning man and the wife living in exhausted self-protection. The help I offered them was completely different from what I would have given without the understanding that came from asking those questions.

4. *Ask a progressive line of questions*, in which each question is based on information uncovered in the previous questions. There should be order and logic to the flow of your questions. Each question should be asked because you are seeking to fill gaps in your knowledge of what has already been uncovered. You accomplish this by continually asking yourself, *What do I not know about what I have just heard?* This challenges you not to make assumptions or settle for incomplete information.

THE REDEMPTIVE IMPORTANCE OF GOOD QUESTIONS

What we have been talking about is crucial for serving as one of the Lord's instruments of change. Asking good questions is vital to helping people to face who they really are and what they are really doing.

As sinners we all tend to recast our own history in self-serving ways. We hide behind the difficulty and pressures of the situation or the failures of others. We look for external explanations, not internal ones. We are more impressed with our righteousness than we are horrified at our sin.

Because of this, we all need people who love us enough to ask, listen, and, having listened, to ask more. This is not being intrusive. This is helping blind people to embrace their need for Christ. It is helping people to see the foolish ways they have lived for their own glory, and the subtle ways they have exchanged worship and service of the Creator for worship and service of his creation.

The forgiving and empowering grace of Christ is for sinners—the transgressor and the weak, the sufferer and the lost. People who do not see their need will not seek his help. But in the Messiah's hands, our questions can become keys that open people's prisons and cause them to rely upon Christ in new and profound ways.

Through our questions Christ changes people. The beaten down become strong in hope. Glory thieves begin to live for the glory of the Lord. The self-absorbed are freed to love God and neighbor. As the Holy Spirit is at work, our questions can be the beginning of God's radical work of change. They are an integral part of what it means to incarnate him to those around us.

LOVE
▶ KNOW
SPEAK
DO

10 | DISCOVERING WHERE CHANGE IS NEEDED

Mike and Marsha had asked if we could talk because "things were such a mess." They both seemed frazzled, so we got together as soon as we could. I brought along someone I was discipling for personal ministry. When I asked what was going on, Mike began to tell the most confusing family story I had ever heard. They had both been married before and had blended two families, each with four older children. Marsha occasionally jumped in with details that only added to my confusion. I don't think I took as many notes in my theology classes at seminary as I did that afternoon! Their story was full of plots and sub-plots. Their attempts to solve problems invariably made them worse. It seemed that their children had made all the wrong decisions as well. It *was* a mess!

At the end of an hour Mike said, "As you can see, Paul, we are in desperate need of help." That was an understatement. I sat there in silence, staring at my pile of notes and the faces of two hurting people who were reaching out for any help they could get. I was so overwhelmed that I couldn't think of anything intelligent to say. I was probably only silent for a few seconds, but it seemed like hours. Finally I told them that I would think and pray about what they had told me, and we would get together to talk again.

After they left, the person I was mentoring said, "Boy, that was encouraging! I can do personal ministry! All you have to do is get people to tell their story and then promise that you'll think and pray. I thought it was much harder than it really is!"

I've thought back many times to that first afternoon with Mike and Marsha. I didn't give them much hope to hold onto, and I wasn't very successful at grabbing hold of their struggles. But given the mountain of confusing details, I think I made the right choice. Personal ministry gets you involved with people who are lost in the chaos of life, whose lives are complicated by their own foolish decisions or the sins of others. Often you will hear about years of attempted solutions that have only made things worse. You will see the destructive work of the Enemy who deceives, divides, and devours, and the impact of poor thinking and deficient counsel.

But personal ministry also allows you to see God at work, as he takes people far beyond their own strength and wisdom. You will witness his plan of redemption being worked out in the context of a person's life. You will have the privilege of connecting people with the resources that are theirs in Christ in a way that transforms heart and life. You will be his ambassadors as you seek to incarnate the love of the Lord Jesus, entering another person's world, being moved by his suffering, and offering the hope of the gospel. You will be part of the great work of God's kingdom.

Personal ministry is not about always knowing what to say. It is not about fixing everything in sight that is broken. Personal ministry is about connecting people with Christ so that they are able to think as he would have them think, desire what he says is best, and do what he calls them to do even if their circumstances never get "fixed." It involves exposing hurt, lost, and confused people to God's glory, so that they give up their pursuit of their own glory and live for his. It is about so thoroughly embedding people's personal stories in the larger story of redemption that they approach every situation and relationship with a "God's story" mentality. We need to be filled with awe at what the Lord has called us to participate in!

As I thought and prayed for Mike and Marsha, two things happened. First, I was able to see God at work in the middle of their chaos. I got excited about helping them to see him. Second, their story began to be less confusing. I began to see how the pieces of the puzzle fit together. I had more questions to ask, but I also had things to say. I had a biblical sense of direction and that made me look forward to getting together with Marsha and Mike.

MAKING SENSE OF THE DATA

Personal ministry is not just about gathering the necessary information, but about making biblical sense of it. In chapter 3 we saw that people do not live life based on the facts of their experiences, but on their interpretation of those facts. The same is true of personal ministry. God created us to be interpreters, so when others tell their stories, we instinctively try to make sense of what we hear. Whatever we say or do in response will not be based solely on what the person told us, but on how we interpreted it.

Biblical personal ministry must be just that—*biblical*. This means that we look at people's lives from the distinct perspective of a biblical worldview. We are concerned with the glory of God, the sinfulness of man, the fallen condition of the world, the reality of the Devil, the grace of the gospel, and the certainty of eternity. Biblical personal ministry is more about *perspective, identity, and calling* than about fixing what is broken.

In the case of marriage, what do struggling couples need? Will they be helped by communication techniques or honest discussions about sex? Do they need a unified front regarding parenting and finances, and healthy ways to deal with conflicts? The answer to all of these questions is, "Yes!" But they need more. They need to live out of an understanding of who they are, who God is, and what he is doing in their marriage. Paul reminds us in 2 Corinthians 11:1–3 that our lives *now* are the training ground for our marriage *then*. We are the bride of Christ. God is preparing us for the perfect marriage to come. For that reason, the big question of our *now* relationships is not whether we will be happy, but whether we will give the love that has been promised to the Groom to someone or something else.

You cannot understand Christian relationships, particularly marriage, any other way. Why would God put the world's most significant, demanding, and difficult human relationship (marriage) smack dab in the middle of the world's most important process (sanctification)? If he did it so that people would realize their individual dreams, it would have made sense to get them fully sanctified before facing the trials of marriage. But God hasn't made a mistake. He is working on a greater dream, so he tries and troubles us. He lets our dreams slip through our fingers so that as we learn to love each other, we grow more deeply in love with him.

When you look at marriage this way, you no longer try to get your spouse to fulfill your dream. You now know who you are (engaged to Christ) and what God is doing (preparing you for the ultimate marriage). As you deal with the stresses of parenting, communication, sex, and finances, you have greater joy than you thought possible in a less-than-perfect marriage. Only from this perspective do the biblical principles for husbands and wives make sense. They are practical applications of what it means to live in a *now* marriage with a *then* marriage focus.

The same is true, of course, for those who are not married. You too are being prepared to be the bride of Christ through the relationships and situations you experience with family, neighbors, coworkers, and church family. Though you may not have an earthly spouse, your life *now* is just as thorough a preparation for your marriage *then* as is true for your married counterparts. You too need a biblical identity, perspective, and calling, and God is committed to helping you get them.

If you do not help people to see their story from a distinctly biblical, Christ-centered perspective, your ministry will do nothing but lob theological platitudes and principles at them. Their hearts will remain unchanged, and any behavioral changes will be temporary. They will not only continue to be at war with others, but also with a God who will not concede his exclusive claim on their hearts.

Biblical personal ministry thrives when good exegesis of Scripture leads to an accurate exegesis of the person's life. This two-sided interpretive process is what makes biblical personal ministry unique. We cannot properly understand people without accurately exegeting Scripture, and we cannot properly apply Scripture without accurately exegeting people. Because the Bible tells us that people live out of their hearts, we are always interested in how the heart's thoughts and cravings are revealed by the choices people make and the things they say and do. It is in the convergence of this two-sided interpretive process that hearts and lives change for the long run.

ORGANIZING THE INFORMATION BIBLICALLY

We cannot allow ourselves to offer counsel to someone on the spur of the moment, with little or no preparation. Unless we take the time to think biblically about what others share with us, we are the blind leading the blind. We must ask ourselves, "What themes, perspectives, promises, and commands of Scripture make sense of this person and speak to this situation?" Our counsel will only be biblical if we filter what we have heard through a sound biblical grid.

Remember, there is never a day when we do not counsel one another. A wife may advise her husband as he is getting ready for work. A parent may coach a child on how to face a difficulty at school. A brother may help his sister talk through some problems with her friends. A boss may confront a worker. Every day we share our interpretations of life with other people, shaping the way they understand their lives. The question is whether our ministry to one another is biblical. In all of this talk, are we asking ourselves what the Bible has to say about it?

Getting to know a person is like going around the house and collecting the laundry. Before long you have a diverse pile of multi-colored clothes, but you'd better sort them before you throw them in the washer, or you will have funny-colored socks! The same is true of getting to know another person. No one ever says, "Pay attention now; I am about to share with you a significant piece of my past." No one says, "Listen carefully, because I am about to reveal the motives of my heart." Instead, we mix history with present circumstances, and emotions with logical reasoning. We interpret the behavior of others as we talk about ourselves. We say things about God as we describe circumstances. It all comes out as a messy pile of isolated facts that need organization and interpretation.

The first step in making sense of things is to organize the information into simple biblical categories. This step is like sorting laundry or assembling a puzzle. When we have finished the task, we can step back and ask, "Where does the Bible say that change needs to take place in this person, in this situation?"

Let's practice organizing data biblically. Imagine that Greta, a woman from church, asks to talk to you. She is concerned about her husband John, who has an increasingly short fuse. He yells at her and the children at the drop of a hat. He is critical and demanding. He is spending more time at work, and most of his home time is spent on the computer. When she asks John what is wrong, he says that life stinks. Greta says that John's dad was a negative guy who thought that people were out to get him. John was not like that when she married him, but Greta is afraid he is turning into his father. When Greta asks John how she can help him, all he says is, "Just give me a little space so I can breathe."

Figure 10.1 is a simple data organization tool to help you sort information as you get to know someone. As you organize the informa-

FIG. 10.1
Knowing a Person Biblically.

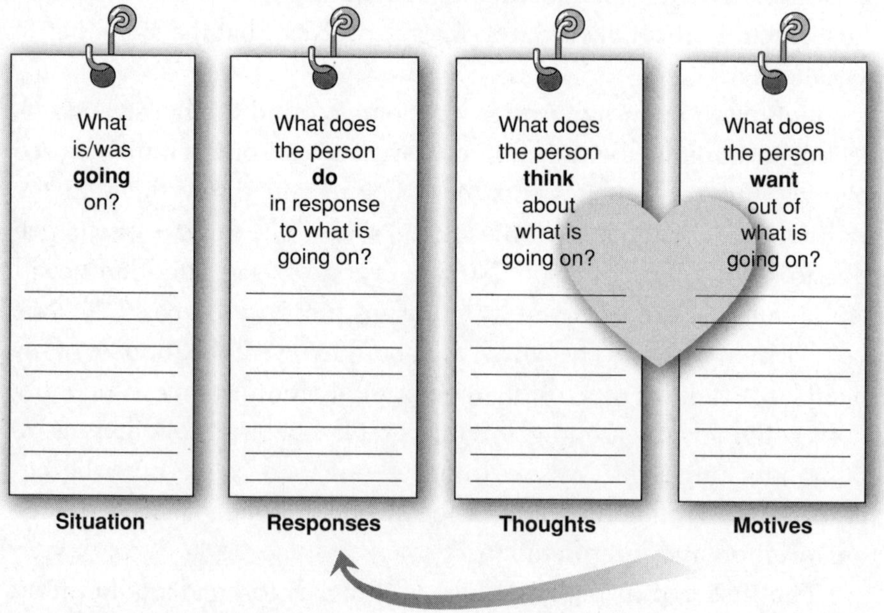

What is/was **going** on?	What does the person **do** in response to what is going on?	What does the person **think** about what is going on?	What does the person **want** out of what is going on?
Situation	**Responses**	**Thoughts**	**Motives**

tion Greta has given you, it will help you to step back to see the big picture in a biblical way. (In this case, you are just beginning to gather information. To truly help Greta and John, you would need to gather much more information by asking good questions.)

The Situation. (*What is going on?*) Here we place all the information that describes the person's world (his circumstances), both past and present. What we know so far about John is that, in the past, he was raised by a negative, cynical father. In the present he is an increasingly angry, critical, distant husband.

The Responses. (*What does the person do in response to what is going on?*) Here we include facts about the person's behavior. We have learned that John is yelling at his family, spending more time at work, and staying on the computer at home.

The Thoughts. (*What does the person think about what is going on?*) This includes information on how the person has been interpreting his world. All we know about John so far in this category is that he says, "Life stinks."

The Motives. (*What does the person want out of, or in the midst of, what is going on?*) This includes what you know about the person's desires, goals, treasures, motives, values, and idols. What does he live for? What really rules his heart? All we know about John at this point is that he says, "Just give me a little space so I can breathe." However, we don't know what he means by "a little space" or why he wants it.

These four categories provide four simple hooks to organize the information you gather from the Johns and Gretas of the world. They also help you identify the kinds of information you still need.

UNDERSTANDING AND USING THE HOOKS

Let me demonstrate how the four hooks simplify the information-gathering process by introducing you to another couple and organizing their information with this tool.

Sharon approached me after the Sunday service. She said that her marriage was a disaster and that she needed to talk immediately. We set up a time to meet and I asked her to invite her husband, Ed. However, Sharon came alone, telling her story emotionally and in great detail. Ed had been unwilling to come, telling her to "get her act together" or he was "out of here."

Sharon told of an increasingly violent relationship. She and Ed were no longer sleeping in the same room or going anywhere together. They had separate bank accounts and had recently agreed that it was best to eat supper separately. Their two young children took turns eating with each parent.

Even before their marriage, they had experienced communication problems. Ed felt that Sharon was always trying to control him. Sharon felt that Ed never paid attention to her viewpoint unless she "made it real clear." Yet Ed said that Sharon was the most beautiful woman in the world and Sharon said that Ed was the best thing that ever happened to her.

Ed was a "mover and shaker" with an expanding import business, and Sharon enjoyed being with people that "matter." She had lived in foster homes all her life and never knew her natural parents. Ed was raised in a working class urban neighborhood. Ed had said for years that Sharon was slowly destroying his manhood. Sharon confessed to two affairs during the marriage. Ed was very angry, and she appeared to be the same.

Sharon made her agenda very clear when we talked. "I am not here to work on me," she said. "I think I am okay. I am here because my marriage is in trouble. Do you think you can get my husband to talk to you? He's the one who needs help!"

Let's use the four categories (Situation, Responses, Thoughts, Motives) to organize what we have learned about Sharon and Ed.

THE SITUATION

For personal ministry to be effective, I must understand Sharon's everyday world. What pressures, opportunities, responsibilities, and temptations does she face daily? Who are the significant people in her life, and what are they doing? What do I know about her past? As I review the facts, I ask myself, *"What is (or was) going on?"* and hang all of the situational information on this hook.

Here are two lists of questions you can use to sort out information about someone's past history and present situation. These lists are not meant to be exhaustive, but "pump-primers" to give you a sense of the kinds of things to listen for and ask.

Historical
- Family of origin. What do I know about this person's childhood?
- Crisis events. What major events (death in the family, divorce, crippling accident, etc.) influenced this person's life?
- Significant relationships. Outside the home, who were the most influential people in this person's life (coach, relative, friend, teacher, pastor)? How did they shape this person's view of herself and her world?
- Significant experiences. These are not the crisis events, but the long-term experiences that shaped the person's life (major family move, going to college, coming to Christ). What is the lasting impact of these experiences?

Remember, this list is not exhaustive. It simply suggests things that may be important to understand about the person's past.

Present
- Life context. What situations and relationships does the person face every day (pressures, opportunities, responsibilities, temptations)?
- Significant relationships. Who are the influential people in this person's life? What impact do they have?
- Present family. What do I know about the family in which she is living?
- Presenting problem. How does the person describe her struggle? What does she say is wrong?

The goal is to get to know Sharon in her world. I need to know the details because my call is to build a bridge of understanding from the Word of God to the details of her life, so that Sharon can understand what God has promised her and called her to do. Let's begin sorting the information with Sharon.

Sharon's Situation
- Troubled marriage
- Husband unwilling to seek help
- Violent relationship
- Separate bank accounts
- Communication problems
- Husband is a "mover and shaker" in an expanding business
- Husband angry—tells her to change or get out
- Many foster homes—never really knew her natural parents

THE RESPONSES

Here I focus on Sharon's behavior. I collect all the information that describes her reactions to what is going on. I am looking for *themes* and *patterns*. What are the typical ways she responds to situations and people? These themes and patterns will give me an idea of what is going on in her heart. Any information that describes Sharon's behavior is placed under the question, "*What does this person do in response to what is going on?*"

Sharon's Responses
- Came for help (for Ed)
- Not sleeping with Ed
- Gets separate bank accounts
- Eats separately from Ed, alternating who gets the children
- Two affairs
- Confessed affairs
- Asked you to get Ed to talk
- Does not move out

- Continues to go to church
- Makes what she wants very clear to Ed (and you)

As you look at this list of Sharon's responses, look for themes and patterns in the way she deals with her problems.

THE THOUGHTS

This category looks at the "heart" that directs Sharon's behavior. I know that, as a human being, Sharon is a meaning-maker. She is always trying to make sense out of her life. She doesn't just respond to the facts of her life, but to her interpretation of those facts. If her interpretations are not biblical, her responses will not be biblical either.

If I have a distorted view of the past, the present, God, the future, and myself, there is no way I will respond properly to what God has allowed in my life. This is one of Sharon's most significant problems. As we seek to minister to people like her, we need to look for the seeds of wrong behavior in distorted and unbiblical thought. We begin by identifying the facts that describe how she thinks about life and placing them under the question, *"What does this person think about what is going on?"*

Sharon's Thoughts
- My marriage is in trouble.
- Ed doesn't pay attention to my viewpoint.
- Ed was the best thing to happen to me.
- I like being with people that matter.
- I am okay.
- Ed is the one who needs help.

THE MOTIVES

There is always something or someone ruling our hearts, and whatever rules our hearts will control our behavior. In this category, we collect all the information that describes what Sharon truly wants, what desires rule her heart, and what idols have taken control. Since

Sharon's behavior is an attempt to get what she wants from people and situations, we need to identify her motives and place all of this information under the question, *"What does this person want out of, or in the midst of, what is going on?"*

Sharon's Motives
- Wants to talk about marriage immediately
- Wants to separate herself from Ed
- Doesn't want to be controlled
- Likes being with people who matter
- Wants Ed to change
- Wants you to know she is okay
- Wants you to know Ed needs help

At this point, what have we accomplished? Instead of immediately responding to the chaotic pile of facts Sharon has shared with us, we have attempted to organize them in biblical categories. Now the information speaks to us, and in many instances suggests further questions to ask Sharon and Ed. This is particularly true in the Motives category; we need to know more about why Sharon wants the things she wants. However, even at this early point in the ministry relationship, the categories help us to put the puzzle together, and start to see where change needs to take place in Sharon and in her marriage.

WHAT ABOUT EMOTIONS?

Perhaps you noticed that emotions were not one of the four organizational categories. How exactly should we think about the role emotions play in our lives?

The Bible paints human emotions with rich and deep colors. From family conflict to political intrigue, from rural farming to life in the big city, from times of national peace to generations of international war, from loyalty and friendship to rejection and betrayal, from affluence and plenty to drought and poverty, from the beauty of a garden to the horror of natural disasters, from freedom and rest to violent slavery, and from pure worship of God to all kinds of idolatry, the Bible captures the full range of human experience. It is filled with stories we can relate to and characters that are like us. Apart from the historical and cultural differences, the biblical world is just like our world in its symphony of everyday experiences.

The Bible is also brutally honest, presenting people and situations with a candor we probably would have softened had we written it. It refuses to gloss over sin's impact on us and our world. But it is also honest for another reason: to demonstrate how the wisdom of the Lord and the transforming grace of Christ are powerful enough to address the deepest issues of human experience. If you read Scripture carefully, you will never get the idea that the work of Christ is for well-adjusted people who just need a little redemptive boost. It never presents any human condition or dilemma as outside the scope of the gospel. Redemption is nothing less than the rescue of helpless people facing an eternity of torment apart from God's love.

What does this have to do with emotions? Everything. As it puts real life experiences on every page, Scripture depicts the full range of human emotions. It captures the violent jealousy of Cain, the bitter tears of barren Hannah, and the fear of Israel as their Egyptian masters close in on them at the Red Sea. It pictures the joy of national victory, the delights of pure worship, and the crushing grief of David over the death of his evil son Absalom. It depicts the death wish discouragement of Elijah, the heartlessness of the Pharisees, and the desperate pleas of beggars for someone's help. It shows us the fury of Christ in the desecrated temple, his grief and pain over his separation from the Father, and his tenderness in seeking out his fearful and confused disciples after his resurrection. It shows Zechariah celebrating the birth of his son and Mary and Martha mourning the death of their brother. The full rainbow of human emotion is depicted in Scripture in a way that only the One who knows the heart could do.

Emotion pervades every aspect of our lives, which is why it is not a separate category by which we sort information about a person. Emotion is a significant aspect of all four categories. Every fact about people is dyed with emotion. It is woven into every situation, response, thought, and motive we have. Emotion is like the weather of our relationships and situations. We may live in the storm of someone's anger or the heat of another's envy. We may find ourselves in the cold, dark night of grief or the warm summer of life, health, and peace. Emotion is an essential part of every relationship and situation in which God sovereignly places us.

Our actions, thoughts, and words also have emotional components. Accurately grasping the themes and patterns of someone's behavior includes recognizing the emotional color of everything that was said and done. Thoughts do not exist in an emotionless void either. If we think our work is impossible, we face the task with frustration and discouragement. If we grasp in our hearts the goodness, grace, and glory of the Lord, we live with joy and hope. You can't fully understand what people are thinking unless you know what they feel as well. Our feelings express our reactions to our interpretations—and we turn around and interpret our feelings as well.

Motives are no different. My emotions are one of the ways my heart expresses what I crave, treasure, and serve. If I live for your affection and you reject me, emotions of sadness and anger will infuse my life. If I treasure personal achievement and succeed, I will be happy, though I may not have joy and my happiness may be fleeting. If we want to know what people really want, we have to learn about their emotional life. Happiness is the result of getting what my heart craves. Discouragement is the emotional response of my heart when the thing I live for moves farther away from me. My heart is filled with fear when I suddenly lose what I am convinced I need. In short, our emotions reflect what we worship. They reveal what has captured our hearts. God gave us emotions as he made us in his image; they are intended to help us live in communion with him. They are a key indicator of whether we are living in joyful covenantal communion with him or in the service of something else.

Our information-organizing model (Situation, Responses, Thoughts, and Motives) does not ignore emotions. Rather, it recognizes that emotions are present in every situation, every response, every thought, and every motive.

LOVING GOD AND PEOPLE ENOUGH TO TAKE TIME

If you understand the story of redemption, you know that God does not seem to be in the fearful hurry that often drives our efforts to help others. Following his example means that we can take the time to ask, listen, think, interpret, and pray. We should not assume that we know more about people than we really do. Following God's example encourages us to take the time to ask biblical questions that help people take a long look at themselves and their lives. It encourages us to follow question with question, assuring them that we really want to understand, and organizing what we learn so that we can think about it from a distinct Scriptural perspective. We do all of this to bring the transforming grace of Christ to people *as they really are* in the midst of *what they are really facing.*

This work of knowing people well is propelled by the two great commands Jesus summarized in Matthew 22:37–40:

> "Love the Lord your God with all your heart and with all your soul and with all your mind." This is the first and greatest commandment. And the second is like it: "Love your neighbor as yourself." All the Law and the Prophets hang on these two commandments.

Because I love God, I want to handle his truth with accuracy, clarity, and specificity. I want to build bridges of understanding from the wisdom of the Word to the details of people's lives. And because I love people, I will not be satisfied with lobbing grenades of general truth at them. Rather, through good questions, committed listening, and careful interpretation, I will enter their world with the understanding necessary to bring Christ's help to where it is really needed. For these reasons, even something as seemingly mechanical as gathering personal information can be fueled by love and become an opportunity to incarnate the presence and grace of the One who is love.

LOVE
KNOW
▶ SPEAK
DO

11 | THE GOALS OF SPEAKING THE TRUTH IN LOVE

From the moment she entered my office, it was clear that Sally was ready for a fight. She glared her way into the room and made tense small talk with me until I prayed. I was the principal of the Christian school her daughter attended, and I had asked Sally and her husband to come and talk about the difficulties her daughter was having at school. I was there as a friend and ally. I was actually quite fond of her daughter and I was concerned that somehow we were missing an opportunity to help her.

I made my first statement, trying to be affirming and warm as I described the difficulties we were experiencing. To my surprise, Sally yelled back at me, accusing me of not loving her daughter and wanting only to rid the school of its "problems." I tried again to quietly share my love and concern, only to have Sally yell at me again, this time sitting forward in her seat and moving closer to my desk. I made one more attempt to help her understand that I was not accusing her daughter (or Sally herself) of anything; my purpose was to share my concerns and look for solutions. As she began to shout a third time, Sally's husband grabbed her knee and said, "Dear, he is not fighting with you."

Sally looked at me for a moment as if she were disoriented. She mumbled, "I'm sorry. I just hate these kinds of meetings. I was sure you were going to tell us what bad parents we are." Perhaps Sally isn't too unusual. Perhaps many of us approach moments of truth speaking with fear and dread. Perhaps for many of us, words like *confrontation* and *rebuke* conjure up images that look like anything but love. Sally had obviously been hurt in previous confrontations and this time had been prepared to defend herself.

Rebuke is the word the Bible uses for bringing truth to where change is needed, yet most of us don't react positively when we hear it. For example, if I called you one night and said that I would like to come over the next morning to rebuke you, how would you respond? Would you run to a friend and say, "The most wonderful thing is going to happen to me tomorrow! Paul is coming over to rebuke me. I can't wait! It has been so long since I've been rebuked." That would not likely be your reaction. Many of us would rather go to the dentist and be drilled without Novocain. When we think of rebuke, we think of harsh words, red faces, ultimatums, and threats. We don't think of an act of patient and committed love. So it is important to consider what a biblical model of rebuke looks like. It is part of the **Speak** component of personal ministry, and we need to know what "speaking the truth in love" is all about.

Leviticus 19:15–18 discusses God's intentions for this aspect of relationships and personal ministry.

> Do not pervert justice; do not show partiality to the poor or favoritism to the great, but judge your neighbor fairly.
>
> Do not go about spreading slander among your people.
>
> Do not do anything that endangers your neighbor's life. I am the LORD.
>
> Do not hate your brother in your heart. Rebuke your neighbor frankly so you will not share in his guilt.
>
> Do not seek revenge or bear a grudge against one of your people, but love your neighbor as yourself. I am the LORD.

The principles of this passage provide a starting point for a biblical understanding of confrontation.

Confrontation is rooted in a submission to the First Great Command. This command calls us to "love the Lord your God with all your heart and with all your soul and with all your mind" (Matt. 22:37). Twice the Leviticus passage says, "I am the LORD." God intends confrontation to be an expression of our submission to him in our relationships with others. From God's perspective, the only reason we confront one another is that we love the Lord and want to obey him. Our failure to confront one another biblically must be seen for what it is: something rooted in our tendency to run after god-replacements. We confront unbiblically (or not at all) because we love something else more than God. Perhaps we love our relationship with this person so much that we don't want to risk it. Perhaps we prefer to avoid the personal sacrifice and complications that confrontation may involve. Perhaps we love peace, respect, and appreciation more than we should. Here is the principle: To the degree that we give the love of our hearts to someone or something else, to that degree we lose our primary motive to confront. But if we love God above all else, confrontation is an extension and expression of that love.

First John teaches us (3:11–20; 4:7–21) that one of the most reliable indicators of our love for God is the quality of our love for our neighbor. The foundation of the Second Great Command is the First Great Command—you cannot love your neighbor as yourself if you do not first love God above all else. Our willingness to gossip, to live in anger, and trim the truth reveals something deeper than a lack of love for people. It exposes a lack of love for God. We no longer serve as his ambassadors in relationships but use them for our own purposes. They become places where our needs can be met. Then, because we are afraid to lose what we crave, we live in silence as our neighbor steps outside God's boundaries.

Love for God is the only reliable foundation for a ministry of truth speaking. Any other motivation distorts the process. We cannot come in anger, frustration, or a spirit of vengeance. We come because we love God and speak on his behalf to someone who may be wandering away. Confrontation has little to do with us. It is all about the Lord, motivated by a desire to draw people back into close, obedient, and loving communion with him.

Confrontation is rooted in the Second Great Command, which calls us to "love your neighbor as yourself (Matt. 22:39). Isn't it interesting that the Old Testament call to love your neighbor as yourself is tied to this call to frank rebuke? A rebuke free of unrighteous anger is a clear sign of biblical love, but I am afraid we have replaced love in our relationships with being "nice." Being nice and acting out of love are not the same thing. Our culture puts a high premium on being tolerant and polite. We seek to avoid uncomfortable moments, so we see, but do not speak. We go so far as to convince ourselves that we are not speaking *because* we love the other person, when in reality we fail to speak because we lack love.

Please don't misunderstand. True love is not offensively intrusive or rude. But the Bible repudiates covering sin with a facade of silence. It teaches that those who love will speak, even if it creates tense, upsetting moments. If we love people and want God's best for them, how can we stand by as they wander away? How can we let them deceive themselves with excuses, blame, and rationalizations? How can we watch them get more and more enslaved by the fleeting pleasures of sin? How can we let a sufferer add to his suffering by the way he responds to his own experience? True love is neither idle nor timid. It is other-centered and active.

The truth is that we fail to confront, not because we love others too much, but because we love *ourselves* too much. We fear others misunderstanding us or being angry with us. We are afraid of what others will think. We don't want to endure the hardships of honesty because we love ourselves more than we love our neighbors. Yet we know that the depth of love in a relationship can be judged by the degree of honesty that exists. Biblical rebuke is motivated by the Second Great Command.

Confrontation is our moral responsibility in every relationship. The passage says, "Rebuke your *neighbor* frankly." This call extends beyond the borders of formal counseling, discipleship, and ministry relationships. It is a call to respond to all who live near us. Rebuke is not something that exists outside a good relationship, brought in only at crisis moments. The Bible presents confrontation as one of the cords of a strong relationship, a normal part of the interaction that makes the relationship what it is.

Often when people hear the words *rebuke* and *confrontation*, they think of a radical moment of truth telling, a long list of stern indictments against a person who is significantly rebellious or who has tragically wandered away. Yet the model here is ongoing honesty in an ongoing relationship. Rather than one big moment of confrontation, the model here is many mini-moments of confrontation. The biblical model recognizes that as we live and work with others, our hearts will be progressively exposed. It calls us to deal with whatever God reveals *as* he reveals it. In each small moment of truth speaking, the progress of sin is retarded and spiritual growth is encouraged. The model in Leviticus fits perfectly with the progressive sanctification model of growth and ministry that the New Testament presents. Here, too, problems are addressed while still in their infancy, before they mature into tragic consequences.

Notice also that the passage says, ". . . so that you will not share in his guilt." There could be no clearer statement of our moral responsibility. Each of our relationships must be pursued in absolute submission to the will and way of the Lord. We have been called to serve as ambassadors of the One who is Lord of every relationship. We must never function as mini-kings, setting our own rules and pursuing our own way.

Rebuke does not mean that our love is conditional. However, the self-sacrificing love of this passage exists at the intersection of patient grace and intolerance for sin. This means that I love you and I will not walk away from you at the first sign of weakness or sin. I will extend to you the same grace I have received. At the same time, however, my love for you does not close its eyes to wrongdoing. It does not stay silent while sin is allowed to grow. The love I am called to extend is the love of the cross of Christ, which stands at the intersection of God's grace and his complete intolerance with sin. His intolerance does not cause God to move away. He moves *toward* me in redemptive love, so that someday I will stand before him without sin. This is what we are called to embody in our relationships. Anything less is to be a moral accomplice in the sin.

How many sermons have you heard on the immorality of self-absorbed silence? How often have you viewed your unwillingness to confront as an act of rebellion in itself? Have you ever considered how often you have chosen to be silent, when God was calling you to be part of his rescue effort? We are called to accept moral responsibility for the things God reveals to us about others. To refuse to speak is to rebel against the Lord we say we love and serve.

Having said this, I should note that this passage does not give you permission to live as if you were someone else's conscience. It does not call you to a self-righteousness that displays a rude and judgmental spirit. This passage repudiates all those things. It is a neighbor-to-neighbor passage. It does not assume two classes of people, the "rebukers" and the "neighbors." The rebukers *are* the neighbors and the neighbors *are* the rebukers. As a neighbor I live in desperate need of the loving restraint God gives me through my neighbors. And as a neighbor I am called to serve others the same way. As long as indwelling sin remains, we all need help and we all need to help others. Sinners minister to sinners with the help of God.

Confrontation is meant to be more of a lifestyle than an unusual event. Confrontation is difficult when it is not a normal part of our experience. Sometimes it is so rare that we lack the necessary understanding, expectations, and skills. Instead, we fumble and fail, only making people dread the next time, like Sally. But from the Bible's perspective, a good relationship always grows in its ability to recognize, confront, and deal with the truth. Each time we speak the truth, we grow in our understanding of our calling and our skill in carrying it out.

Often there is so little honest conversation between parents and teenagers that moments of rebuke are extremely uncomfortable. At one point in our family, there were important things we needed to discuss with our daughter. We decided to make weekly appointments to talk with her about them. The first time was very difficult, but each time got easier. Soon the ground we gained spilled over into our informal conversations. All our interactions began to be more comfortable and honest. This passage envisions a "constant conversation" model where the daily intervention of honest rebuke is a regular part of all relationships.

There is also a payoff for more formal discipleship and counseling situations. The person who has made honest, humble, loving rebuke a part of his daily relationships (as a giver and a receiver) will be clear and comfortable when he confronts a person in a more structured setting. The skills of family leadership and ministry also make us effective in the church of Christ. Perhaps we confront poorly or not at all because we do not have a ministry mentality or communication maturity at home. If we have avoided confrontation or been more angry than constructive in our rebukes, how can we expect to be ready when God gives us opportunities in the church?

We fail to confront in love because we have yielded to subtle and passive forms of hatred. Embedded in the passage is a contrast between love and hatred. If you tried to illustrate this passage, it would look like this: At the center is a high plateau of love, based on a commitment to honest rebuke. On either side is a dark valley of hatred. One is the valley of passive hatred and the other is the valley of active hatred. Both are temptations and both are wrong! Leviticus 19 is clear that we must find a way to lovingly confront sin when we see it in others. If we fail to do so, we cannot console ourselves by saying, "Perhaps I am not loving this person as God wants me to, but at least I do not hate him!" There is no neutral ground between love and hatred. Our response to the sins of others is either motivated by Second Great Command love or by some form of hatred.

One subtle form of hatred is favoritism, granting favor to some but refusing it to others because of a standard we have set up in our own minds. It may be based on economic status, physical appearance, race or ethnicity, doctrinal differences, self-righteousness, revulsion over particular sins, or something else. Some people live outside the circle of our favor (and therefore our ministry) simply because of who they are. This can even happen in families. I fear that there is much more hatred in our families and churches than we think.

A second form of passive hatred is bearing a grudge. We keep a record of what someone has done against us. We go over it again and again, each time growing more angry and giving ourselves more reason to despise the offender. Our anger grows even when no further sin has been committed; it becomes the interpretive grid through which we assess everything the person does. No matter what he does, he cannot do anything right in our eyes. Everything is distorted by the anger and bitterness through which we view it, destroying any possibility of dealing with sin in godly way.

This passage does not offer an exhaustive discussion of passive hatred, but it does warn us of the myth of "neutral ground" and indicate what passive hatred looks like. We are constantly dealing with the sins of others, as they are with us. The issue is whether our responses are motivated by biblical love or by self-righteous, prejudiced, and grudge-bearing hatred.

We fail to confront because we have yielded to more active forms of hatred. Here we not only act as the judge, but as the jailer and executioner as well. This passage says that there are three ways our hatred actively reveals itself: injustice, gossip, and revenge. All three have been present in all of our lives at some point, and all three responses destroy, or at least distort, the biblical ministry of rebuke. God ordained rebuke to restrain sin until our redemption is complete. We either position ourselves to be part of that work or we stand in the way.

Injustice perverts God's system of restraint. It doesn't protect, correct, or restrain the sinner. It hurts and mistreats him.

Gossip doesn't lead a person to make humble confession before God or others. When I gossip, I confess the sin of another person to someone who is not involved. Gossip doesn't restrain sin; it encourages it. It doesn't build someone's character; it destroys his reputation. Gossip doesn't lead a person to humble insight; it produces anger and defensiveness.

Revenge is the opposite of ministry. Ministry is motivated by a desire for someone's good; revenge is motivated by a desire to harm him. We have forsaken our call to bring the person to the Lord so that he can see himself as he really is, and given ourselves instead to a quest to settle the score.

What is so terribly serious about all this is that we have been called to incarnate the glory of Christ's love on earth—to love as he has loved us so that people would know we are his disciples. The ultimate apologetic for the reality of the gospel is the loving unity of the body of Christ, a unity so deep, resilient, and pervasive that it can only be compared to the unity of the Trinity. (See John 13–17.) Our call is to find satisfaction in our relationships, not because people please us, but because we delight in displaying God's love to a hopeless world.

What a difference it makes to see that being sinned against is not an occasion for vengeance but for God to be revealed! Instead of assuming God's position as judge, we ask how we can incarnate his love to the people involved in the hurtful situation. Too often we forget that there is nothing more wonderful than to be Christ's ambassadors. We participate in the most important work of the universe.

We can do this because sin's mastery over us has been broken as we have been united with Christ's life, death, and resurrection (Rom. 6:1–14) and indwelt by a Holy Spirit who battles the flesh on our behalf (Gal. 5:16–26; Rom. 8:1–11). Because of this, we can say "no" to powerful emotions (passions) and compelling desires (Gal. 5:24) and turn in a new direction. We do not have to give the parts of our body to favoritism, grudges, gossip, injustice, and revenge. Rather, we can offer ourselves to the Lord for his use. The cross of Christ not only provides redemption, but the resources we need to be part of his work.

Confrontation flows out of a recognition of our identity as the children of God. The passage repeats the phrase, "I am the LORD." It reminds us that we have been chosen by him, and our lives are no longer our own. Everything we are and have belongs to him, and we will find our greatest joy in relationships when we recognize that they, too, belong to him. We are the Lord's. They are the Lord's. The situation is the Lord's. Loving confrontation is rooted in an awareness that we are God's children, and our goal is to be active in his purposes for us. To do less is to forget who we are.

Proper biblical confrontation is never motivated by impatience, frustration, hurt, or anger, but is one way God prevents these things from damaging our relationships. Failure to make loving rebuke part of our relationships gives the Devil a huge opportunity. I have met many couples who have lost all the tenderness, appreciation, patience, respect, sensitivity, and romance in their relationship. These precious commodities had been destroyed by a failure to confront sin biblically. Their marriages had become a cycle of accusation, recrimination, and revenge. Bitterness and anger had sucked the life out of their love until the spouses could barely remember what once attracted them to each other. They never intended it, but their refusal to confront sin in God's way and their daily habit of devouring each other had gutted their relationship. The sweet, hopeful couple of the past had become two isolated, angry, and hopeless people who wanted out of their marriage.

A humble, honest lifestyle of rebuke protects us from ourselves. As sinners living with sinners, we need something to retard the progress of sin in our relationships. Early in our marriage Luella and I decided that we would not let the sun go down on our anger (Eph. 4:26). We promised each other that we would not go to bed angry. At first we would lie in bed, propping our eyes open, waiting for the other person to ask for forgiveness so that we wouldn't have to. But as time went on, we saw how this principle restrained our sin, strengthened our relationship, protected our love, and matured us both. We have been married for over thirty years and we are still sinners, yet we love each other more than ever, and we don't carry yesterday's baggage into today's encounters. Each anniversary we thank the Lord for rescuing us from ourselves.

Confrontation does not force a person to deal with you, but places him before the Lord. The most important encounter in confrontation is not the person's encounter with you, but with Christ. Rebuke does not force a person to face your judgment; it gives him an opportunity to do business with God. It is motivated by a desire for the person to receive the grace of conviction, confession, forgiveness, and repentance—to experience the grace we also have received. Confrontation does not enforce legalities; it ministers the restraining, forgiving, restoring grace of Christ to someone who has turned from him. It is not motivated by punishment, but by the hope that the Lord would free this person from the prison of his own sin to know the freedom of walking in fellowship with him.

BIBLICAL CONFRONTATION MEANS STARTING WITH YOUR OWN HEART

Since personal biblical ministry involves building relationships that encourage and support God's work in hearts, it is impossible to serve without somehow being touched by the sin and struggle of those we serve. The angry person will get angry with you, the distrustful person will question your trustworthiness, and the discouraged person will probably receive your best counsel with cynicism and doubt. Since personal ministry is about incarnating the presence of Christ, we want to respond in the right way to the things we experience in the relationship.

If we are going to be faithful to Christ in such circumstances, we must begin by examining our own hearts. Are there thoughts, motives, or attitudes (self-righteousness, anger, bitterness, spirit of condemnation, vengeance) that would get in the way of what God intends to do? As instruments of Christ's grace, we must confess that we need that grace just as much as the people we are helping. We need God to provide the love, courage, compassion, and wisdom we will need to represent him well.

Sadly, this step of preparation is often neglected. The result is that the rebuke is not effective, not only because the receiver was unteachable but because the ambassador was unprepared. If I do not start with my own heart I will tend to:

Turn moments of ministry into moments of anger. If I do not face the ways the person has made me angry, my words will be shaped more by my anger than by the good God wants to do through me.

Personalize what is not personal. If I do not deal with my heart, the horizontal offenses (against me) will seem more significant than the person's vertical life (relationship with God). I will become increasingly sensitive to how the person is treating me. Before long, I will take offense at things that are not personal, but are simply indicators of where basic changes are needed in the person's heart.

Be adversarial in my approach. This follows directly from personalizing what is not personal. The more I am hurt and fail to deal with it, the more I assume a "stand against" posture rather than a "stand with" posture when I encounter the one who hurt me. It is tragic but true: we *do* sometimes become the adversaries of people we are called to help. It happens with friends, spouses, parents and children, and pastors and their flocks. When it does, we get in the way of what the Wonderful Counselor is seeking to do.

Confuse my opinion with God's will. The last thing a person needs in confrontation is my opinion. He needs to see himself from a biblical perspective, and he needs a sense of calling. (What is God calling him to do in response to what is happening inside and around him?) My job is to hold the mirror of the Word of God in front of him so that he can see himself accurately. However, when I fail to deal with my own heart, my words will be driven by my feelings, desires, and opinions. If I start by examining my own heart, I help ensure that my agenda is the same as the Lord's.

Settle for quick solutions that do not address the heart. When I do not face my own sinful attitudes, my ministry to this person will be shaped less and less by Christ-like love and more and more by other attitudes. I will be less and less excited by what God can do (and by the privilege of being part of it), and more and more eager to get out of the relationship. Rather than being motivated to persevere until God has accomplished all that he intends, I will find the person irritating and the relationship burdensome. I will be attracted to quick, superficial solutions that allow me to move on. My responses are not driven by love for God or for the person, but by a love for self.

Take a careful look at your own heart. These things *do* happen to people in ministry. They impact the fellowship of the body of Christ and subvert the good God is seeking to do in our families. Are there sinful attitudes you have not faced that can hinder the ministry God has planned for you? Parents, are your daily interactions with your children shaped by Christ-like patience? Counselors, are you incarnating the character of the Lord? Pastors, are there people in church that you have given up on? Brother and sisters, do you have friendships that are tense or broken? Husbands and wives, is your marriage reduced to casual conversation and household plans? It is impossible to speak the truth in love when I am not dealing with the thoughts, feelings, desires, and attitudes that stand in the way.

Remember, God has ordained that difficult person to be in your life. It is not a sign of God's inattention but his covenant-keeping care. Humbly embrace the fact that the Wonderful Counselor is working on everybody involved. Humbly acknowledge the ways God is using this person to expose the areas where you need to grow. Embrace the fact that God can transform the heart of that person without neglecting you—and vice versa! Most of all, celebrate! You are experiencing the jealous grace and glory of the Lord. Through you, he is fighting for that person's heart and through him, he is holding tightly onto yours. He will not let either of you go, and he will not forsake the work he is doing in each of you. Remember, it is impossible to celebrate God's work of transformation without confessing your need for more. No one is more ready to communicate God's grace than someone who has faced his own desperate need for it.

BIBLICAL CONFRONTATION
STARTS WITH THE RIGHT GOALS

Once we have prepared our hearts, we can consider what God wants to accomplish when we confront someone. What is God seeking to do through our humble, loving, honest words of rebuke? The best way to answer these questions is to ask, "Why do people need to be confronted?" The answers will direct us toward the proper set of goals.

We all need the ministry of loving, honest rebuke because of:

The deceitfulness of sin. Sin blinds our hearts. We may have the occasional blind spot or be completely in the dark spiritually, but as long as indwelling sin exists, we need one another to help us see ourselves clearly.

Wrong and unbiblical thinking (Num. 11; Ps. 73). None of us thinks in a purely biblical way. We hold distorted, self-aggrandizing, or self-excusing perspectives on God, others, and ourselves. We fail to properly understand our past and present, and all this shapes our behavior.

Emotional thinking. We don't do our best thinking in the middle of suffering, difficulty, and distress. We don't think clearly when our emotions are raging. We forget what we've learned about God *and* ourselves when we find ourselves in trouble. It is a sweet grace to have someone come alongside us and help us remember what we need to remember.

My view of life (God, self, others, the solution) tends to be shaped by my experiences. Because I am the one who interprets my experiences, my conclusions will be reinforced by each new situation. I will interpret each new circumstance in a way that convinces me that I am right in my way of looking at things, oblivious to the impact of spiritual blindness, sinful desires, and wrong thinking. I need the intervention of truth from someone who really loves me, who can confront and correct the distortions in my view of life.

Our loving, honest rebuke can be equal to these challenges only if we pursue two goals. The first is to be used as one of God's *instruments of seeing* in the lives of others. I am not trying to advance my own opinion. I want to help people see themselves in the mirror of God's Word. I want to help them see what God sees.

The second goal is to be used by God as an *agent of repentance.* The biblical definition of repentance is a change of heart that leads to a change in the direction of my life. Joel 2:12–13 pictures this as not rending the garments (the external behavior of remorse in Old Testament culture), but rending the heart (heartfelt remorse for my sin accompanied by a desire to change). Our goal is not to pressure people into behavioral changes, but to encourage heart change that impacts the life. Repentance means turning to go in the other direction, and that turning must begin with the heart.

My goal is that through the things I say (message), the way I say them (methods), and the attitudes I express (character), God will change the heart of this person. Think of it! Think that God is connecting you with people so that he might complete his work in their lives! You are called to be more than a husband, wife, parent, counselor, neighbor, or friend. You have a *kingdom worker* identity. You have been chosen to pursue relationships with a sense of *redemptive calling*. You have been given the opportunity to see God miraculously transform people, up close and personal. Let that calling motivate you to give yourself to kingdom work. Look for ways to bring people to true heart repentance, and watch the harvest of change the Lord will produce.

DON'T LEAVE THE GOSPEL AT THE DOOR

A mistake we often make when we seek to lead someone to repentance is to emphasize the law over the gospel. Yet Paul says (Rom. 2:4) that it is God's kindness (goodness) that leads us to repentance. He also says (2 Cor. 5:14) that it is the love of Christ that compels us to no longer live for ourselves, but for him. The grace of the gospel is what turns our hearts, because the gospel is God's magnificent promise of forgiveness in Christ. This draws us out of hiding into the light of truth, where true confession and repentance can take place.

Confronting people should not only confront them with failure and sin, it should also confront them with the gospel. We cannot forget this! We need to remind people of their identity in Christ (2 Peter 1:3–9; 1 John 3:1–3). We need to remind them of God's amazing promise of forgiveness (1 John 1:5–10), and the wonderful gift of the indwelling Holy Spirit (Eph. 3:20), who gives us strength to obey. These truths give believers the courage to examine their hearts, confess their sin, and turn to Christ. If we are speaking as agents of repentance, the law is not enough. We must come with the gospel as well.

In Romans 8:1–17, Paul presents the gospel as a *comfort* and a *call*.

> Therefore, there is now no condemnation for those who are in Christ Jesus, because through Christ Jesus the law of the Spirit of life set me free from the law of sin and death. For what the law was powerless to do in that it was weakened by the sinful nature, God did by sending his own Son in the likeness of sinful man to be a sin offering. And so he condemned sin in sinful man, in order that the righteous requirements of the law might be fully met in us, who do not live according to the sinful nature but according to the Spirit.
>
> Those who live according to the sinful nature have their minds set on what that nature desires; but those who live in accordance with the Spirit have their minds set on what the Spirit desires. The mind of sinful man is death, but the mind controlled by the Spirit is life and peace; the sinful mind is hostile to God. It does not submit to God's law, nor can it do so. Those controlled by the sinful nature cannot please God.
>
> You, however, are not controlled by the sinful nature but by the Spirit, if the Spirit of God lives in you. And if anyone does not have the Spirit of Christ, he does not belong to Christ. But if Christ is in you, your body is dead because of sin, yet your spirit is alive because of righteousness. And if the Spirit of him who raised Jesus from the dead is living in you, he who raised Christ from the dead will also give life to your mortal bodies through his Spirit, who lives in you.
>
> Therefore, brothers, we have an obligation—but it is not to the sinful nature, to live according to it. For if you live according to the sinful nature, you will die; but if by the Spirit you put to death the misdeeds of the body, you will live, be-

cause those who are led by the Spirit of God are sons of God. For you did not receive a spirit that makes you a slave again to fear, but you received the Spirit of sonship. And by him we cry, '*Abba*, Father.' The Spirit himself testifies with our spirit that we are God's children. Now if we are children, then we are heirs— heirs of God and co-heirs with Christ, if indeed we share in his sufferings in order that we may also share in his glory.

Paul begins by encouraging us with the *comfort* of the gospel (vv. 1–11). This comfort is rooted in two powerful realities. First, the work of Christ has removed the sentence of condemnation that was on our heads because of our sin. Jesus fully paid the penalty for our sin— past, present, and future. This comfort deals with the guilt of sin and should draw us out of the darkness of hiding and into the light of his grace. We do not need to give in to fear, denial, blame-shifting, self-righteousness, or rewriting our own history. These are all attempts at self-atonement, which is no longer needed because Christ has made full atonement for our sin. As we come to Christ in confession, we need not fear his wrath and rejection. Because Christ met the requirements of the law and died as an acceptable sin offering, we will never face condemnation! As we help people to see the gravity of their sin, we also comfort them with the fact that Christ's work has satisfied God's anger.

People need to hear the comfort of the gospel again and again. They need to be reminded of who they are in Christ and what they have received in his life, death, and resurrection. It is *not* safe to assume that a Christian who attends a good church understands this. People often live with huge gaps in their understanding of the gospel. One gap is in understanding how the comfort of the gospel radically changes our approach to life in the here and now. Daily confession of sin is essential to a gospel-driven lifestyle. It makes no sense to rationalize, blame-shift, or rewrite history to make myself look better. This is a denial of the gospel. Self-examination and confession flow out of a deep confidence that Christ's work is effective for me today. I come to him confident that he forgives me.

The second comfort of the gospel is the Holy Spirit, who lives within every believer to combat the way sin renders us incapable of doing good. Before our salvation, we were controlled by our sinful nature. We were unable to think, choose, desire, act, or speak as God ordains. But now things are different because God lives inside us! We are no longer under the control of the sinful nature. God knew that our condition was so desperate that it was not enough to forgive us. He needed to live within us in all his power, grace, and glory, so that we no longer have to live as slaves to sin's passions and desires. Because the Spirit controls our hearts, we can say "no" to sin and turn in another direction.

Paul puts it this way: "The Spirit gives life to your mortal bodies." We are now dead to the controlling power of sin and alive for the purpose of obedience. We can follow God because the Spirit gives us the life, power, and desire to obey. It is our job, as Christ's ambassadors, to take these truths to people, lest they be controlled by the fear that God requires them to do what they cannot do. Sometimes God does call people to massive life change. As one man said, "You are saying that I can no longer be me!" In a real sense, he was right. God was calling him to turn almost every area of his life in a new direction. This can be terribly intimidating unless we help people look at God's call through a gospel lens.

But this is not all that Paul wants us to understand about the gospel. The gospel is not only a comfort, it is also a call, as summarized in verses 12 though 17. Paul reminds us that the work of Christ and the presence of the Holy Spirit leave us with an obligation to get serious about sin and see it as God does—as a life and death matter. We have no right to say that, because we have been given blanket forgiveness, it doesn't matter how we live. To Paul, grace leaves us obligated to deal rigorously with the sin that grace addresses. If God was so serious about sin that he sacrificed his own Son and filled us with his own Spirit, how can we be any less serious about our sins of heart and behavior?

The ongoing work of God in the believer's life is to eradicate sin ("put to death the misdeeds of the body"). As a believer, I am obligated to participate in the Holy Spirit's search-and-destroy mission. I have no right to live "according to the sinful nature" any longer. This denies the gospel and my identity as a child of God. I can never say, "I don't want to;" "I would if I could;" "It is too hard;" or "It is okay, because I am forgiven." The only proper response to the comfort of the gospel is to accept its call and follow Christ in obedience. I am called to accept my sonship, realizing that true sons of God are those who are "led by the Spirit" and not the sinful nature.

As we root our truth speaking (confrontation and rebuke) in the gospel, our goal is that hearts would be changed by the work of Christ that the gospel declares. First, we want the promises of forgiveness and power to give people real hope for change. Second, we want the call of the gospel to cause people to accept responsibility for their sin and accept God's call to obey. The heart that has embraced both the hope (comfort) and the obligation (call) can receive honest words of confrontation. The person can see the gravity of his sin and the grandeur of God's call to obey in light of gospel truths. He is ready to live as a true child of God, as someone who can be honest about himself and follow God in faith and obedience.

In the push and pull of personal ministry, it is easy to emphasize one side of the gospel over the other. For example, if you were talking to a husband who had verbally abused his wife for years, it would be tempting to emphasize the call of the gospel over the comfort. However, it is the comfort of the gospel that gives this man the courage to step out from behind his denials and rationalizations to confess his sin.

On the other hand, if you were talking with his wife, you might be tempted to emphasize the comfort of the gospel to the exclusion of the call. Yet it is the call of the gospel that exposes the bitterness, self-righteousness, and vengeance that are powerful temptations for those who have been sinned against. Everyone needs both sides of the gospel—all the time! These two aspects of the gospel (the grace of justification and the grace of sanctification) do not stand in opposition to each other; rather, they complement and complete each other. Together they express God's grace in Christ; they depict what the gospel produces in those who live in its light. Figure 11.1 illustrates a balanced gospel and the dangers of gospel imbalance.

Fig. 11.1

A Balanced Gospel Perspective.

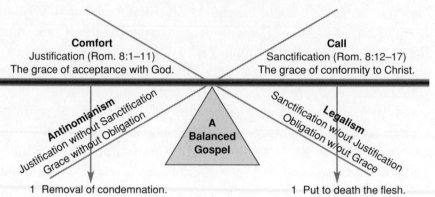

This is the goal of confrontation: not to force behavioral change, but to encourage people's new natures with the gospel. We seek to open people's eyes to the full glory of Christ's grace as they see the gravity of their sin. The gospel is what turns idolaters into worshipers of God. It's what makes the self-righteous humble and willing to listen. The gospel gives practical courage to the fearful and discouraged, and helps the weak to live with confident perseverance. The gospel turns victims into helpers and the self-absorbed into those who love to serve. True biblical confrontation confronts people with much more than their sins and failures. It confronts people with Christ. He really is "the Way, the Truth, and the Life!" Hope for change always rests on him.

LOVE

KNOW

▶ SPEAK

DO

12 | THE PROCESS OF SPEAKING THE TRUTH IN LOVE

You can't have a relationship without some kind of confrontation. It happens every day. A mom wakes her daughter for school and talks to her about the state of her room. A brother confronts his sister, who took something from him without permission. A wife talks to her husband about his busyness. A pastor confronts a wayward man in his congregation. A married son approaches his mother about her interference in his marriage. An elder confronts a deacon about his prickly attitude. A woman talks to her friend about her tendency to gossip. An elderly man confronts his son who seldom visits.

We confront one another every day, but the question is, *Whose agenda drives our confrontation?* Are we trying to get people to do what pleases us? Or are we confronting them as ambassadors, using God's Word to lead them to repentance?

Effective biblical confrontation often begins before we speak. How we live with one another from day to day sets the stage for the way our words will be received. There is no separation between our daily lives and God's redemptive work. We don't advance our own wills in "normal" situations and self-consciously serve the Lord in "ministry." This divided world is a fabrication of the Enemy.

The Lord owns every one of our relationships. He has placed us in each one for the advancement of his kingdom and the sake of his glory. His agenda is so much bigger and better than ours! By his grace he is taking lost, suffering, blind, deceived, self-absorbed, fearful, and rebellious people and molding them into the likeness of his Son. He displays his glory by transforming the thoughts and intentions of our hearts.

This display of glory is taking place wherever his children—his ambassadors—live, work, and relate. Every situation, conversation, relationship, trial, or blessing belongs to him. None of it belongs to us. We cannot be satisfied with pleasing ourselves in what we say and do, but must ask what would please him.

People who approach life this way are ready to serve as God's instruments of change. They see beyond their own agenda and are motivated by his. They are convinced that there is nothing more worthwhile in life. People who live this way speak the truth to others out of a recognition of their own need and out of thankfulness for the help God faithfully sends their way.

UNDERSTANDING THE STEPS OF THE CONFRONTATION PROCESS

Our goal is to do more than read people a list of charges from Scripture or tell them what we think of them. We want to help people understand what is wrong and lead them to repentance. To that end, we will consider four steps in the confrontation process, with one real life situation in mind.

Jim and Dan are close friends. Dan comes to you concerned that Jim is doing things that are unbecoming of a Christian. He has admitted to cheating on his hours at work and to occasionally "borrowing" office supplies. He has talked about "chilling out" with co-workers at local clubs that Dan thinks should be off limits to a Christian. Dan has also been hurt that Jim has violated his confidence when he has shared personal things. Dan has tried to talk to Jim about his relationship with God, but Jim has been resistant, saying only that he is "discouraged with God" right now. Jim has said more than once that he is considering changing churches and moving away. You are concerned for Jim, know him well, and have a relationship of mutual trust. You decide to talk with him.

What will you say? What does it look like to lead Jim to repentance? How will you take the truth of Scripture to the specific places where change is needed? How will you encourage a hunger for heart change and not just for change in the situation? How will you love Jim with humble, honest, sight-giving, repentance-producing rebuke?

The following four steps frame the confrontation process:

1. CONSIDERATION

The question to ask yourself is, "What does this person need to see (about himself, God, others, life, truth, change) that he does not see, and how can I help him see it?" This question alone can refocus our confrontation. Our goal is not to communicate a list of offenses, but to help people see themselves. Often when people tell their story, they are not in it! They focus on the difficulties of the situation and the attitudes and behavior of others. They don't include their own thoughts, desires, choices, and actions. While we are sensitive to the realities of suffering and being sinned against, our goal is to encourage people to look at their behavior and examine their hearts with biblical eyes.

Imagine a mother confronting her daughter about cleaning her room. The step of consideration encourages her to do more than express irritation or issue an ultimatum. The mother wants to help her daughter see that the way she treats her possessions is a reflection of her heart. This focus can also help the elder confronting a deacon about his bad attitude. He wants to do more than tell the man to keep his sighs to himself. He wants to help him recognize, own, and repent of his anger and impatience.

This first step calls me to forsake my agenda and take up the Lord's. I am not permitted to unload on you everything I have always wanted to say, or to simply recite my complaints. All that I say, and the way I say it, must have godly change as a goal. Otherwise, I forsake my identity and my calling.

Five questions can help people see what God wants them to see. The order is important because it teaches us to think biblically about why we do the things we do and how God changes us. The questions are appropriate for young children and mature adults and for informal and formal ministry.

1. *What was going on?* This question focuses on the situations or circumstances that people are facing. Their responses are important for two reasons. First, you want them to see that circumstances did not force them to do what they did. Second, you want to understand the details of their world in order to speak truth into it. Just because you "know" a person doesn't mean you thoroughly understand all his struggles. If you make assumptions, you are filling in the gaps of your knowledge out of your own experience, not his.

2. *What were you thinking and feeling as it was going on?* This question takes people's eyes off the situation and asks them to examine their hearts. It reminds them that our hearts always interact with what goes on around us. We are never just victims, but incessant interpreters whose interpretations precede and shape our actions. We also experience powerful emotions that direct our behavior.

3. *What did you do in response?* This question comes after the question above because our behavior is shaped by our heart's response to the situation. As you combine the information from the first two questions, you can help people see the connection between their interpretation of their circumstances and their response. By asking this question at this time, you help people to admit that their behavior was not forced by the situation ("It was the only thing I could do!") or by others ("She made me so angry!"). Lasting change depends on seeing this connection. Without it, people revert to blame-shifting.

   If we fail to expose the connection between interpretation and response, we give Satan a huge opportunity. He is the teller of plausible lies. Just as he did in the Garden, Satan works with partial and distorted truths. His lies have power because they begin with something true. For example, I could not walk into a room of strangers and convince them that I was an Olympic gymnast. That would be a lie, and not a plausible one. However, if I dressed in a fine suit, carried a nice leather briefcase, and learned some specialized vocabulary, I could probably convince strangers that I was an architect. My attire and conversation would give the second lie plausibility. This kind of lie is the Enemy's specialty.

Returning to our example, it is true that everything has not worked out for Jim as he dreamed. He has faced tough situations and difficult people. The Enemy has material to work with. He can tempt Jim to believe that his behavior was *caused* by these pressures. If Satan is successful here, it won't be hard to convince Jim that what needs to change is not himself, but the people and situations around him.

By asking these questions in this order, we are attempting to break through well-defended strongholds in the person's heart. We seek to expose self-excusing arguments and self-atoning lies and help people, maybe for the first time, to see that their behavior reveals more about their own hearts than it does about the difficulties of their situations. If people do not see things at this level, they may decide to do some things differently, but in their hearts they will still be convinced that most change needs to take place outside them. The change will be temporary, because it is not rooted in the heart.

4. *Why did you do it? What were you seeking to accomplish?* If the second question uncovers thoughts, this question seeks to reveal motives. In asking this question, we are teaching that the heart is always serving something. In Matthew 6 Christ uses the metaphor of treasure to express this worship orientation. Human life is one big treasure hunt. We all have things that are valuable to us (acceptance, possessions, achievement, a certain lifestyle, God's glory, vengeance, love, independence, health). In some way, we all seek to get those things from our situations and relationships. Our behavior always expresses these motives—or idols—of the heart. Notice that questions two and four connect behavior to the thoughts and motives of the heart (Heb. 4:12).

As you make these connections, you help Jim to see that what he sets his heart on shapes his response to suffering *and* blessing. In many ways, Jim's struggle is with blessing. He works for a solid company. In the body of Christ he is surrounded by people who really love him, and to whom he can talk. Yet Jim is not getting what he craves and so he is sullen and discontent, even angry with God. Jim needs to see that his struggle is essentially a struggle of worship. To the degree that he seeks life from the creation, he will be dissatisfied and angry with God. Change will only take place as Jim recognizes the god-replacements that rule his heart, condition his emotions, and control his behavior. His insight, confession, and repentance need to be heart-deep.

At some point Jim needs to confess that he has been living for his own glory rather than the Lord's. Lasting change takes place when people are not only shocked by the evil in their world, but by the degree to which they have lived as glory thieves, demanding for themselves what belongs only to the Lord. What lasting good does it do to teach self-absorbed idolaters how to establish a peaceful coexistence in their marriage? What lasting good is it to get a depressed person up and running, when the core of that depression goes unaddressed?

The Wonderful Counselor is a jealous god. He is not satisfied with the outside of the dish being polished when the inside is left unchanged (Matt. 23:25). Biblical personal ministry always moves toward issues of glory and worship. The most basic question in all personal ministry is, "For whose glory are you living?"

5. *What was the result?* This question not only seeks to uncover consequences (Gal. 6:7), but the way these consequences are a direct result of the thoughts and motives of the heart. The seeds planted in the heart grow into some kind of fruit in the person's life. We are all quite skilled in denying our own harvest. ("If you had these kids, you'd yell too!" "He just pushed my buttons!" "I didn't mean to say that.") We need to help people examine the fruit in their lives and see the connection between their harvest and the thoughts and motives of their hearts.

We want to be used by God to give people two things. The first is a harvest mentality, where people understand that every day they plant seeds and harvest fruit from the seeds they have planted. The second is an investment mentality that acknowledges Christ's teaching that our lives are shaped by the treasure in which we invest. Every day we invest in something, and live with the return on previous investments. Our goal is that people would "own" their harvest and the return on their investments.

As we help people to consider these things, it is important to remember that acquiring personal insight is generally a process. It may not take place in one sitting, or even in your presence. As long as people are willing to be part of the process, you can work to refocus their attention toward the heart and its fruits.

It can be helpful to have people respond to these questions in journal form. I typically ask people to identify two or three situations or relationships that are a regular source of struggle. I then ask them to journal about those struggles using the five questions listed above for two or three weeks. Then I take the journal and read it, highlighting themes and patterns. The next time we meet, I return the journal and ask them to read it in my presence and respond. Again and again, God has used this simple method to open people's eyes to what is going on in their hearts.

Once I was talking with a man who was very angry but did not see it. He had driven away all of his friends, family, and coworkers, yet he saw himself as unjustly forsaken. Whenever I attempted to talk to him about his anger, he got irritated. So I asked him to do a five questions journal for three weeks. When he brought me the journal, I underlined all the roots and instances of anger with a red marker. By the time I was done, that journal was almost solid red! The next time we got together, he read the journal for a few minutes, and then, with eyes moistened with tears, said, "The man who wrote this journal is a very angry person!" That window of personal insight became a doorway to change for that man. He began to see the ways he had lived a selfish and demanding life, never allowing people to meet his expectations. He began to see how his judgmental attitude made him very hard to be around. For the first time in years, he began to live with his eyes wide open.[1]

When you encourage this kind of change, you are doing the work of an ambassador. You are incarnating the presence of the Messiah who gives sight to those in spiritual darkness. When Christ gave sight to the blind during his days on earth, he also gave us a metaphor for his work with every blind sinner who comes to him in humility. Seeing is the beginning of the change process. It is the beginning of grief, not only for the things I have experienced, but for the ways I have stolen glory that belongs to God and demanded to be the center of my world—and others' as well. This kind of insight smashes our idols and exposes the self-serving arguments and lies that have hidden that idolatry for too long.

The confrontation process begins with giving people insight not only into their behavior, but into the system of worship that directs it. This step is essential and cannot be rushed.

2. CONFESSION

This is the next logical step in the confrontation process. If people have looked at themselves in the mirror of Scripture, they should have identified sins of heart and behavior that need to be confessed. Jim should be seeing the spirit of entitlement that allows him to steal from work without feeling guilty. He should be realizing how he has looked at a life of blessing and seen nothing but want. Along with these insights about his heart, he should be able to see the many responses that have flowed from them.

The problem is that sinners find confession difficult. We all have ways to take ourselves off the hook. When the light of truth shines on us, we instinctively deny, recast history, explain away, accuse, blame, defend, argue, rationalize, or hide. Yet confession is essential to the change process. It is the time when people finally admit what is in their hearts and take responsibility for what they have done. Therefore, we should never assume that people are confessing to the Lord, nor should we allow our words of confrontation to do their confession for them. We should call people to confession that is not weakened by "buts" and "if onlys." Confession reminds people that their hearts and lives belong to the Lord, and misplaced worship lies beneath sins of behavior. True confession flows out of worship and results in a deeper, fuller worship of God.

As Christ's ambassadors, we seek to lead people to speak humble, specific words of confession to the Lord. We also need to encourage them to identify people who have been affected by their sins and seek their forgiveness. We should lead them to pray, to admit their sin, and to seek God's forgiveness and help.

To do this we have to deal with our own hearts as well. As we have seen, we will be affected by the sins of the people we serve. In more formal counseling sessions, the know-it-all, controlling, argumentative person will be rude, dismissive, and adversarial. After a few sessions, it is easy to hope for a cancellation! Or perhaps a brother or sister in Christ frequently seeks your advice but never seems to take it, yet still calls you in self-inflicted emergencies. We need to admit that we too are sinners, and that our responses do not always reflect the character of Christ. Unless we are honest and repent of our sin, we will not call someone away from his sin; instead, we will subtly become part of the cycle.

If we do not deal with the common temptations of ministry (self-righteousness, unbiblical judgment and condemnation, bitterness and anger, impatience, a lack of gentleness) we will subvert the confession process. Have you ever noticed that the way we sin against people in ministry has a pseudo-confessional quality to it? Harboring bitterness against people is actually *confessing their sin to myself*, over and over again. Anger is akin to *confessing their sin to God*, dissatisfied that he hasn't done something and placing myself in his position as judge. Gossip is *confessing their sin to someone else*. Each of these can exist in subtle form in our hearts, subverting the ministry God wants to do through us. We aren't always heartened by the fact that God will convict people, lead them to repentance, forgive them, and draw them into renewed communion with him. There are times when we are like Jonah, who became angry after the repentance of Nineveh.

But Jonah was greatly displeased and became angry. He prayed to the LORD, "O LORD, is this not what I said when I was still at home? That is why I was so quick to flee to Tarshish. I knew that you are a gracious and compassionate God, slow to anger and abounding in love, a God who relents from sending calamity. Now, O LORD, take away my life, for it is better for me to die than to live." (Jonah 4:1–3)

Basically Jonah is saying, "This is exactly why I did not want to go to Nineveh. I just knew you would forgive these people! They don't deserve your forgiveness; they deserve your judgment! Now they have gotten off scot-free!" I wish I could say that I have never felt that way about people, but I have. Often the people who need our ministry most are the hardest ones to serve. In those times it is very easy to be in the way of, rather than a part of, God's plan to lead them to heartfelt repentance. As we call others to confession, we need to confess the sins in our own hearts at the same time.

3. COMMITMENT

Consideration and confession make up the "put off" aspect of the confrontation process (see Eph. 4:22–24). Commitment is the first step of the "put on" phase of repentance. Questions to ask here might include, "Where is God specifically calling this person to radical new ways of living and thinking? What biblical desires would God want to control Jim's heart as he deals with his church relationships and his job? In what new ways is God calling him to love and serve others? What steps of restitution is God calling Jim to make? What new habits should he insert into his daily routines? Is he committed to these things?"

Don't soften God's call for concrete commitments of heart and life. People's commitments should be God-ward and not simply horizontal bargains with the goal of an easier, better life. God is worthy of their worship even if their circumstances remain the same. If the confessed sin was against God, the commitments must be made to him as well. If the person has lived for her own glory, a new way of living must be rooted in a zeal for God's glory and a resolve to live for him.

Biblical commitment runs deeper than learning the things that have been destructive to me, and doing the things that will make them better. "What's in it for me" commitments are essentially old idolatries in a new form.

In both the Old and New Testaments, God repudiates this kind of surface commitment. He is unwilling to settle for anything less than our hearts. (See Isa. 1:10–20; 29:13; and Matt. 23.)

4. CHANGE

It is easy to assume that change has taken place because the person has gained insight and made new commitments. This may tempt us to stop the confrontation process prematurely. But change has not taken place until change has taken place! Change—not personal insight or commitment—is the goal of confrontation. Insight and commitment are simply steps toward a life lived in the worship of God. We must help people to apply insights and commitments to their lives. If commitment focuses on the "what," change focuses on the "how."

How will Jim demonstrate his thankfulness to God and to others? How will he incorporate new habits into his daily routine to break down the distance from his friends and church family? Change applies new commitments to the situations and relationships of daily living.

If we want our words to be instruments of change in confrontation, we need a sense of direction. These four steps provide a road map.

1. *Consideration.* What does God want the person to see?
2. *Confession.* What does God want the person to admit and confess?
3. *Commitment.* To what new ways of living is God calling this person?
4. *Change.* How should these new commitments be applied to daily living?

HOW TO CONFRONT BIBLICALLY

As in all other aspects of personal ministry, confrontation must not only be shaped by biblical goals, but by biblical methods as well. We need to constantly scour Scripture for the theology and methodology of ministry it reveals. For example, when Paul instructs members of the body to minister to one another, he says, "Speak the truth [content] in love [method]." The two are equally important. Truth that is not spoken in love ceases to be truth because it is twisted by other human agendas. Love that is not guided by truth ceases to be love because it is divorced from God's agenda. Once we understand the goals of confrontation and the steps of the process, we can ask *how* Scripture calls us to confront one another.

It bears repeating that we are not advocating a "reading the riot act" form of confrontation, where the receiver is silent and the confronter lays out a list of offenses. In Scripture, the more common style of confrontation is interaction. The confronter stands alongside the person, helping him to see, telling stories, asking questions, drawing out answers, and then calling for a response. There is a more conversational structure. Christ winsomely employed this method of confrontation in his parables. (See Luke 7:36–50; 14:1–14.) He spoke so that people might see, and in seeing, might confess, and in confessing, might repent. He confronted powerful attitudes, beliefs, and actions, yet in a way very different from our tense scenes of confrontation.

Another example of interactive confrontation is found in 2 Samuel 12:1–7.

> The LORD sent Nathan to David. When he came to him, he said, "There were two men in a certain town, one rich and the other poor. The rich man had a very large number of sheep and cattle, but the poor man had nothing except one little ewe lamb he had bought. He raised it, and it grew up with him and his children. It shared his food, drank from his cup and even slept in his arms. It was like a daughter to him.

"Now a traveler came to the rich man, but the rich man refrained from taking one of his own sheep or cattle to prepare a meal for the traveler who had come to him. Instead, he took the ewe lamb that belonged to the poor man and prepared it for the one who had come to him."

David burned with anger against the man and said to Nathan, "As surely as the LORD lives, the man who did this deserves to die! He must pay for that lamb four times over, because he did such a thing and had no pity."

Then Nathan said to David, "You are the man!"

Nathan was called to confront the king with his murder and adultery, but he did not burst into the throne room and read off a list of charges. His goal was to help David see what he had done and lead him to repentance, so the way he confronted David looks very different from what we often do. Nathan's approach is noteworthy in at least a dozen respects.

1. Note the severity of the issues. Nathan is not just providing "spiritual guidance." David has committed murder and adultery.
2. Note the degree of spiritual blindness. David is the God-anointed king, yet he has not only committed adultery with Bathsheba and murdered her husband, he has brought her into the palace to live with him. The more outrageous the sin, the more fundamental the blindness that covers it. This is why you should not settle for lecturing or reading charges. You are not simply dealing with the person's sin, but with self-protective blindness that keeps the sin from the person's view. The person you are called to confront will tend to be both willfully blind and blindly willful. If he is going to confess and turn, he needs to *see* what he has done. We need a style of confrontation that helps him do that.
3. There is no evidence that Nathan enters the throne room with flashing eyes, bulging veins, pointed finger, and words blaz-

ing. ("David, you are a murderer and adulterer!") In fact, you might find Nathan's patient manner unsettling.

4. Nathan stands before David and tells him a story, an extended metaphor crafted to open the eyes of David's heart.

5. Notice that the story is built on subject matter related to David's life (sheep). If we pay attention, we can learn many things about a person that will help us when the time comes to confront. The metaphors do not have to be dramatic or earthshaking. Sometimes using a little element from a person's life to illustrate a biblical principle or reveal a sin is more effective than a long, dramatic story.

   The angry man I mentioned earlier simply did not see what he was doing to his family. He was the head of a computer department for a large corporation and he wanted the same response from his family that he got from the computer. He did not want conversation or relationship, just immediate action in response to clear commands. I used the metaphor of "pressing the button again" to help him see what he was doing. His way of life at home was devoid of the self-sacrificing love and patience God calls husbands and fathers to display, but he did not see it because his family was "in order." God used the button metaphor to open his eyes.

   Weeks after I first used it, this man said to me, "You know, you have really spoiled my job for me! Every time I sit down at my computer, I think about what I have done to my family, and I ask for the Lord's help." My response was, "Praise the Lord!" When you use pieces of a person's life as tools to help him see, they will continue to confront the person long after you are done speaking. This helps people to continually recommit themselves to what the Lord wants to show them.

6. In Nathan's interactive style of confrontation, the focus is on the story, with the goal of stimulating David to see what he has not seen.

7. Notice that the story is short on details, yet very specific in application. The story is not the goal; it is a means to the goal. It

must be pointed enough to cut through layers of blindness and expose the heart.

8. The story accomplishes its goal, resulting in a heart reaction: "David burned with anger" (v. 5).

9. Notice that David is the first person to speak after the story is completed. He has gotten the point of the story and says, "The man who did this deserves to die!" (v. 5). The story leads David to confront himself, even before he realizes the application to his life.

10. Nathan follows David's self-confrontation by specifically applying the story to his sins of adultery and murder (vv. 7–12).

11. David then speaks clear words of confession that are free of blameshifting or excuse making (v. 13).

12. Nathan ends by assuring David of God's forgiveness and the consequences of his sin (vv. 13–14).

The wise ministry of this prophet presents a wonderful model of biblical confrontation. The Gospels put this same model before us in the ministry of Christ. Again, because Jesus seeks to open people's eyes and lead them to repentance, the confrontation is interactive. He tells stories, asks and answers questions, guides a person's thinking, enters into conversation, employs imaginative metaphors, and waits for self-confronting responses, all with the goal of personal insight and heart repentance.

In truth speaking, the principle is to start with interaction. This includes:

Two-way communication. The person being confronted must be invited to talk. This is the only way to know if he has understood what you are pointing out; if he has owned what needs to be admitted and confessed; and if he is committed to new ways of living.

Use of metaphor. A metaphor is a familiar thing used to communicate a less familiar idea. God employs an extensive list of metaphors to help us see and know him. Metaphors such as rock, fortress, sun, shield, door, and light teach us that God is solid, stable, unmoved, unchanging, someone upon which we can stand.

In confrontation, we want to find things in a person's life that illustrate truths or reveal sins he needs to see. We need to ask the question, "What do I know about this person's background, job, interests, and experiences that can provide metaphors for me to use?" The metaphor may be a single comparison ("You're pushing the button again!") or an extended story ("The kingdom of God is like a man sowing seeds . . .").

Self-confronting statements. Here you encourage the person to make connections between your examples and his own life. Don't make connections for him! *His* heart needs to embrace what God is showing him and, without pressure, be ready to confess and turn from sin.

Summary. Here you summarize all that God wants to teach the person and call him to respond in heartfelt commitment. Make sure the issues are clear and don't assume the person's agreement. Stop and ask for specific commitments. Communicate the general principles of Scripture in a way that is concretely applicable to this particular person, so that he walks away not only with a clear sense of conviction, but a clear sense of calling as well.

Confrontation should always begin with interaction, but there will be times when you are called to minister to someone who is stubborn, rebellious, and proud. The person will not participate in the give-and-take of interactive confrontation, so he needs to hear God's will pronounced and be exhorted to respond. This style of confrontation, declaration, is what we most often associate with confrontation, but it should be reserved for those who refuse to do the self-examination that interactive confrontation requires. It is for the stiff-necked and the hard-hearted. We should always begin with interaction (engaging a person in heartfelt self-examination) and only move to declaration ("Thus says the Lord—therefore repent") when the person has refused to listen and consider. (See Matt. 18:15–20; 23:13–39; Amos 6.)

It is a sweet grace when we are surrounded by people who love us enough to confront us—who are unwilling to let us stay lost, blind, confused, rebellious, and wandering away. It is a sign of God's covenant faithfulness when he sends people to help us see and repent. He heals our spiritual blindness most often in everyday moments of growing awareness and progressive conviction. He uses husbands and wives, brothers and sisters, fathers and mothers, elders and deacons, neighbors and friends to do his kingdom work. He calls us, wherever we are, to help each other see and pursue a life of faith.

It is tragic when we are too busy to see the need around us. It is terrible when we see wrong going on but trim the truth because loving, humble rebuke takes us beyond the borders of our safe lives and casual relationships. These responses are the fruit of self-love that has replaced a love for God. The ministry of loving, humble, biblical truth speaking always begins with examining our own hearts.

We have been called to participate in the most important activity in the universe. God is taking rebellious, self-absorbed people and changing them into those who pursue holiness for the sake of his glory, even as they suffer in a fallen world. To this end he has called us to call sinners to repentance, incarnating his presence and work.[2]

LOVE
KNOW
SPEAK
 ▶ DO

13 | ESTABLISHING AGENDA AND CLARIFYING RESPONSIBILITY

I was only eighteen when I asked my wife to marry me. I really loved her, but I didn't yet know *how* to love her. We were committed Christians and we wanted to do marriage God's way, but we lacked wisdom and maturity. We needed someone to apply the principles of Scripture to the realities of our particular relationship. Thankfully, we received much counsel on how to take the things God says about marriage and work them out in our life together. Now, more than thirty years later, we continue to learn a little more each day about what it means to apply God's truth to our lives.

Change always demands a deeper understanding of the things of God and a more careful application of those truths to our lives. Since change is a lifelong process, it won't be over until we are in the presence of the Lord. So, as we encourage people to change, dealing with the needs of the moment is not our highest priority; rather, it is answering God's call to "Be holy, because I am holy" (Lev. 11:44). As we call people to do what God has called them to do, we must keep this ultimate destination in view.

After thirty years, I am still learning what it means to love Luella "as Christ loved the church" (Eph. 5:25). We are still learning how to embed our story in the larger story of redemption. I am still asking Luella to forgive me, and we still have misunderstandings. We still need to be rebuked and still benefit from accountability. We still help each other identify areas of spiritual blindness where we step outside God's boundaries.

At the same time, we have grown wiser and our marriage is easier.

We live with a confidence we didn't have in the early years. We have experienced the truthfulness of the Word and the faithfulness of our Lord. We have seen again and again that his grace is sufficient in our times of greatest weakness. We have learned that living for his glory results in our good. We have identified idol after idol and their effects on our relationship. Yet with all this change, we are still changing! And we have learned that keeping the final destination in view is the only way to solve the problems of today.

You will see the truth of this principle often in personal ministry. Seldom will you deal only with a person's original problem; instead, you will also tackle layers of difficulty that have been created by "solutions" that addressed the need of the moment but did not keep God's ultimate purpose in view. When you are facing difficulty, disappointment, or crisis, it is easy to be captured by the problem in front of you. It is hard to be committed to long-term goals when you are putting out fires. That is why we not only need the practical wisdom of specific application, but someone to faithfully remind us of our ultimate destination.

Paul captures this principle of "long view living" in 2 Corinthians 11:1–3.

> I hope you will put up with a little of my foolishness; but you are already doing that. I am jealous for you with a godly jealousy. I promised you to one husband, to Christ, so that I might present you as a pure virgin to him. But I am afraid that just as Eve was deceived by the serpent's cunning, your minds may somehow be led astray from your sincere and pure devotion to Christ.

Paul understands the Christian life eschatologically. This means that today is preparation for tomorrow, and tomorrow is preparation for something else yet to come. Paul is saying, "I know I have hovered over you, but you need to understand why. I am afraid that you will forget who you are and to whom you have been promised." To Paul, the only way to go through life properly is to understand that we are engaged. We have been betrothed to Christ, and our life now is preparation for the great wedding to come.

The difficulties now, the suffering now, the disappointments now, and the blessings now are all preparation for the wedding *then*. Our experiences today do not reflect God's inattention or unfaithfulness, but his jealous love. He is exposing our wandering hearts and foolish minds and the ways we trust our passions more than the principles of his Word. He is calling us to forsake our own glory for his, and teaching us that the idols we pursue will never satisfy us. He is making us wise to temptation and aware of a lurking enemy. He is teaching us to live for treasures that moth and rust can't destroy and that thieves can't steal. He is teaching us what it means to live in a way that recognizes our identity as his children. He is teaching us to live open, approachable, and humble lives.

In other words, your whole life is premarital counseling! You belong to a groom whose name is Immanuel, and God is preparing you for the wedding for which you were created and redeemed. Everything you face today is premarital preparation—living *now* with *then* in view.

In contrast, sin produces in all of us a tendency toward "now-ism," which means we forget three things: who we are (betrothed to Christ); what he is doing now (preparing us for the final wedding); and what we are supposed to be doing (remaining faithful to him). When we focus only on what we want now, we fail to solve our problems and we also cause more difficulties. A common factor in depression is self-absorbed now-ism. Anger is often fueled by a self-righteous now-ism. Fear and anxiety are strengthened by an obsession with the here and now. Maturity and perseverance are weakened by a "now" mentality.

Teaching others how to solve *now* problems with *then* in view is one of the most important things we can do, because it is not something we sinners do well on our own. We tend to be shortsighted and self-absorbed. We forget that God's primary goal is not changing our situations and relationships so that we can be happy, but changing us through our situations and relationships so that we will be holy. We need people who love God and us enough to come alongside and help us deal with our spiritual myopia.

This is one reason why the Bible does not present divorce as a solution to marriage problems, though it may be a result. Unrepented adultery may provide biblical grounds for release from the marriage covenant, but divorce does not solve the problems that led to it. Divorce changes relationships, situations, and locations, but it doesn't change the heart. People who use divorce as a solution often repeat the same problems in subsequent relationships because the one thing that needed to change remained unchanged: them! They were blinded by their own now-ism. But if they see their marriage *now* as a training ground for their marriage *then*, the trials God sends their way make perfect sense. As you solve marriage problems with *then* in view, you won't deal with trouble by separating from your spouse. You will learn how God wants to change you so that you can better live with him or her. Your *now* response will be shaped by a *then* perspective.

QUITTING TOO SOON

Most of us are tempted to think that change has taken place before it actually has. We confuse growth in knowledge and insight with genuine life change. But insight is not change and knowledge should not be confused with practical, active, biblical wisdom. In fourteen years of seminary teaching, I have met many brilliant, theologically astute students who were incredibly immature in their everyday life. There was often a huge gap between their confessional and functional theology. Students who could articulate the sovereignty of God could be overcome by worry. Students who could expound on the glory of God would dominate classroom discussions for the sake of their own egos. I have counseled students who could explain the biblical doctrine of progressive holiness while nurturing secret worlds of lust and sexual sin. I have seen many men who were months away from ministry who had not yet learned how to love people. Students who could explain the biblical teaching of God's grace were harsh, judgmental legalists.

In short, we must not confuse insight and change. Insight is a beginning, a part of the whole, but it is not the whole. We do want people to see, know, and understand, but we also want them to apply that insight to their daily life. God opens our eyes so that, in seeing him, we would follow him more closely. This means that personal ministry should not end too soon. If holiness is God's goal, we must be willing to help others through the process of change.

For many people, it is much easier to know what is wrong than how to change it. I may have confessed a selfish, idolatrous heart and seen its fruit in my relationship with my wife. But it will be harder for me to think clearly and creatively about how to repent and actually love her in specific ways. I may understand the major themes of Scripture, but I may not know how to use them in certain situations and relationships. We all need people to stand alongside us as we apply God's Word to our lives.

INGREDIENTS NEEDED TO ENCOURAGE CHANGE

Have you ever had personal insights that did not lead to lasting change? Has the theology you have learned always had a practical impact on you? Have you ever made commitments that somehow got lost in the frenetic pace of life? Have you ever known that certain changes needed to take place, but you didn't know how to make them? Have you ever lost sight of your identity in Christ amid pressure, trial, or suffering? Have you ever benefited from someone holding you accountable?

The final aspect of our model, **Do,** teaches us how to apply truths we have learned, personal insights we have gained, and commitments we have made, to our daily lives. Here we teach people to be dissatisfied with the gap between their confessional and functional theology. We lead them to live out their identity as children of God, claiming the rights and privileges of the gospel. **Do** trains people in the decisions, actions, relationships, and skills of Christ-centered, biblically informed living. We have a wonderful opportunity not only to teach people how to solve their problems biblically, but to turn their lives around for the long run.

Here, as always, it is vital to keep the heart in view. People who begin to follow Christ by faith in practical ways will increasingly expose their hearts. If they are willing to examine them, they will see where they tend to doubt or don't require themselves to think biblically. They will see where they are tempted to run after god-replacements and live for their own glory. And they will discover whether they are ready to find hope and help in Christ or if they prefer to give in to self-atoning patterns of excuse making, blame-shifting, and rewriting their own history. As the heart is revealed, people can learn how to live a "changed and being changed" life.

To help people in these areas, you pursue four objectives:

1. *Establish your personal ministry agenda.* This provides a sense of direction.
2. *Clarify responsibility.* As people apply truth to life, the issue of who is responsible for what will always arise.
3. *Instill identity in Christ.* Change is a hard process, and people need to be reminded of the resources that are theirs as children of God.
4. *Provide accountability.* Change demands patience and perseverance, so we all need the encouragement, insight, and warning that a system of oversight provides.

In this chapter, we will look at the first two objectives.

KNOWING WHERE YOU'RE GOING

If you are driving somewhere new and you find yourself lost, you don't want directions from someone who just moved to the community and doesn't know the area. Nor do you want directions from a person so familiar with the area that he doesn't provide the details you need to find your way. As we help people chart a course of change in their lives, we need to avoid the same pitfalls. We need to remember that it is impossible to lead a person to change if we don't know where we are going, and that what is obvious to us may be anything but obvious to another.

> ▶ OBJECTIVE 1:
> ESTABLISH YOUR PERSONAL MINISTRY AGENDA.

This is as important in informal personal ministry as it is in more formal counseling situations. An agenda is simply a plan for accomplishing a goal, a map that shows us our destination (the changes that need to take place) and how to get there (How? Where? When? With whom?). Our goal is more than denouncing sin or solving the problem of the moment. We need to know what specific changes God is calling this person to make in this situation.

What should Harry do about the job that takes him away from his family eighty hours a week, thus threatening his marriage? How will George deal with his enslavement to pornography? How will Anita confront her father for the abuse she endured at his hands? How can she learn to forgive him? What will Bob do about those deeply ingrained ways of thinking that contribute to his suicidal depression? How will Fran learn to live as a child of God, rather than a "failure and a loser"? What actions should Bill and Dorothy take to protect their rebellious son from himself? How will Andy restore the trust he has destroyed in his marriage? How will Lisa defeat the fear that has paralyzed her? How can Dick live with gospel hope after a crippling injury? What does it look like for Stephanie to love, lead, and parent three demanding toddlers?

Biblical personal ministry needs to answer questions like these. We need to apply the principles, perspectives, commands, and themes of God's great redemptive story to the concrete realities of a person's life. We cannot leave people to themselves or advise them from a distance. Yet all too often, our ministry is weakest here. We fail to recognize that, on their own, people often have a hard time applying biblical truths to their lives. We need to establish a biblical sense of direction (agenda) for our ministry at this stage. Otherwise, our counsel will be weakened by:

- Personal bias
- Ignorance
- Poor theology
- Misunderstanding of Scripture
- Improper application of Scripture
- Fear of man
- Emotional thinking
- Pressure of the moment.

God has chosen us to be his ambassadors in this person's life! The Holy Spirit is enlivening the person's heart and empowering our words. The Savior is loving and changing others through us. Nothing we can do is more important or will have more lasting results. In view of the holiness of our calling, we should not speak without preparation. We should ask questions that help us think clearly about how to accomplish God's goals for change in this person. Here are three agenda-setting questions.

What does the Bible say about the information that has been gathered? This is not simply asking, "Where can I find a verse on _____?" We want to examine things through the lens of the great themes of Scripture, to understand how a distinctively biblical worldview shapes our response to the issues in the person's life. We are asking, "What has God taught, promised, commanded, warned, encouraged, and done that addresses this situation?" This protects our ministry from personal bias, unbiblical thinking, and a crisis-driven impulsivity that can lead us into trouble.

Going through this process demands humility on our part. One of the most harmful errors we can make in ministry is to assume that we have "arrived" spiritually and theologically. None of us has fully grasped the grandeur and practicality of Scripture. None of us has a completely uncorrupted Christian worldview or mastered the gospel in all its applications and implications. All of us are people in process, called to minister to other people in process. We must confess our own blindness as we lead others to recognize theirs. We all need the Holy Spirit as our Teacher just as much as the day we first believed. Rich and powerful discoveries in Scripture await all of us, discoveries that are brand new even from old, familiar passages.

Moments of ministry are opportunities for us to sit at the Lord's feet and learn new and deeper things. The needs of the people we serve drive us deeper into Scripture to discover new treasures. We should be thankful for another opportunity to use the tools God has given us more carefully, skillfully, and efficiently. We should not assume that we have arrived!

What are God's goals for change for this person in this situation? This question applies God's call to "put off" and "put on" (Eph. 4:22–24) to the specifics of a person's thoughts, motives, and behavior. What does God want her to think, desire, and do? Answering these questions marks out our destination. At this point, we need to recognize that our agenda will not always be the same as the Lord's. For example, I may not want what God wants for the child abuser I am helping. I may not want what God wants for an incredibly self-absorbed person who is bitter at the world. I may not want what God wants for the angry person whose anger has spilled over onto me. I may be a Jonah who resents God's mercy to the modern day Ninevites he calls me to serve. Asking this question keeps me from confusing God's agenda with my own. I cannot lead a person if I don't know where we are going, and I must only lead people where God is calling them.

This question takes the general commands, themes, perspectives, and principles of Scripture and fashions them into specific steps of change. The goals we establish must address the What? How? When? and Where? of change. We need to present biblical goals that fit the context in which a person lives and works. You can only do this if you have processed the person's situation through sound biblical thinking and concrete goal setting.

What are some biblical methods for accomplishing God's goals of change? After establishing biblical goals, we need to determine the best biblical means of accomplishing them. Often people have a sense of what is wrong, but the way they seek to correct it complicates matters further. Let's say you are ministering to a husband who confesses that he has not encouraged his wife as he should. It would not be biblical to advise him to bombard her with flattering but insincere words. To provide the how, you must know God's Word, the situation, and the person's heart motives well.

God will often surprise us at this point. The Bible presents a lifestyle that is radically different from anything we would concoct on our own. The Bible not only lays out a surprising picture of what is wrong with us, but a surprising agenda for correction as well. We always need to ask: How should this person put off what needs to be put off, and put on what needs to be put on? To what steps of obedience is God calling him?

APPLYING THE THREE QUESTIONS

Let's return to the "Sharon and Ed" example in chapter 10 as a way to understand how these three questions help us set biblical goals. We saw that Sharon and Ed's relationship was marred by abuse, infidelity, isolation, manipulation and retaliation. Though Sharon was "the most beautiful woman in the world" to Ed, and Ed was "the best thing that ever happened" to Sharon, their marriage was on the verge of collapse. There is more than one way to minister to Sharon and Ed, but whatever we do must be shaped by clear biblical thinking and concrete biblical goals. For our purposes here, we will focus the questions on Sharon.

What does the Bible say about the information gathered?
- Sharon's marriage is her primary human relationship (Gen. 2; Eph. 5). Is she living this way?
- Relationship struggles reveal our hearts (Luke 6:43–45; Mark 7).

- It is easier to see another's faults than to see our own (Matt. 7:3–5; Heb. 3:12–13).
- God calls us to peace (Matt. 5:9; Rom. 12:14–21).
- God calls us to be agents of reconciliation (2 Cor. 5:16–21).
- Forgiveness is the way to peace and reconciliation (Luke 17:3–4; Eph. 4:29–5:2).
- God gives Sharon and Ed everything they need to work on their marriage (2 Peter 1:3–9).
- God clearly describes how a husband and wife should relate to each other (Eph. 5:22–33).
- The core issue in marriage is not what Sharon wants and the best way for her to get it, but what God wants and the best way to pursue it.

In each of these principles and themes is material that could revolutionize this marriage. Imagine the difference if Sharon and Ed quit blaming each other and humbly admitted that the things they have done reveal the true thoughts and desires of their hearts. Imagine the fundamental changes that would take place if they admitted what really is ruling their hearts and setting the agenda for their marriage. Even better, imagine what would happen if biblical attitudes became their daily personal agenda. When we actually apply biblical perspectives to people's daily lives, they rearrange them from the inside out.

As you help Sharon and Ed, these perspectives remind you how deep the problems in this marriage are. Helping this couple to develop a few communication skills will not make things better. There is almost nothing in this marriage that does not need to be rebuilt! The problems are first vertical, then horizontal. God has been removed as the ruler of Sharon and Ed's hearts and as the agenda setter for their marriage. Their highest commitment is to their own personal happiness, and they are angry that their mate has not delivered! As you look at this marriage biblically, you know you must begin by calling them to repent of the god-replacements that control their hearts and shape their marriage.

What are God's goals of change for Sharon?
- ◆ To move from blind self-righteousness to humble self-awareness
- ◆ To move from bitterness to forgiveness
- ◆ To move from seeking vengeance to seeking to do good
- ◆ To move from self-protection to loving and sacrificial service
- ◆ To move from angry withdrawal to productive communication
- ◆ To move from separation to the pursuit of reconciliation
- ◆ To entrust Ed to God and quit being Ed's "messiah"

Each of these is more a category than a goal, and each would involve many specific changes. For example, Sharon has been a willing partner in a vengeful, "Oh, yeah? I'll show you!" marriage. God calls her to look for ways to do good even in the face of evil. This agenda will lead to a myriad of changes in the way she responds to Ed.

Fɪɢ. 13.1
Clarifying Responsibility.

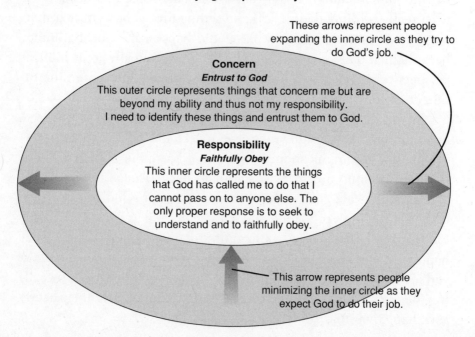

These arrows represent people expanding the inner circle as they try to do God's job.

Concern
Entrust to God
This outer circle represents things that concern me but are beyond my ability and thus not my responsibility. I need to identify these things and entrust them to God.

Responsibility
Faithfully Obey
This inner circle represents the things that God has called me to do that I cannot pass on to anyone else. The only proper response is to seek to understand and to faithfully obey.

This arrow represents people minimizing the inner circle as they expect God to do their job.

What are biblical methods for accomplishing God's goals of change?

- Help Sharon to see herself in the mirror of God's Word.
- Have Sharon keep a focused journal using the questions from chapter 10. This will help her see how the themes of her heart play out in her actions and reactions.
- Encourage Sharon to do the two circles exercise (Figure 13.1), with particular focus on her relationship with Ed. This will give Sharon a clear understanding of her God-given "job description" and a grasp of the things she must entrust to God.
- Study Psalm 73 and 1 Peter 1 with Sharon to help her escape the discouragement, anger, and fear that result not only from Ed's failure but her own self-absorption and now-ism. Teach her how to set her eyes on what is unseen and eternal.

As we seek to encourage change in the hearts and lives of others, we want to help people not only to confess their sin but to repent as well. This is why we ask, "How can I stimulate the kind of change that needs to take place in this person?" These three questions provide a simple model that sets goals at the convergence of broad biblical themes and personal application. They help us to pay attention to the process of ministry. We are more than watchmen giving warning; we are actually tools of change in the hands of the Redeemer.

▶ **OBJECTIVE 2:**
CLARIFY RESPONSIBILITY.

One of the most important questions in life is, "Who is responsible for what?" As you deal with this question in ministry, you will tend to encounter three classes of people.

The first group is made up of people who are *irresponsible*. They fail to recognize and shoulder their God-given responsibilities. Next, you will encounter those who are *overly responsible*. These people take responsibility for things that God has not assigned or equipped them to do. The third class of people is probably the largest of the three. These people are *genuinely confused* about which things are their God-given jobs and which things they can entrust to him. Sometime they are mini-messiahs, trying to do things that only God can do. At other times, they ask God to take care of responsibilities he has clearly placed on them. All three groups need to understand their responsibilities in order to apply change meaningfully to their daily lives.

Figure 13.1 is a simple tool for clarifying responsibility. Let's start with the inner circle, the Circle of Responsibility. This circle represents a particular person's biblical job description. These are the things that God, in his Word, calls this person to do in his present situation and relationships. A man, for example, needs a clear sense of what God calls him to do as a husband, father, neighbor, relative, son, worker, and member of the body of Christ. God is calling him to deny himself, take up his cross, and follow Christ (Luke 9:23–25), and to no longer live for himself, but for the Lord (2 Cor. 5:14–15). The response of faith in this case is obedience. Our job is to help this man find specific ways to respond, in the obedience of faith, to this call to discipleship.

In this circle, we ask the person to list what he thinks are his God-assigned duties in each role God has given him (as a father, employee, etc.) Next, we help him examine his list in light of Scripture, to discover whether the things he listed really are what God has called him to do. Often there are discrepancies between our lists and God's! When we see this, we can gain a better sense of what God actually expects of us—and will enable us to do by his grace.

The outer circle, the Circle of Concern, represents those things that are important to a person (the love of a spouse, a child's salvation), yet beyond his ability to bring about. Therefore, they are not his responsibility. Here we are calling a person to recognize his limits and to remember God, who is faithful to his promises (Ps. 145:13) and sovereign over all things (Acts 17:24–28). The response of faith in this case is to entrust these matters to God in prayer.

People confuse these circles in two main ways. First, they allow the inner circle to expand into the outer circle, so that they function as mini-messiahs, trying to do what only God can do. Second, they shrink the inner circle and, under the guise of trusting God, neglect to do what God calls them to do. We want to help them avoid both pitfalls.

Imagine how helpful this exercise would be for Sharon, who has clearly been very confused about the issue of responsibility. Sometimes she has acted as if she were lord, master, and messiah, attempting to do what only God can do (expanding her Circle of Responsibility inappropriately). At other times she has been unbiblically passive, waiting for God to do the very things he has clearly assigned to her (shrinking her Circle of Responsibility inappropriately). Sharon would greatly benefit from having the issue of responsibility clarified for her.

If Sharon lives as a mini-messiah (with too large a Circle of Responsibility), there will be two negative effects. First, since she is trying to do God's job, she will experience discouragement, frustration, and failure. After all, she is not qualified! Second, because she is focusing on God's job, she will tend to leave undone the things that God, in his Word, has given her to carry out. Sharon has experienced both problems as she has sought to make changes in her marriage.

As another example, Alicia is concerned about her teenage son, Matt. He is increasingly rebellious, irresponsible, unkind, and selfish. He is missing more school than he is attending. Alicia has told Matt and her close friends that her goal is to "turn Matt into a responsible Christian if it is the last thing I ever do." This is the goal of a mini-messiah, although Alicia doesn't realize it. She has improperly expanded her Circle of Responsibility to cover things that belong in her Circle of Concern. Though she can do certain things to help, challenge, discipline, and encourage Matt (things that are within her Circle of Responsibility), she cannot control Matt's heart (a matter that belongs in her Circle of Concern). Only God can do that. Alicia is taking God's job as her own and she will experience failure and frustration as a result.

Having too small an inner circle—attempting to give back to God what he has called me to do—will have two negative results as well.

First, I will waste time and prayer if I wait for God to do something he has assigned me to do. I will think God has failed me when, in fact, I have failed him! If overly responsible people are mini-messiahs, people who shrink their inner circle are "spiritual vacationers." They have abandoned their God-assigned workplace and are lounging around, expecting him to do their job. God will empower me to do the things he has called me to do, but he will not do them for me! Therefore, I will be waiting for something I will not receive. And as I am waiting, the second negative result will surface: things will worsen because of what I have left undone.

What would happen, for example, if Alicia had the opposite reaction to Matt's rebellion and made her Circle of Responsibility too small? What if Alicia said to her friends, "I've decided to let go and let God deal with Matt. I can't parent him any more; God is just going to have to do a miracle." It is true that only God can change Matt's heart, but it is also true that God positions and uses people to accomplish his miraculous plan. He has given Matt a mother because Matt needs a mother, and because he intends to bring his truth to bear on Matt through her. Alicia should daily entrust Matt to the Lord, while she continues to do the things God has called her to do as a parent. God wants Alicia to live out an active, obedient trust, not a passive one.

A passive response may appear to be the "spiritual" thing to do, but it is just as unbiblical as living like a mini-messiah. It is the response people often make when facing a broken relationship. Let's say that Dave knows that he has a broken relationship with his friend Alec. Alec hardly calls any more and hasn't asked for Dave to pray for him, as he used to, in months. Dave knows that their problems go back to a public disagreement he had with Alec a year ago. Dave says that he has "dealt with it in his heart" and is now waiting for God to restore the relationship. That response reveals that Dave's Circle of Responsibility is too small. The Bible clearly calls him to take steps to be reconciled to Alec (Matt. 5:23–24).

Many Christians also take a "passive trust" approach to seeking guidance and direction from the Lord. They think that knowing

God's will comes as God reveals his secret plan to them; then they will know what to do. But guidance is really a matter of obedient, active trust. I examine the options before me using the principles, themes, and perspectives of Scripture. Then, to the best of my knowledge and ability, I apply biblical wisdom and make a decision. My decision is not based on reading God's mind, but on things he has clearly revealed in his Word. As I step forward, I entrust myself to the Lord, knowing that he rules over everything and will place me where he wants me. This is the biblical model of guidance. Too many people have their "Christian divining rods" out in hopes of discovering the secret will of God. Meanwhile, the Bible in their hands is unopened—the thing God has said will be a "lamp to their feet and a light to their path"!

TRUST AND OBEY

The Christian life can really be boiled down to two words: trust and obey. I must always entrust the things that are out of my control to God (Circle of Concern), and I must always be faithful to obey his clear and specific commands (Circle of Responsibility). Romans 12:14–21 is a wonderful passage to use to explain this "trust and obey" lifestyle.

> Bless those who persecute you; bless and do not curse. Rejoice with those who rejoice; mourn with those who mourn. Live in harmony with one another. Do not be proud, but be willing to associate with people of low position. Do not be conceited.
>
> Do not repay anyone evil for evil. Be careful to do what is right in the eyes of everybody. If it is possible, as far as it depends on you, live at peace with everyone. Do not take revenge, my friends, but leave room for God's wrath, for it is written: "It is mine to avenge; I will repay," says the LORD. On the contrary:

"If your enemy is hungry, feed him;
   if he is thirsty, give him something to drink.
In doing this, you will heap burning coals on his head."

    Do not be overcome by evil, but overcome evil with good.

What is powerful about this passage is that it lays out the "trust and obey" lifestyle in the context of mistreatment. God clearly explains our duties in the face of wrong treatment:

- Bless those who persecute you (v. 14).
- Be tender and compassionate (v. 15).
- Commit to living in harmony (v. 16).
- Do not be proud (v. 16).
- As far as you can, live at peace with everyone (v. 19).
- Meet your enemy's need (v. 20).
- Overcome evil with good (v. 21).

In making my responsibilities under mistreatment clear, Paul also makes it clear that there are things that I must not take as my responsibility. For example, I must not retaliate or seek revenge. These are things that only God has the right and the power to do. They are, in fact, things he has promised to do. I must not load them onto my shoulders.

At the same time, it is wrong to be passive in the face of mistreatment, waiting around for God to do something. God calls us to be obediently active, looking for ways to do good, make peace, and meet needs. In the process, we continue to entrust the person who has wronged us to God's just and merciful hands. In short, we must do what God has called us to do in a spirit of joyful submission, and, in a spirit of humble trust, let God do what he alone can do.

Few areas are more confusing to people than the area of personal responsibility. They need practical clarity to help them through the process of change. We can help them first by providing a clear sense of direction as we think biblically about God's agenda. Second, we can help by clarifying the issue of responsibility and applying the "trust and obey" lifestyle to their daily situations and relationships.

Holding onto God's grace and glory is the only way to deal with the disappointment and loss that is so much a part of life. As we hold these themes before people, we not only participate in God's kingdom work of lasting change, we also introduce them to the Person who offers the highest human satisfaction that can be found.

LOVE
KNOW
SPEAK
▶ DO

14 INSTILLING IDENTITY WITH CHRIST AND PROVIDING ACCOUNTABILITY

As we continue examining the ways God can use us to help people change, think about your own life for a moment. Aren't you also a person in need of ministry? Whether you are an influential Christian leader or a brand new believer, if you examine your life, you will see that you too need the ministry of others.

This chapter examines the fact that encouragement and accountability are important parts of the truth application process. Scripture makes it clear that we were never created to live in isolation. God designed us to live in community, first with him and then with one another. According to the Bible, personal change is a community project. In fact, it is in the process of change that we really begin to see our need for one another. My need for others is not because I am a moral or intellectual cripple in a world of healthy people. Rather, God created us to be dependent on each other to live life righteously, just as he created us to be dependent on his revelation to interpret life accurately.

▶ OBJECTIVE 3:
INSTILL IDENTITY IN CHRIST.

THE IMPORTANCE OF KNOWING WHO YOU ARE

People need encouragement as they pursue the hard work of change. They need truths that will motivate and strengthen them.

The gospel motivates us not only with the presence of Christ and the surety of his promises, but also with our brand new identity. In passages like Romans 6:15–17 and 1 John 3:1–3, Scripture lays out this new identity for us. We learn that we are not only forgiven, but have in fact been adopted into the family of God. We are children of the King of Kings! The God of the universe is our Father!

Another way the New Testament describes this dramatic new identity is to say that we are "in Christ." This means that we have been fully united to him and received all he has promised us. This goes far beyond the fact that we have been forgiven and are going to heaven. Something more fundamental has happened. Paul describes it in Ephesians 2:6–7: "And God raised us up *with Christ* and seated us *with him* in the heavenly realms *in Christ Jesus,* in order that in the coming ages he might show the incomparable riches of his grace, expressed in his kindness to us *in Christ Jesus.*" John 15 captures this identity with a metaphor, saying that as believers we are like branches attached to a vine. We can only bear fruit because of our union with Christ the Vine. We have life because we are "in" the Vine.

All of this is important in times of change because we always live out of some kind of identity, and the identities we assign ourselves powerfully influence our responses to life. As people pursue the process of lifelong change, they need to live out of a gospel identity. They, like us, need to be reminded of who they are again and again.

In the press of everyday life, it is easy to forget who we are. As we try to replace old behaviors with new ones, it is easy to take our eyes off our status as children of God. In fact, the longer we struggle with a problem, the more likely we are to define ourselves by that problem (divorced, addicted, depressed, co-dependent, ADD). We come to believe that our problem is who we are. But while these labels may describe particular ways we struggle as sinners in a fallen world, they *are not* our identity! If we allow them to define us, we will live trapped within their boundaries. This is no way for a child of God to live!

There is a radical difference between saying, "I am a depressed person," and saying, "I am a child of God 'in Christ' and I tend to struggle with depression." The second statement does not pretend that the war isn't raging, but it is infused with hope. It says, "Yes, I wrestle with depression every day, but I am not alone. I do not rest on my own strength and wisdom. I have come to understand that my Creator and Savior is also my Father. I am beginning to grasp how rich I really am because of my place in his family, and I am learning to live out of the riches he has provided, rather than the poverty of the identities I used to assign myself." It is never a waste of time to remind people of who they are in Christ. Doing so stimulates hope, courage, and faith.

One of the best identity passages in the New Testament is 2 Peter 1:3–9. Study it until it has mastered you! This passage should be a tool you can use wisely, practically, and well with others.

> His divine power has given us everything we need for life and godliness through our knowledge of him who called us by his own glory and goodness. Through these he has given us his very great and precious promises, so that through them you may participate in the divine nature and escape the corruption in the world caused by evil desires.
>
> For this very reason, make every effort to add to your faith goodness; and to goodness, knowledge; and to knowledge, self-control; and to self-control, perseverance; and to perseverance, godliness; and to godliness, brotherly kindness; and to brotherly kindness, love. For if you possess these qualities in increasing measure, they will keep you from being ineffective and unproductive in your knowledge of our Lord Jesus Christ. But if anyone does not have them, he is nearsighted and blind, and has forgotten that he has been cleansed from his past sins.

Let's examine the important points of this passage.

- Peter acknowledges in verse 8 that there will be people who know the Lord, but whose lives are ineffective and unproductive. Maybe their home is a war zone. Perhaps they are consumed with bitterness or are resistant to those in authority. Whatever the issue, their lives have not produced the good fruit you would expect from someone with the full rights and privileges of a child of God.

◆ Peter says in verses 5–8 that these people do not produce the expected fruit because they are missing essential character qualities (faith, goodness, knowledge, self-control, perseverance, godliness, brotherly kindness, and love). But Christ lived, died, and rose so that they *would* possess these qualities.

◆ When we see Christians who do not exhibit Christian character or produce good fruit, we ought to ask why. What is missing? Peter's answer is, "These people have forgotten who they are" (v. 9). They have lost sight of their identity in Christ, so they do not realize the resources that are theirs. Because of this, they fail to live with hope, faith, and courage. Their problems worsen and new layers of difficulty are added. This heightens their potential to walk through life with a problem-based identity. There are probably more people living like this than we would ever imagine. When I work through this passage with people, I am frequently impressed by how often they respond as if they have never heard these truths before. Their sense of who they are has usually been shaped by their problems.

◆ Another significant aspect of our identity is that in Christ we have been given "everything we need for life and godliness" (v. 3). As children of God, we are rich! We don't just have *some* things; we have all we need! God supplies his children with everything they will ever need to do what he has called them to do.

Notice the tense of the verb in verse 3. Peter says that everything "has been given." The verb is in the perfect tense, which refers to an action in the past that has continuing results into the future. The giving has already been done; it is not something we have to wait for. As a result of the work of Christ, everything we need for "life and godliness" has been placed in our storehouse. The two words here are not redundant; Peter is making an important distinction. God has not only provided all we need for eternal life, but for godliness as well. Godliness means living a God-honoring life from the time I am accepted into God's family until the time I join him in eternity. We have been given everything we need to think, desire, speak, and behave in a God-honoring way. What an awesome provision!

This gospel identity and its amazing resources are a powerful defense in the war for our hearts. As people step out in new obedience, the Enemy will come to them and say, "You don't have what it takes to do this. If only you had _____ or _____, then maybe you could, but you don't." In these moments, the war for the heart is a war of identity. How people respond to Satan's attacks depends on the identity they have embraced. Unfortunately, many people leave God out of the story when they talk about their troubles. They are preoccupied by the sins of others and the difficulties of the situation. But if there is no God in their story, there will be no biblical sense of identity, because biblical identity is always rooted in him. The Enemy knows that he doesn't have to tempt us to forsake the faith to get a victory. He wins daily skirmishes with us by clouding or attacking our identity.

When you forget your identity and the riches that are yours in Christ, you live like a poor person. In Philadelphia, it has been reported that 3,500 homeless people live on the streets. Their lives are little more than finding something to eat and somewhere to sleep. At the end of the day, they are happy simply to have a place to lay their head in peace. They don't ask for more.

Many people in the midst of a struggle live as if they were spiritually homeless. They live the same survivalist, distracted, fearful, escapist, and "for the moment" existence. They do not think about growth and change or pursue the good things that are their inheritance as children of God.

They just try to get through the day. They live as if they were poor, when, in fact, they are amazingly rich.

When we live with a poverty identity, the problem is not that we ask too much of the Father, but that we settle for too little. We settle for hammering together some kind of spiritual survival with the hope that things will be better in eternity. But the Bible never presents our life on earth as a meaningless time of waiting for the good stuff that comes later. The biblical model of waiting is not simply about what you will get at the end of your wait, but about who you will become *as* you wait. God has promised you real, abundant life in the here and now. We have a Father. We have a home. We are rich. We *struggle* a great deal, but we can *expect* much as well.

◆ In verse 4, Peter tells us what to expect of the great provision God has made for us in Christ. God's purpose is not that we would be personally happy (nice job, marriage, family, church, neighborhood, vacation, retirement), but that we would become participants in his divine nature! In doing this, God is addressing my most significant need. This need is not external or emotional, but moral. What we need most is a heart ruled by the Lord rather than by "evil desires." We need to be progressively freed from our slavery to the god-replacements that imprison us in self-absorbed pursuit of our own glory.

Peter's point is that if my heart is ruled by evil desires, I will participate in the "corruption of the world" rather than the work of Christ. I will not have a harvest of good fruit. Too many Christians think they do what they do *because* of what they have experienced. Peter reverses the order. Rather than the corrupt world causing us to have evil desires, Peter says that our evil desires cause the corruption of the world! Scripture, in all its earthy honesty about the trouble we experience in this world, always brings us back to the heart. And it comforts us with the gospel promise of the heart-transforming, life-changing grace of Jesus Christ.

A subtle monasticism still exists in the church today. The theology of the monastery taught, "It's an evil world out there, so the way to be pure is to separate from it." Yet history records that the monastery duplicated all the ills of the surrounding society. Why? Because they made a tragic mistake: They let people in! And as sinful people came in, they brought with them the full range of evil desires, corrupting the very environment that was their hope of purity.

Peter's model is very different. It is an inside-out model. God has made ample provision for the progressive change of my heart, so that as I deal with the problems of life in a fallen world, I can do what is right and reap a harvest of good fruit. Peter is saying that the most significant thing God saves us from is ourselves! Because of his abundant grace, we no longer have to live enslaved to ourselves, but for "him who died for us and was raised again" (2 Cor. 5:15).

If we apply these truths to Sharon and Ed (from chapter 10), we see that they are both trapped in their own heart environment. Sharon is convinced that Ed is her greatest problem; Ed is convinced that Sharon is his. Neither one wants help for him- or herself. It's not that they want too much from their Father; they are willing to settle for far too little! Their marriage has been corrupted by their own desires, many of which were in place before they got married. If they fail to deal with these heart issues, their marriage will either be locked into a cycle of blame and recrimination, or they will divorce and repeat their mistakes in new relationships. This is why identity issues are so important. They are not icing on the cake. They *are* the cake.

◆ Finally, Peter tells us what will happen when we start living out of our identity in Christ (vv. 5–8). It will change the way we live. We will not settle for a little bit of Christian character. We will not see our relationships and situations as dangers to be avoided, but as opportunities to experience what already belongs to us in Christ. We will be expectant and active because we have a progressive growth paradigm for life. We will not give in to patterns of avoidance, escape, or defense. We will not settle for a slightly better marriage, or marginally honest relationships. Each day we will want to experience more of the resources that are ours as children of God. This expectant, progressive model of change is critical for people applying new insights and commitments to their lives. Let me illustrate.

Imagine that I get a call one afternoon from a bank officer who informs me that I have inherited $50 million from a distant relative. I get off the phone quite excited to tell Luella of our newfound fortune. I then run down to the bank, produce the requisite documents and withdraw $10,000 to take Luella out to eat (in Paris, for the weekend of her life!). Six weeks later, Luella, who does the finances in our family, is still struggling to stretch dimes into dollars. Confused, she says to me, "Paul, I thought you said we were rich beyond anything we thought we would ever experience. Yet we are living as if we are as poor as we have ever been. Why aren't we living out of the inheritance you were given?"

Imagine me saying to Luella, "Do you know how hard it is to get down to that bank and draw out that money? First, the bank is in the center of the city. The traffic is unbelievable and the parking is worse. When you get to the bank you have to stand in one of those long, Disney World lines, and when you finally get to the counter, they treat you more like a criminal than a customer. [The bank has a fingerprinting pad next to each teller window for those who make major withdrawals.] It's too much of a hassle!"

If you were Luella, wouldn't you be thinking, *You're rich! How can anything keep you from the inheritance you have been given and the life it would give us? You need to keep going to that bank until you have received everything that is rightly yours!*

Peter ties our ability to persevere through difficulties to our grasp of our identity in Christ and the resources that come with it. If we really understand it, we will make every effort to obtain more and more of what is ours in Christ. He has promised to progressively conform our sinful hearts to the likeness of our Savior, Jesus Christ.

As we apply new insights and make new commitments, this is the identity we need. But just like heroes of our faith, we will tend to forget who we are. Moses said, "Who am I, that I should go?" and Gideon said, "But Lord, how can I save Israel?" We need to be continually reminded of our status as children of God and our spiritual resources in Christ.

Philippians 2:1–12 is another helpful identity passage, particularly because of its "if-then" construction. Verse 1 gives us the "ifs" by listing four redemptive realities in the life of every believer:

- If you have been encouraged by your union with Christ
- If you have experienced the comfort of Christ's love
- If you have enjoyed fellowship with his indwelling Holy Spirit
- If you have experienced God's tenderness and compassion

Verses 2–12 give us the "thens" by detailing how we should live in light of the grace we have been given as children of God:

- Then be one in spirit and purpose (v. 2).
- Then do nothing out of selfish ambition or vain conceit (v. 3).
- Then consider others better than yourselves (v. 3).
- Then look not only to your own interests, but also to those of others (v. 4).
- Then make sure your attitude is the same as Christ's (vv. 5–8).

The if-then structure of this passage provides a practical description of what it means to live in light of my identity in Christ, including the radical heart changes that God is progressively working in me by his grace. Imagine what would happen to Sharon and Ed's marriage if they began to live this way! Think of the changes that would take place if humble, unified, loving service replaced proud, self-interested, demanding disunity. They do not have to live as they are living. They have already been given something better in Christ.

▶ OBJECTIVE 4:
PROVIDE ACCOUNTABILITY.

THE GIFT OF LOVING ACCOUNTABILITY

Like the concept of confrontation, the concept of accountability tends to carry negative connotations. People can conjure up intrusive images when they hear the word. Yet the biblical picture is very loving in at least two ways. First, as we help restore people to where God wants them to be, we are called to "carry each other's burdens" (Gal. 6:2). We are also told to fight the deceitfulness of sin by "encouraging one another daily" (Heb. 3:13). We must love people enough to do more than expose wrong, pronounce right, and walk away. Accountability requires a willingness to roll up our sleeves and get alongside people as they fight the war between sin and righteousness.

In personal ministry we call people to exercise faith in new and deeper ways—to forsake things they have done for years and do things they have never done before. We call them to new motives, purposes, and goals. We call them to make peace where there has been war, to serve where they have demanded and controlled. We call them to give up things that have been precious, and to do all these things not just once, but with long-term commitment and perseverance.

Yet as people step out in faith, they are often still confused and afraid. They have committed to a new and better way, but they are not yet ready to be on their own. The disciples provide a wonderful example of this phenomenon. They had been with Jesus for three years and seen the glory and power of his presence. They had learned much about the kingdom of God, but in many ways they were still wobbly and uncertain. In his last few moments with them before the cross, Jesus recognized that they were not ready to be on their own.

(See John 16:12–16.) Their fear and confusion at his crucifixion (which Jesus had warned them was coming) reveal what spiritual babies they were. Confused and afraid, they hid together, wondering what to do next. Even after they saw the resurrected Christ, they were still asking the wrong questions (Acts 1:7–11). But Jesus didn't leave his wobbly disciples alone. He sent the Holy Spirit to guide, teach, encourage, warn, convict, and strengthen them.

God calls us to the same ministry by the power of the same Holy Spirit. He calls us to stand with people as they step out in faith, obedience, and courage. This is the ministry of accountability. It is not about lying in wait to catch them doing wrong. The purpose of accountability is to assist people to do what is right for the long run. It provides a presence that keeps them responsible, aware, determined, and alert until they are able to be on their own. It directs eyes that have just begun to see, and strengthens weak knees and feeble arms. We seek to encourage flagging faith and to keep God's goals before people's eyes. We help them to understand when they need to flee from sin and when they are called to stand and fight.

Like all personal ministry, accountability is incarnational. By standing alongside people, we incarnate the presence of the Holy Spirit who is not only *with* them but *in* them. We preach the gospel of an ever-present Redeemer who doesn't just command, but enables. He doesn't just convict; he forgives and restores. Biblical accountability is not fearful, abusive, or intrusive. It is loving, sacrificial, ambassadorial, incarnational, and holy. How could we serve Immanuel ("God with us") and do anything less?

By contrast, accountability is not about being a private detective, trying to do the work of the Holy Spirit, being someone else's conscience, forcing someone to obey, chasing someone who is running, or looking for someone who is hiding. Accountability provides loving structure, guidance, encouragement, and warning to someone who is fully committed to the change God is working in his life. *The person who makes accountability work is always the person being held accountable.* He doesn't see our presence and help as scary or intrusive. He doesn't run and hide from it. Rather, he is glad to know that as others stand with him, God stands with him. Accountability works because he is a seeker, not a runner. The runner doesn't need accountability; he needs rebuke. Accountability is help for those who are committed to change.

WHAT ACCOUNTABILITY PROVIDES

Accountability provides help on a practical level in ways like these:

Accountability provides structure. Life is often messy and chaotic. Change seems easier to discuss than to actually achieve, so accountability provides an outside system of structure ("Do these things during this period of time") that can be immensely helpful to someone attempting something for the first time.

Accountability provides guidance. Often a person will want to do what is right but won't be sure how to do it. It is a great benefit to have someone provide practical, ongoing wisdom as to the *where, when,* and *how* of change.

Accountability provides assistance. There are times when a person is afraid to make the needed changes alone (for example, a difficult talk with a wife, friend, or child) and needs someone to help him do it.

Accountability provides encouragement. Change is hard, beating at the borders of people's faith, courage, and hope. People are often tempted to question their commitments or even quit. They need someone they trust alongside them, who knows their inner struggle and can encourage them to continue. They need someone to incarnate the presence of the One who is their help and hope.

Accountability provides warning. Sometimes people confess their need for change, but begin to rebel against it when they realize the cost and work involved. These people need to be warned of the consequences of their disobedience and rebellion. They need to be reminded that they will reap what they sow (Gal. 6:7).

Accountability brings ongoing help to the person who is fully committed to the "put off/put on" process. Ask yourself three questions as you seek to provide such accountability:

1. What kinds of ongoing help will this person need?
2. How often will I need to be in contact with him or her for change to continue?
3. Are there other resources in the body of Christ that would be helpful during this period? How can I connect this person to these resources?

Change in a fallen world can be burdensome. As people bring new insights and commitments to their lives, they need to be reminded of their identity in Christ and the presence of the indwelling Holy Spirit.

THE SIMPLICITY AND GRANDEUR OF PERSONAL MINISTRY

If you were to summarize this book, what would you say? Perhaps you would describe it as a book of strategies for personal change. Maybe you would say it is about counseling in the local church. Some might say it explains how to bring Scriptural principles to the problems of life. Others might say it is about the necessity of personal ministry in the body of Christ.

All of these answers would be correct, but this book is first of all a call to live a daily ministry lifestyle rooted in God's Word. We have laid out a whole Bible, whole life, whole body lifestyle. This lifestyle doesn't look to the Bible as an encyclopedia for problem solving, but finds in God's great story a perspective that transforms the way we deal with the circumstances of life.

Second, this book is rooted in the belief that God has called and positioned all of his children to live as his ambassadors. His claim is on all of our time and each of our relationships as we serve as his representatives.

Finally, this lifestyle is not simply for the few who are privileged to minister as a career. God's kingdom work involves every member of the body of Christ. Whether you are a child, a spouse, a neighbor, a relative, a pastor, an employer or employee, a teacher, a student, or a friend, all of your relationships must reflect your ambassadorial calling. You must always seek to faithfully represent his message, methods, and character. God sends unfinished people to unfinished people with the message of his grace so that he can reclaim every heart for his glory.

CORE TRUTHS OF AN AMBASSADORIAL LIFESTYLE

We have seen that eight principles and perspectives characterize this ministry lifestyle.

Truth #1. We need God and his truth to live as we were meant to live (Gen. 1:26; 2 Tim. 3:16–17). We need to forsake any delusion of autonomy or self-sufficiency. We cannot figure life out on our own nor do what God calls us to do. Our utter dependence on the Lord is not rooted in the Fall, but in our humanity. We were created to worship the Lord and depend on him.

Truth #2. Each of us has been called by God to be his instruments of change in the lives of others, beginning with our families and the church (Eph. 4:11–16; Col. 3:15–17). Ministry is not an activity that takes place outside our primary relationships. Rather, God intends to use us *in* these relationships as he does his redemptive work.

Truth #3. Our behavior is rooted in the thoughts and motives of our hearts. People and situations only prompt our hearts to express themselves in words and actions (Prov. 4:23; Luke 6:43–45; Mark 7:20–23; Matt. 23:25; James 4:1–10). Without denying the sad realities of suffering and being sinned against, we must reject any view of human behavior that forgets the heart. Instead, we affirm that God changes people's lives as his grace transforms their hearts. Thus, in personal ministry, no matter what the difficulty, the heart is always our target.

Truth #4. Christ has called us to be his ambassadors, following his message, methods, and character (2 Cor. 5:14–21). Our calling allows us to represent the Lord of the universe to people around us! God is taking lost, confused, discouraged, rebellious, and self-absorbed people and making them into people who are empowered by his grace and motivated by his glory. Nothing is more important!

Truth #5. Being an instrument of change involves incarnating the love of Christ by sharing in people's struggles, identifying with their suffering, and extending God's grace as we call them to change. We should seek relationships that are more than mutually fulfilling. We are to build relationships in which God's work of personal transformation can thrive. We do this by sharing the love Christ has poured out on us. We do it by coming to those who suffer as fellow sufferers who offer God's comfort and compassion. And we do it by coming as sinners to other sinners, extending to them the grace that has transformed our hearts—and can do the same for theirs.

Truth #6. Being an instrument of change means seeking to know people by guarding against false assumptions, asking good questions, and interpreting information in a distinctly biblical way (Prov. 20:5; Heb. 4:14–16). We cannot be content with casual relationships among God's people. We want to really get to know people and discover where change is needed. We learn to ask questions that cannot be answered without self-disclosure. And we filter everything we learn about people through the grid of Scripture. Our goal is not only to know others biblically, but to help them know themselves in the same way.

Truth #7. Being an instrument of change means speaking the truth in love. With the gospel as our comfort and call, we can help people see themselves in God's Word and lead them to repentance (Rom. 8:1–17; Gal. 6:1–2; James 1:22–25). When we confront people with the truth, we want to be instruments of seeing and agents of repentance. It is easier for people to see problems in people and situations than it is to see them in themselves. That's why we lovingly hold the Word of God before them, so they can see themselves clearly and repent. Our prayer is that the words we speak will expose and change their hearts as they respond to the comfort and call of the gospel.

Truth #8. Being an instrument of change means helping people do what God calls them to do by clarifying responsibility, offering loving accountability, and reminding them of their identity in Christ (Phil. 2:1–14; 2 Peter 1:3–9; 1 John 3:1–3; Gal. 6:2). We must not confuse insight with heart and life change. Acquiring biblical insight is a necessary part of the process, but it is not, in itself, change. Change comes when people identify the specific things God is calling them to do and begin doing them by faith. We encourage this process by standing with people, offering the wisdom, guidance, and encouragement of biblical accountability. Lastly, we encourage change by helping people live out of an accurate sense of their identity as the children of God, with all the rights and privileges that this identity entails.

These are the biblical principles and perspectives that shape our ministry to others. The King has called us, and he will prepare us for his work. We have been bought with a price, and our lives do not belong to us. Receiving grace means becoming a conduit of grace to others. Suffering commissions us to comfort other sufferers. Being changed is to become an ambassador for change to others. There could be no more meaningful life this side of Glory! We should be deeply grateful to be included in the plan. But perhaps you wonder if you'll ever be able to live the lifestyle this book describes. Maybe you are dizzy with all the details, strategies, and skills. Perhaps you are overwhelmed by what you've seen about your own heart.

Two things always come to my mind as I finish teaching this material. First, I am hit with the utter simplicity of biblical personal ministry. It is not a secret technology for the intervention elite, but a simple call to every one of God's children to be part of what God is doing in the lives of others. It is living in humble, honest, redemptive community with others, *loving* as Christ has loved, and going beyond the casual to really *know* people. It is loving others enough to *speak* the truth to them, helping them to see themselves in the mirror of God's Word. And it is standing with others, helping them to *do* what God has called them to do. It is basically just a call to biblical friendship! It is almost embarrassingly simple: *Love* people. *Know* them. *Speak* truth into their lives. Help them *do* what God has called them to do.

At the same time, there is a grandeur to personal ministry that cannot be captured with words. God is painting his grace on the canvas of human souls. One day we will stand with him in Glory and see that canvas completed, and we won't be able to do anything but worship. What is our part in all of this? We are God's brushes. He wants to soak us on the palette of his grace and paint more of his goodness on yet another soul. The question is, "Are we soft brushes in his hands?" A hard, dried-out brush doesn't pick up the paint well and mars the surface it was meant to beautify. I hope this book will help you become a soft brush in the hands of a Redeemer who will continue to paint until his canvas is complete.

As we stand before him on that last day and see the awesome beauty of the universe's most glorious canvas, God's voice will penetrate the sounds of our worship with these wonderful and mysterious words: "Well done, good and faithful servants!" Then we will know that each moment of ministry was worth it. We will know that we have been part of the most important, lasting, and beautiful thing that has ever been done—redemption. We will experience the reality of the words of the hymn:

> Who are these like stars appearing,
> > these before God's throne who stand?
> Each a golden crown is wearing;
> > who are all this glorious band?
> Alleluia! Hark, they sing,
> > praising loud their heav'nly King.
>
> Who are these of dazzling brightness,
> > these in God's own truth arrayed,
> clad in robes of purest whiteness,
> > robes whose luster ne'er shall fade,
> ne'er be touched by time's rude hand?
> > Whence come all this glorious band?

These are they who have contended
      for their Savior's honor long,
wrestling on till life was ended,
      foll'wing not the sinful throng;
these, who well the fight sustained,
      triumph through the Lamb have gained.

These are they whose hearts were riven,
      sore with woe and anguish tried,
who in prayer full oft have striven
      with the God they glorified;
now, their painful conflict o'er,
      God has bid them weep no more.

These, like priests, have watched and waited,
      off'ring up to Christ their will;
soul and body consecrated,
      day and night to serve him still;
now in God's most holy place
      blest they stand before his face.[1]

These are the rewards awaiting God's faithful. May they encourage you in your service to the King!

APPENDIX 1: OPENING BLIND EYES: ANOTHER LOOK AT DATA GATHERING

Celia had come to counseling to "get help with relationships." She called herself "rejection going somewhere to happen" and tearfully described her inability to find just one "faithful friend." God seemed far off, yet Celia plaintively maintained that she was "not such a bad person," surely not bad enough to deserve the "punches in the stomach" that she had received.

I sympathized with Celia but also endeavored to get her to look at herself. Since rejection was a theme in her life, I suggested that we ought to ask if there was anything she was doing to contribute to the problem. Celia immediately became defensive. As a counselor, what should I do next? I needed to know more about Celia, but more importantly, Celia needed to see more about herself. There were walls of personal blindness that needed to be penetrated or Celia would never be a true counselee. Celia was hurt, frustrated, and exhausted, but because of her personal blindness, she was not yet a seeker.

One of the tragic effects of the Fall is personal blindness of heart—it is universal. It is one of the things that makes biblical counseling so difficult. It radically alters the data-gathering process.

Because sin is deceitful and fallen people are so naturally blind to issues of self, data gathering must always pursue two goals. First, the process must give the counselor the information needed to provide wise biblical counseling. But an even more fundamental purpose is that we would be the Messiah's instruments to open eyes that have been blind for too long.

Opening blind eyes is at the heart of Christ's messianic mission. Looking forward to the coming Messiah, Isaiah says, "Then will the eyes of the blind be opened and the ears of the deaf unstopped" (Isa. 35:5). God promises further, "I will lead the blind by ways they have not known, along unfamiliar paths I will guide them; I will turn the darkness into light before them and make the rough places smooth. These are the things I will do; I will not forsake them" (Isa. 42:16).

The Messiah is the One who is able to open the eyes of blind sinners and make them see. Isaiah describes the sinner this way:

> So justice is far from us,
>   and righteousness does not reach us.
> We look for light, but all is darkness;
>   for brightness, but we walk in deep shadows.
> Like the blind we grope along the wall,
>   feeling our way like men without eyes.
> At midday we stumble as if it were twilight. . . . (Isa. 59:9–10a)

In the Sermon on the Mount, Christ commissions us to be part of his messianic mission to shine the light of truth into the darkness of sin. This is exactly what we should be seeking to do in counseling. Our goal is not only to expose the darkness that exists in relationships and situations but the darkness of the heart, so that the gospel can be applied.

All counselees in some way "grope along . . . feeling [their] way like men without eyes." Our data gathering needs to take this need seriously. I want to help counselees see themselves in the mirror of God's Word. I will ask questions that they would never ask and probe in places they would not know to probe. My questions will flow out of biblical perspectives on people and their problems. Here I image the Messiah as I seek to end the groping in darkness. I am not simply announcing my conclusions but helping blind eyes to see, with biblical clarity and depth, the heart's thoughts and motives.

This appendix focuses on the "eye-opening" function of data gathering. We will examine the nature of the blindness that all sinners experience and look at what we must bring to our role as God's instruments.

THE MASKS OF SPIRITUAL BLINDNESS

The difference between physical and spiritual blindness is that the former is blatantly obvious while the latter often goes unnoticed. A physically blind person is immediately confronted with his condition. Often, a spiritually blind person not only fails to recognize his blindness, he is convinced that he has excellent vision. A fundamental part of being spiritually blind is that you are blind to your blindness.

Spiritual blindness is the condition of every sinner, every counselee. Yet few will realize its impact on the way they view themselves, God, others, and their situations. They are like those described in Romans 1, who think that they are wise when really they are fools. They assume that they think well when the thinking of their heart is actually foolish and futile.

Spiritual blindness is deceptive. As John wrote to the church in Laodicea, "You say, 'I am rich; I have acquired wealth and do not need a thing.' But you do not realize that you are wretched, pitiful, poor, *blind* and naked" (Rev. 3:17). Spiritual blindness is deceptive because it masquerades as other things. If we are going to be God's instruments to open blind eyes, we must recognize the typical masks that spiritual blindness wears. The following is a representative list.

THE MASK OF AN ACCURATE SENSE OF SELF

Celia thought she knew herself. She was offended at the suggestion that she might bear some responsibility for what was happening in her life. It is only as one looks intently into the perfect mirror of Scripture that a person will see himself as he actually is (James 1:22–25).

Most of our counselees will have distorted views of themselves because the mirrors into which they look are like carnival mirrors. They reflect the real you but with a distortion. You see yourself, but not as you really are.

So it is with many counselees. Their sense of self has been developed by looking into the carnival mirror of others' opinions, or a cultural view of success, or pop psychology, or past experience (the list could go on). The counselee is unaware that he has a distorted sense of self. He has the Word of God, but he has used it more as an encyclopedia of religious thought or a devotional tool. Even when listening to the Word preached, he will miss the revelation of self that is there. He hears stories or principles expounded but does not see himself mirrored in the passages.

THE MASK OF BEING SINNED AGAINST

Celia was able to recount—in Technicolor detail—stories of constant abuse at the hands of others. Her focus was on how others behaved toward her.

There is no more powerful metaphor to describe how spiritual blindness masquerades as a sense of being sinned against than the "plank and speck" metaphor of Matthew 7. Imagine a person literally obsessed with a piece of dust in another's eye while walking around with a plank jutting out of his own! He is gripped by a sense of being sinned against, not of being a sinner. Thus, to him, the change that is needed is change outside himself.

THE MASK OF TRIALS AND TESTING

Celia did not have an accurate sense of herself and her sin, so she tended to call the natural consequences of her own choices and actions *trials*. Paul says, "Do not be deceived: God cannot be mocked. A man reaps what he sows. The one who sows to please his sinful nature, from that nature will reap destruction; the one who sows to please the Spirit, from the Spirit will reap eternal life" (Gal. 6:7–8).

Since most of our counselees do not have a harvest mentality, they tend to look at the things they harvest not as the result of their planting, but as painful trials they do not deserve.

Also, because sinners tend to exchange worship and service of the Creator for worship and service of the created thing (see Rom. 1:25), they tend to miss the good things that the Creator is doing in a situation. Instead, they focus on the loss of some created thing. A trial is a trial to me because it puts what is valuable to me at stake. Manna falling from heaven became a trial to the Israelites because they were not focusing on the covenant love its provision represented, but on its taste as compared to the menu of Egypt!

Counselees in their blindness will call the consequences of their own behavior "trials" and the good things from God's hand "testings." They will be blind to the fact that God sends trials for their redemptive good. Rather than seeing themselves as loved by God and being conformed to the image of his Son through circumstances, they see themselves as singled out for difficulty. To them, life isn't fair. Suffering is without redemptive purpose and a sign that God does not love them.

THE MASK OF NEEDS

Celia saw herself as needy. She viewed herself as one who had spent most of her life living without. She often said, "If only I had had _____, then I would have been able to _____." Her understanding of needs was as cloudy as the culture's around her. Yet her interpretation of her life rested heavily on this term. Essentially she was saying that her life's problems were the direct result of her neediness. She carried with her the classic, "If only . . ." interpretation of life.

What Celia didn't see was that her neediness was really more about sin's tragic effect, which turns us from worshipers of God to those who live "gratifying the cravings of our sinful nature and following its desires and thoughts" (Eph. 2:3). Her neediness revealed much more about who she was than what she was missing. Celia's sense of need revealed the lusts of her heart more than it revealed the betrayal of others. And what she *actually* needed was the one thing she never craved—God. If you really want to understand what is important to a person, find out where he feels needy. Values become desires, desires become demands, and demands get expressed in counseling as "needs."

Celia was blind to the fact that she was the sun in the center of her universe and that all of life was viewed from the vantage point of what it offered her. She was blind to the fact that she carried this "needs" perspective into every room she entered, and it shaped every situation and relationship. She came into situations loaded with silent demands and responded with angry criticism to anyone who seemed to ignore her needs. She thought that her neediness proved the selfishness and unwillingness of all around her when, in fact, it demonstrated the depth of her own self-centeredness.

THE MASK OF WISE COUNSEL

Like all counselees, Celia had many voices around her. Like Job, much of the counsel she received was not helpful; and it was not helpful because it was not biblical. Yet Celia found comfort in the words of her counselors, if only for a season.

Although she was coming for counseling, Celia often repeated to me the "wisdom" she had gleaned from those around her. But Celia only quoted people who agreed with her view of life and supported the decisions she made. She did not quote anyone who disagreed with her.

Another scriptural term for the spiritually blind is "fools." Celia's wise counsel was really foolishness. It only appeared wise to her because she was blind to the real issues in her life. Proverbs says that the fool has "no desire to get wisdom" (Prov. 17:16). Celia thought she was on a quest for wise counsel when really she was on a quest for support of her point of view.

THE MASK OF PERSONAL INSIGHT

Celia, like all human beings, was always seeking to make sense out of her life. She wanted it organized into categories that would help her understand what had gone on and what she should do about it. She spent much of her time analyzing things and felt it had been helpful. But her search was not open-ended: if I began to question Celia's interpretations, there would soon be an air of tension in the room.

Spiritual blindness can even masquerade as wisdom! To be intellectually bright and actively analytical does not necessarily mean that you are wise. True wisdom begins with humility, the recognition that I do not have in myself all that I need. I need to be a seeker after the truth that is found only in God's Word. Real insight does not result from being analytical but from being biblical. Listen to the words of the psalmist:

> Your commands make me wiser than my enemies,
>   for they are ever with me.
> I have more insight than all my teachers,
>   for I meditate on your statutes.
> I have more understanding than the elders,
>   for I obey your precepts.
>   (Ps. 119:98–100)

Celia was blind to the fact that her insight revealed more about her heart than her situation. Her insight was born out of desires that distorted her interpretations of what was going on around her. It was more a desire-driven perspective than an objective analysis. Thus, it was more an expression of idolatry than an expression of faith. Yet none of this was obvious to Celia because blindness often wears the mask of insight.

THE MASK OF A SENSE OF VALUES

Celia thought she knew what was important, but the more I listened to her, the more I was convinced that what moved her were not the things of prime importance. Here again Celia was blind. She had evaluated her situation and acted in a way consistent with her values, yet her problems continued. This left her frustrated and confused.

The treasures that motivated Celia all had to do with human relationships. She saw friendship, respect, acceptance, and love as most important and did all she could to avoid rejection, loneliness, and the low self-image she said resulted. But the more Celia examined people and their reactions, the more she tried to please them and the angrier she got. She entered her relationships with a long list of silent demands, yet she was unaware of how judgmental and unforgiving she was when people failed to live up to them. Matthew 6 says that whatever is my treasure will control my heart, and what controls my heart will control my behavior. In other words, I will live to gain, maintain, and enjoy the things of value to me.

Celia's problem was her values. She had put her identity in the hands of people. She kept meeting frustration and failure because the God who had called her to himself was working on something different. His focus was not so much on the relationships but on Celia, that she would be conformed to his Son's image.

Counselees often do not recognize their blindness because it is masked by a passionate sense of right and wrong. The angry man who has hurt his family for years with his violent responses sees only what he has lost by being separated from them. To him what is important is his right to see his kids and to live in the home he pays for. He keeps saying in counseling, "This is not right, it just isn't right!" Yet he is blind to the changes he needs to make in order for the family to be properly restored.

A wife's focus is on the coldness and distance of her husband. She wants the counselor to turn him into a man who cherishes her, yet she is blind to the constant stream of criticism that has driven him away. She is irate when the counselor begins to focus on her as someone who needs change. She is utterly blind to the eternally valuable things God wants to work in her.

THE MASK OF THEOLOGICAL KNOWLEDGE

Celia knew a lot about Scripture and the doctrines of the faith. There were few biblical-theological terms that I could use with which she was not familiar.

Unfortunately, Celia's theological knowledge did four things for her.

First, it produced a level of confidence in her interpretations of life. She assumed that her ideas and actions flowed out of her beliefs. Second, it produced in her an assessment of maturity. Celia thought of herself as a mature believer and was offended if someone treated her as someone needing basic biblical teaching. Third, in counseling her knowledge gave Celia an "I already knew that and I already tried that" attitude. Fourth, it produced in her a sense that her problems were not her fault. She "knew what was right and did what was best." Hence, the cause of the difficulty had to be outside of her. Her knowledge obscured personal responsibility and conviction of sin.

The fact was that Celia had not been able to apply her theology to everyday life in a way that made sense of her struggles. She was a lady without wisdom, blind to the fact that she was not spiritually mature. Spiritual maturity results from practicing truth in everyday life, not from knowing truth in one's mind (Heb. 5:11–14). But Celia was convinced that her Christian counselors kept telling her things she already knew.

Coupled with this sense of theological adequacy was Celia's tendency to ask the wrong questions. Celia's questions did not lead her to a deeper understanding of her situation, a fuller hope in God, or a practical agenda for change. There is a principle here that we will consider more fully in a future article. It is this: insightful people are insightful not because they have the right answers but because they have asked the right questions. If you do not ask the right questions, you will never get to the right answers. Celia constantly found herself in an analytical cul-de-sac, leading to a loss of hope and a struggle with depression.

Here is an example of Celia's wrong questions. She would say, "I pray and I pray. I read my Bible. Yet God isn't helping me. He isn't answering my prayers." Then she would ask this question: "Why isn't God working in my life?" This is a bad question, based on an unbiblical assumption, which cannot lead in a good direction.

Celia's question led her to two answers. Sometimes she would conclude that God wasn't active because he simply didn't love her. He had better things to do than worry about her puny life. On other occasions she would conclude that God was not active in her life because she was such a miserable sinner, and his inactivity was a punishment for her iniquity. Bad answers to a bad question will produce a harvest of bad fruit. Like Job's infamous counselors, Celia did not build the bridges from her theology to her situation that would lead to biblical interpretations of life.

To ask Celia's question biblically, one must start with the following biblical assumption: God is ever active in my life (Ps. 46; Rom. 8:18–39). To ask why he isn't working is to assume something that is untrue. True conclusions cannot come from false assumptions. A better way of asking the question is to say, "God is redemptively active in my life, so what is he doing and why don't I recognize it?" This question can lead to greater insight, biblical change, and a harvest of good fruit.

THE MASK OF PERSONAL HOLINESS

Although Celia did not speak of herself using the biblical language of holiness, that is precisely what she thought she possessed. She believed that she wanted the right things and that she did the right things; she could not figure out why things were so wrong. Her belief in her personal holiness rested on a legalistic self-righteousness that had nothing to do with God's call to "Be holy, because I am holy" (Lev. 11:44).

Celia was blind to the fact that she was a classic Pharisee. Like a Pharisee, she reduced God's law to a doable human standard. The things Celia emphasized required no reliance on Christ—they were behavioral standards that made no demands on the heart. Celia saw the gospel as having to do with Heaven and Hell. She felt no need for the present redemptive power of Christ in her life because the "righteousness" she had attained was humanly attainable.

Celia consistently emphasized lesser things and prided herself in accomplishing them, yet she ignored the weightier matters of the law. She prided herself in her neat home, in her punctuality, in her memory of every friend's birthday, the Christian books she had read, her financial vigilance, and her willingness to volunteer. Yet she was jealous, angry, judgmental, bitter, vengeful, and lacking in mercy.

Christ said to his disciples, "Unless your righteousness surpasses that of the Pharisees and the teachers of the law, you will certainly not enter the kingdom of heaven" (Matt. 5:20). To the Pharisees he said, "You give a tenth of your spices—mint, dill and cummin. But you have neglected the more important matters of the law—justice, mercy and faithfulness. You should have practiced the latter without neglecting the former" (Matt. 23:23). The righteousness of the scribes and Pharisees was not enough *because it was not righteousness*. It was ugly, prideful, human *self*-righteousness. This kind of righteousness always emphasizes what is humanly doable and ignores what can only be accomplished through the bountiful streams of the grace of Christ.

Perhaps this is the epicenter of spiritual blindness. At its core, to be spiritually blind means to think you are righteous when really you are not. This makes the grace of God and the obligation to change non-issues. If I am righteous (so I think), I do not need Christ and I do not need change. This is clearly demonstrated in Luke 18 with the story of the two men in the temple. The Pharisee stood in the temple and told God that he did not need him. He was there to announce that he was okay, distancing himself from the sinner and listing his righteous acts before the Lord.

Similarly, Celia would come to counseling and recite her list of good deeds, asking me to agree that she was okay. By missing the important issues of the heart and emphasizing doable behaviors, she saw herself as being clean, yet inside were "dead men's bones."

THE MASK OF REPENTANCE

Celia, like many counselees, thought that being in counseling was an act of repentance. This is not always true. Many of those we counsel tend to see the talking they do as confession and their staying in the counseling process as repentance. But for Celia counseling was really more like penance. She was blind to the fact that she was really participating in an act of self-atonement. I call this "Protestant absolution." The counselee confesses, examines issues, participates in an ongoing discussion of self and the situation and, week by week, leaves the counseling time feeling atoned, cleansed, and right. Yet all of this is happening without any substantive heart or behavioral change. The counselees see themselves as repentant, but in reality there are times when counseling becomes a way to *avoid* working on the issues on God's agenda.

Celia's life did not bear the fruit of repentance. First, she was not becoming a self-starter. She continued in sinful and destructive behaviors though we talked about them on numerous occasions. She would grudgingly admit wrong when confronted, but her confessions seldom resulted in new ways of responding. Second, Celia remained defensive. She continued to have a hard time receiving my biblical evaluation of her. She accused me of not understanding her, of not believing her, or of taking another's side. Third, Celia did not have a teachable spirit. It was hard for her to admit her need to be instructed from Scripture and to learn to apply it to her life. She would debate my theology, my interpretation of a passage, or my application of a biblical principle to her life. Fourth, Celia completed her counseling homework in a perfunctory manner, without enthusiasm, insight, or the changes that were the goal of the assignment.

Yet Celia saw very little of that. She was blinded by her legalistic attendance at counseling, her willingness to discuss personal issues, and her study of assigned Scripture passages. Unfortunately, all of these things (which she thought indicated repentance) masked the bitterness and self-righteousness that controlled Celia's heart.

Repentance is presented in Scripture as a radical change of heart that results in a radically different way of living. As the heart turns and moves in a different direction, the life does as well. Anything short of this is simply not repentance. Many people come to counseling with the goal of self-atonement, though they may not realize it. They want support for what they are doing. They want to feel good about themselves, and they find that they do feel better after their counseling sessions, so they continue. But they have not submitted to God's radical call to repentance. They are not praying with the psalmist in Psalm 139:

> Search me, O God, and know my heart;
>   test me and know my anxious thoughts.
> See if there is any offensive way in me,
>   and lead me in the way everlasting.
>   (Ps. 139:23–24)

Being "in counseling" kept Celia blind to her stubborn, unrepentant heart. She thought of herself as one who had confessed everything she needed to confess. She saw herself as repentant. "Why else would I be in counseling?" she would say. Shocking as it may seem, spiritual blindness even wears the mask of repentance!

It is vital to remember the profound effect that spiritual blindness has on every sinner and his view of life. Our data gathering needs to be motivated by the counselee's need to see. Further, we need to remember that spiritually blind people do not think they are blind because their blindness wears many masks. We need to recognize these masks and pursue a data gathering process that opens the counselee's eyes to who he really is. We commit ourselves to be God's means of opening blind eyes and to see this as a necessary data-gathering function.

APPENDIX 2: WHAT THE COUNSELOR BRINGS TO THE PROCESS OF DATA GATHERING

In our last appendix, we looked at the problem of spiritual blindness and its power to deceive. We saw that spiritually blind people do not know that they are blind, so we as counselors must become familiar with the various masks spiritual blindness wears. Spiritual blindness is always a factor in the counseling process, so as biblical counselors, we must be prepared.

But it's important to remember that this is not a problem that applies only to counselees. When we heed the Bible's warning that *every one* of us is a sinner and by nature spiritually blind, we realize how much we as counselors need the mutual, person-to-person ministry that the New Testament depicts at the heart of church life. Because my deceitful heart easily blinds me to my own sin, I need other believers who love me enough to show me my life from God's perspective. They need the same thing from me. Our human nature requires a redemptive agenda for every one of our relationships. Hebrews 3:12–13 summarizes it this way: "See to it, brothers, that none of you has a sinful, unbelieving heart that turns away from the living God. But encourage one another daily, as long as it is called Today, so that none of you may be hardened by sin's deceitfulness."

Notice that, according to this passage, the thing that calls me to this daily personal ministry is not a *situation*—that is, a sin or problem requiring change that I have observed in you. Rather, what calls me to involvement is a *condition*—indwelling sin and its power to blind and harden the heart. As long as sin remains, spiritual blindness will exist and require us to be committed to relationships that promote honest, loving, mutual ministry.

This is especially important for Christians with a biblical counseling ministry. Counselees depend on us to enter their world with a godly perspective that will help them break through their own blindness. We will never be able to offer that to them unless we have submitted our own lives to the searchlight of Scripture, guided by Christian brothers and sisters who can help us to know our own hearts aright.

Counselors who have made that commitment will develop the following qualities essential to helping counselees.

YOU CAN BRING OBJECTIVITY

Many counselees are blinded by their subjectivity—the way their view of life is shaped by the things they want. When their requests are selfish at root, they can't see it. They are unaware of their tone of voice, the look on their face, the way their version of the story is subtly shaped by their desires. They don't see the times when they criticize others for things they excuse in themselves, when they refuse to forgive others' sins and are defensive when people confront them. If they've become absorbed in a victim mentality, they will not see it. Neither will they see when their acts of service become manipulative, exposing to others (not to themselves) the lack of faith that fuels their whole system.

As a counselor, don't harden your heart against these people. There but for the grace of God go you! Your counselees need help to see themselves clearly, and this is where your biblical objectivity as a counselor is so essential.

When a counselor enters the counselee's world, he is not blinded by the self-interest that dominates the counselee. (At least not to the extent that he has submitted himself to the discipling ministry of the Word and others.) He is able to "restore" his counselee because he is not "caught" in the counselee's spiritual trap (Gal. 6:1). He can speak with biblical objectivity.

A spiritually blind counselee, by contrast, has lost such an objective perspective, if he ever had one. He is locked into one (unbiblical) perspective; this starting point affects the way he experiences everything else that happens to him.

For most counselees, their starting point is their own experience. They tend to view all of life through the lens of their own personal history, assumptions, and desires. The interpretation they've made of their lives thus far will also color all future interpretations. It will even color the way they understand Scripture. People who interpret life through the lens of their own experience will do the same with God's Word. Personal experience, not Scripture, controls their view of the world.

Such a person needs someone whose vantage point is different, someone who starts with Scripture and moves toward life. Scripture must become the basis for interpreting life, and not vice versa. As a biblical counselor, you want to bring that biblical perspective to your counselee, because when God's truth becomes the lens through which everything is examined, life changes. In marriage counseling, for example, the counselor can break through the perennial "He said-She said" with "What has God said?"

Ralph and Shirley had been married for fifteen years. It was almost impossible for them to discuss anything without the conversation disintegrating into a war of accusations. Shirley was convinced that the best years of her life had been spoiled by Ralph's avoidance of issues and willingness to compromise with the world. Ralph saw Shirley as self-righteous, harsh, and judgmental. In their conversations, they lobbed the grenades of bitterness that they had warehoused in their hearts against each other. They were trapped in the polar-opposite views of their life together and therefore unable to solve their problems. Shirley and Ralph needed the radical intervention of a biblical perspective at three levels.

On the behavioral level, they needed to ask, "What has God said about the way we talk to each other?" Their communication did not promote love, understanding, hope, and solution. It was one of their major problems. The clear communication principles in Ephesians 4:25–5:2 would, if heeded, bring both new perspective to this problem and lasting change.

On the thoughts level, Shirley and Ralph needed to ask, "What has God said are *his* goals for who we are as his children?" The New Testament, in passages such as Romans 8:28–29, Galatians 5:16–26, Colossians 3:1–14, and 2 Peter 1:3–9, teaches that God's goal for Ralph and Shirley is more than Shirley's desire for personal ministry fulfillment or Ralph's desire for a respectful wife. God's goal is that they would increasingly become participants in his divine nature. Ralph and Shirley did not see that the way they fought about the Christian life demonstrated that they had little vision of (or commitment to) what God was really seeking to accomplish in them through all he had brought into their lives. He was seeking their conformity to the image of Christ.

Finally, on the desires level, they needed to ask, "What is it that God wants our hearts to crave?" Ralph craved "just a little bit of respect." It was the silent demand in every encounter with Shirley. Shirley craved "a husband who wanted to serve the Lord as much as she did." Questions flowing out of James 4:1–10, Philippians 3:1–16, and Colossians 3:1–17 exposed the "He wants-She wants" cast of their relationship. This was the source of their inability to solve their problems.

Shirley and Ralph needed the help of someone who would start from the vantage point of Scripture and interpret what was going on in their relationship. They needed someone to model how to ask the right (biblical) questions that lead to the solutions that can be found only when people examine their behavior, thoughts, and desires in light of Scripture.

When I do my data gathering, I try to frame my questions in a way that the counselee never would. The most searching questions a counselee might ask himself are still impacted by his blindness. Certain questions will never be asked, but they should be. There are other questions he will ask about others that he should ask about himself. I want my questions to deal with the same set of facts as my counselees' questions, but in a way that helps them think about their lives biblically.

YOU CAN BRING WISDOM

In Romans, Paul talks of sinners' foolish hearts as being darkened. A fool is a spiritually blind person. He thinks he sees, is wise, and understands, when really he is blind, foolish, and confused. The description of the fool in Proverbs portrays a person who:

- Is convinced that he is right (12:15).
- Quickly shows his annoyance (12:16).
- Is hotheaded and reckless (14:16).
- Spurns discipline and correction (15:5).
- Wastes money (17:16).
- Delights in airing his own opinions (18:2).
- Is quick to quarrel (20:3).
- Scorns wisdom (23:9).
- Is wise in his own eyes (26:5).
- Trusts in himself (28:26).
- Rages and scoffs, and there is no peace around him (29:9).
- Gives full vent to his anger (29:11).

A fool needs the intervention of God's Word because his choices, responses, perspectives, actions, and attitudes announce to all that he is blind. He needs the lens of biblical wisdom to help him see and understand as God does.

The biblical counselor can offer God's wise perspective through Scripture. He brings more than just opinion, research, experience, or training. He brings a confidence in (and a submission to) the Word of God that will expose and penetrate the counselee's blindness. The biblical wisdom he offers will be pure, peace-loving, considerate, submissive, full of mercy, full of good fruit, impartial, and sincere (James 3:17). In short, he is, by God's grace, the fool's exact opposite.

Many of those we counsel reveal their foolishness in a distorted sense of proportion and distorted values. They lack a biblical value system that can help them, on a practical level, to know what is really important and what is not. Only Scripture can help a counselee understand how the things in his life really interrelate.

The counselor can ask questions that require the counselee to look at life outside his subjective perspective. He can ask him what is really important, and what the true relationship is between various things in his life from God's point of view. These questions can challenge the counselee's old, familiar view of life by encouraging him to submit to God's view.

Let's look again at Ralph and Shirley. Ralph is convinced that Shirley is his problem, and all the questions he asks himself flow out of that interpretation. Shirley is convinced that Ralph is her problem, and she has done all of her diagnostic thinking from that perspective. Together they share the belief that their problem is that they are too different in their approach to life and their goals. However, the principles of Proverbs indicate that the anger, disunity, and hopelessness that Ralph and Shirley experience are not the result of being different, but the result of the foolish ways they have dealt with their differences. Scripture further tells us that these responses flow out of the desires of the heart that they bring to each of their encounters. Sameness and agreement are not the essential ingredients of unity. Rather, love (for God, above all else, and for my neighbor as myself) is what causes one to be humble, gentle, patient, and forbearing in the face of difference and provocation (Eph. 4:1–2).

If Ralph asked questions of *himself* that flowed out of Proverbs' description of a fool (listed above), he would develop a new agenda for solving his marital difficulties. Here are a few examples of the questions Ralph could ask himself:

- Where have I been so convinced that I am right, that I have been unwilling to hear Shirley's perspective or to re-examine my own viewpoints?
- How do I typically respond when Shirley challenges my thinking or decisions (Prov. 12:15)?
- When do I tend to become quickly irritated and annoyed, responding impulsively out of anger?
- What impact does this anger have on Shirley and her willingness to be open and honest in conversation (Prov. 12:6; 14:6; 15:1)?
- What do I want from Shirley that I perceive she is not giving me, thus making me angry? What "treasures" do I think Shirley is taking away (Matt. 6:19; James 4:1)?

Such questions would lead Ralph to face *himself* before God, to see his need for Jesus' mercy, and to seek that mercy. He would begin to identify the many different things he can do to see concrete change take place.

A person who develops a thorough and consistent biblical view of life can escape the hopelessness of his old value system and the paralysis, confusion, or misguided enthusiasm that it often creates. When Ralph learns to see things biblically, he sees fresh, new options for change. He is no longer trapped by his own subjectivity. He no longer believes that he is stuck in an impossible, no-win marriage. He begins to see the thoughts and desires of his heart that are at the roots of his problems, and he sees how those desires have shaped his response to Shirley in every situation. He no longer insists that he is trapped or that he is right. Rather, he sees the "put offs" and "put ons" of heart and behavior that will change his marriage.

YOU CAN BRING THE GOSPEL'S CLARITY

People by their very nature are interpreters, always seeking to make sense of life. It is not unusual for counselees to feel very confused when they are unable to understand *what* is happening, *why* it is happening, and *what to do* as a result.

There are also many confused counselees who do not *know* that they are confused! They think that their interpretations are insightful and their actions logical. They do not see themselves and their situations with clarity.

One of the most significant areas of spiritual blindness that I observe in counseling is a blindness to the realities of the gospel in a counselee's life. The person is confused and paralyzed because he has left significant facts out of his interpretive system.

The gospel gives us three essential perspectives on the human struggle. Without an awareness of these perspectives, life will make no sense, or it will be understood unbiblically and therefore incorrectly. The gospel gives us a true sense of self, of God, and of process.

SENSE OF SELF

Our response to any situation is always shaped by our understanding of our identity. Consequently, we need the gospel to inform and correct our definition of who we are and what our struggles are really about. What the gospel teaches me is that my struggle is deeper than the problems of my past, the difficulties in my present relationships, and the situations I face daily. Peter says that the corruption in the world is caused by evil desires of the heart. This is where change needs to take place.

Many of the people I counsel have little sense of the presence and power of indwelling sin. They have little sense of the thoughts, desires, and choices of the heart at the root of their personal difficulties. So they continue to blame people and situations, blind to the heart's struggle that they bring to every situation of life. The gospel presents the war within (Rom. 7 and James 4) as the primary target of God's redemptive concern (2 Peter 1:3–4).

SENSE OF GOD

Here, too, I am amazed that often my counselees have little sense of the ever-present, always active, all-powerful, promise-keeping Redeemer who is the God of the gospel. The gospel presents God as my ever-present help in trouble (Ps. 46), who is ruling over all things (even the apparently chaotic and purposeless) for my sake (Eph. 1:22–23). He is working in every situation to deliver me from bondage to sins of the heart, to help me experience the riches of the grace he has lavished on me in Christ, and to conform me to his Son's image (Rom. 8:28–39; Eph. 1:3–7). He is the Forgiver, Reconciler, Deliverer, Comforter, and Restorer.

Because of his incessant redemptive activity, each situation in life, even those that are dark, confusing, and scary to me, is sanctified, full of meaning and purpose, and infused with hope.

Counselees often have little sense of the God of the gospel who rules his world in such a way that he is not far from each one of us. He has done this so that, at any moment, we can seek him and reach out and find him (Acts 17:26–27). They tend to have little hope when they reach the end of their own wisdom and strength. Their functional God is small, weak, uncaring, and distant—not one to whom you would entrust the fine china of your life. Their responses to life and their confusion are directly related to their sense of who God is.

SENSE OF PROCESS

The gospel not only declares that God is active, it describes what he is doing and how he is doing it. This sense of redemptive process is missing in many people I counsel. They do not have a progressive sanctification model for understanding their life and problems.

God has instituted a process with the goal that my "love may abound more and more in knowledge and depth of insight, so that [I] may be able to discern what is best and may be pure and blameless until the day of Christ, filled with the fruit of righteousness that comes through Jesus Christ—to the glory and praise of God" (Phil. 1:9–11).

His primary goal is not that I would experience present personal happiness. His goal is nothing short of my becoming a participant in his divine nature (2 Peter 1:4). Further, the very relationships with which I struggle and the difficult situations from which I would like to escape are the instruments he is using to produce the heart change that will result in a life that is fruitful to his glory. Suffering should not come as a surprise and it should not be received as an indication of his distance and lack of care. It is a tool of his redemptive love. Our counselees need to cultivate their confidence in God's active, progressive sanctification process so that they can make biblical sense of their problems.

Without an understanding of indwelling sin and the struggle within, without an understanding of the presence, character, and activity of God and his sanctifying process, life will not make sense. Counselees will be confused because they lack the wisdom, insight, and practical, agenda-setting understanding that come when we view ourselves and our situations from the vantage point of the gospel.

Sally lived for the acceptance of people, but this was not what brought her to counseling. She came because she was depressed over a series of broken relationships. However, Sally was blind to her demanding ways, fear, and manipulation of people. She was blind to the condemning and vengeful responses she had to those who failed her. She did not see that she smothered people with her neediness. Her friends were her life-giving, functional gods. As she sought counsel, she felt alone, forsaken by God and people. Confused and unable to understand why all of this was happening, she became increasingly self-absorbed and depressed. She saw no hope of lasting change taking place. From where she stood, it looked as if every good thing she had attempted to do had blown up in her face.

Sally talked of how God must hate her. She had stopped reading her Bible and praying, and her church attendance had become sporadic at best. She believed that she had been unfairly singled out for suffering. All she wanted was for it to stop.

Clearly, the gospel was not making sense out of life for Sally. She had no functional sense of the God of the gospel who is sovereign, holy, forgiving, restoring, reconciling, ever-present, and ever-active, ruling over all things for her sake and lavishing on her the glorious riches of his grace in Christ Jesus (Eph. 1:3–9).

She did not see herself as the sinner for whom the gospel is intended, so she did not see the idolatrous heart that caused her to enter situations and relationships loaded with selfish expectations and silent demands. She did not see how these idolatrous expectations set up the constant disappointment she experienced, and she had no sense of the system of covert and overt vengeance that was her response to people who caused her pain. She did not see that she was playing god as both lawgiver and judge.

Finally, Sally had no sense of the gospel process of progressive sanctification. There was no recognition of the hand of God in her circumstances. He was at work in each situation and relationship, but he was not committed to giving her the acceptance she craved. He *was* at work to expose her sinful heart and behavior and, through these experiences, to form in her the image of Christ. The very circumstances that served as Sally's examples of

God's "unfaithfulness" were, in fact, administered by his loving, covenantal care for her good! Sally was confused because she left essential facts out of her appraisal of her life—the facts of the gospel.

Sally represents everyone we counsel. If their eyes are blind to the realities of who they are as sinners, the character and activity of God, their inheritance as his children, and the process of redemption (sanctification) that is going on, there is no way that our counselees will interpret what is happening correctly. There is no way that they will behave in a biblically appropriate manner.

This is a core distinctive of biblical counseling. Biblical counselors do not see the Bible as an encyclopedia of life principles that need only be followed to have a happy life. Rather, Scripture gives us a radical view of life that has its roots in the gospel; every biblical perspective and principle is rooted there.

This view of life is that we are a people chosen by a sovereign, loving God who, in Christ, has forgiven us and adopted us into his family. He is at work in each situation to conform us to the image of his Son, supplying all that we need to do what he has called us to do. Therefore, we do not buy into the false hope of becoming independently strong, "healthy," aware, and happy individuals. All that we do and all that we hope for is rooted in the fact that we are weak vessels of clay that have been filled with the all-surpassing power of God's presence. We look to the future with hope, preparing for a time when there will be no more sickness, sorrow, sin, or death, for we will be with Christ and like him eternally. That is why, even in the dark days of personal suffering, we do not lose heart (2 Cor. 4:7–18).

You cannot extract Christ from the principles of Scripture without doing violence to them. All that God calls us to do is rooted in what Christ is doing. If the counselee does not have the gospel at the heart of his interpretive system, the principles of the Bible will make no sense to him and he will not respond appropriately.

The clarity that we bring to the life of the counselee is the gospel itself. The gospel is what we want them to see, perhaps for the first time. Every problem can be faced through the manifold provisions of Christ. Consider Paul's prayer for the Ephesians:

> I pray also that the eyes of your heart may be enlightened in order
> that you may know the hope to which he has called you, the riches

of his glorious inheritance in the saints, and his incomparably great power for us who believe. That power is like the working of his mighty strength, which he exerted in Christ when he raised him from the dead and seated him at his right hand in the heavenly realms, far above all rule and authority, power and dominion, and every title that can be given, not only in the present age, but also in the one to come. And God placed all things under his feet and appointed him to be head over everything for the church, which is his body, the fullness of him who fills everything in every way.

(Eph. 1:18–23)

Paul is praying that these Christians would view themselves and all of life in terms of the radical truths of the gospel. His prayer is that they would be able to see the power and riches that are their inheritance in Christ.

Our counselees will not live as God has called them to live if they are blind to the power and the presence of Christ at work in their lives. Instead, their lives will be "ineffective and unproductive" (2 Peter 1:8–9).

This gospel clarity should shape our data gathering as we too pray for "the eyes of [our counselees'] hearts to be enlightened." So we ask questions that flow out of the gospel, causing our counselees to look at things they have not considered. As they answer these questions, the clarity of the gospel will begin to drive away the clouds of confusion.

Earlier we saw that one element in spiritual blindness is that people ask the wrong questions—which lead to wrong answers. In our data gathering, we can begin to teach our counselees how to start with biblical truths and ask questions based on those truths. For example, if the Bible says that God is redemptively active in my life "in all things" (Rom. 8:28), I do not ask questions that assume that he is not and wonder why. I may ask, "What is the good that God is doing in these painful events?" or "What keeps me from seeing the good that God is doing?" or "Where does my agenda (plan) for my life and God's plan differ?" or "What are my treasures (the things most valuable to me)? Are these the things that God says are most valuable and that he is working to produce?" These questions flow out of biblical truths and lead to biblical self-awareness and biblical change.

A husband who is discouraged by what is happening in his family and is tempted to believe that God is absent needs to personalize these questions. What are his goals for his family? Are these God's goals? What are the typical ways he has sought to accomplish these goals? Has he functioned as an instrument of God or as one who owns his family? Where is he not experiencing God's "absence," but rather harvesting what he has sown? Where is the hand of God discernible in his family? Has he, as a husband and father, been in a conflict of agenda with God? Where? What does he want most out of each of these relationships? Are these what God wants for him? Where is he trying to do God's job, trying to produce what only God can produce? Where has he failed to recognize his own themes of weakness, temptation, and sin in his responses to his wife and children? When does he tend to get angry, lashing out with condemning, accusatory, and threatening words? Where does he tend to struggle with discouragement and hopelessness? What does this say about how he thinks about himself, God, others, and his situation? These are questions that flow out of biblical truths and lead to biblical awareness and biblical change.

YOU CAN BRING PURPOSE

Everyone who comes for counsel comes for a reason. They have an agenda, something they would like to see accomplished. But as a counselor you must remember that spiritual blindness will prevent counselees from seeing when their agenda is narrow, selfish, or too temporary ("this-worldly") in nature. They will need your help to see when their purpose for counseling reveals that they have exchanged the worship and service of the Creator for worship and service of the created thing (Rom. 1:25).

The man who is separated from his wife comes to counseling because he wants his family back. The wife comes because she wants a husband who really loves her. The teenager comes because his car has been taken away "until he gets his act together." The depressed young man just wants a little bit of happiness. The pastor wants to understand why he is not more successful in ministry.

Each has a reason for coming to counseling, yet none of them sees the self-orientation of their purpose. In reality, they want little more than the particular piece of the created world that would make them happy. Yet they are children of a God who wants much, much more for them and who sacrificed his own Son in order to secure it!

Such a counselee comes to counseling blind to the fact that his agenda is colored by fear, self-interest, control, personal happiness, or a desire for some other aspect of creation. His problem is not that he wants too much from the Lord, but that he is willing to settle for too little. He seeks the temporary pleasures of the created world when God wants him to become nothing less than a partaker "in the divine nature" (2 Peter 1:4).

The counselee needs someone to come alongside him who is armed with purpose—but not the narrow purpose of self-interest. He needs someone who has a redemptive purpose that is not crippled by self-interest and a desire for personal gain. He needs someone to introduce him to God's grand, redemptive agenda, which is higher, fuller, and deeper than anything he would have wanted or planned for himself.

Peter says that God is working on more than giving me a happy marriage and good kids. As Paul says at the end of Ephesians 3, he is "able to do immeasurably more than all we ask or imagine." In our counseling, we do not want to be shortsighted; we do not want to settle for too little. We want to be used of God to move people from being joyful because it seems as though God is fulfilling their plans to the place where they have forsaken their personal dreams for the greater joys of participating in what God has planned for them.

The biblical counselor wants what God wants for the counselee. His agenda is formed by Scripture—to help the counselee invest in things that will not fade or perish. To accomplish that, he needs to help the counselee uncover his heart's true intentions while opening his eyes to God's glorious purposes for him. As a counselor, I want the questions I ask to accomplish this goal. I want them to open my counselee's eyes to what he is really living for and to create in him a hunger for more than the temporary pleasures of this life. I want to greet the counselee's agenda with redemptive purpose.

Our data-gathering methodology must take this goal seriously. How can our questions accomplish it? This will be the focus of the next appendix.

In our counseling, we are representing the Messiah. What is his work?

> To open eyes that are blind,
> > to free captives from prison
> > and to release from the dungeon those who sit in darkness.
> > > > > (Isa. 42:7)

Can we as his servants be committed to anything less?

APPENDIX 3: STRATEGIES FOR DATA GATHERING

Psalm 36:2–4 powerfully depicts the reality of spiritual blindness and its effect on the way a person lives his life:

> For in his own eyes he flatters himself
>   too much to detect or hate his sin.
> The words of his mouth are wicked and deceitful;
>   he has ceased to be wise and to do good.
> Even on his bed he plots evil;
>   he commits himself to a sinful course
>   and does not reject what is wrong.

This reality of the human heart moves the biblical counselor to see the data-gathering process not only as a means by which the counselor comes to know the counselee, but also as a way to help the counselee see himself with new biblical clarity. Sin is not just about willfulness; that is, a conscious stepping over God's boundaries. Sin is also about blindness; that is, not seeing what needs to be seen to live as God has called me to live. The sinner is both *willfully blind* and *blindly willful*. Thus we as counselors are always dealing with spiritual blindness in our counseling, whether we realize it or not.

This is where Psalm 36 is so instructive. First, it gives us a sense of how spiritual blindness functions: "In his own eyes he flatters himself too much to detect or hate his sin" (v. 2). The spiritually blind person thinks more highly of himself than he ought to think (see Rom. 12:3), and this self-righteousness blinds him to the sin in his life. He does not hate his sin because he does not see himself as capable of such things. Instead, he defends, excuses, rationalizes, recasts, and explains his sin away. A spiritually blind person will not have a biblical sensitivity to or revulsion from sin.

Psalm 36 also points out that if I am not sensitive to my own sin, actively hating it and fleeing from it, I will pursue it all the more. Spiritual blindness leaves us with no internalized system of restraint. In my blindness I will continue to lie and deceive. I will live foolishly and will not do what is good. Even in my quiet meditations, my thoughts will go toward things outside of God's will for me. The psalmist's summary is this: the spiritually blind person will not reject what is wrong. This is true of *all* sinners. All of us struggle with pockets of spiritual blindness, and in those places, none of us sees, hates, or rejects our sin.

This is the spiritual reality we have been considering in the previous two articles. Now we will learn strategies a biblical counselor can use to break through spiritual blindness.

THREE STRATEGIES IN DATA GATHERING

Second Corinthians 10:3–5 structures the way I use the data-gathering process to expose spiritual blindness in those I counsel. As he discusses his ministry goals, Paul says:

> For though we live in the world, we do not wage war as the world does. The weapons we fight with are not the weapons of the world. On the contrary, they have divine power to demolish strongholds. We demolish arguments and every pretension that sets itself up against the knowledge of God, and we take captive every thought to make it obedient to Christ.

My purpose is not to do a thorough exegesis of this passage, which has been most often applied to spiritual warfare and apologetics, but to observe its implications for the way we think about spiritual blindness and practical strategies for change.

LOCATE THE STRONGHOLDS

First, the metaphor of a stronghold is helpful. A stronghold is a place that has been fortified against attack. It is strongly built and actively defended. Because of this it is particularly hard to bring down. Let me give you an example of how this manifests itself in a counselee's life.

Susan did not see herself as a sinner. She saw herself as needy and her needs as consistently unmet. Her neediness was her stronghold. It provided safety from facing the responsibilities of biblical living; it provided an excuse for the way she lived, and it allowed her to consistently place blame on others. Her neediness was a fortress to which she would regularly retreat.

Not only did Susan hide behind her neediness, she actively defended it. She became angry and defensive whenever she believed that I was attacking her view of life. She would fight back, accusing me of being like all the other insensitive men in her life. In defending her neediness, Susan was *willfully blind*. Every sinner has strongholds of spiritual blindness, places where the blindness is fortified to provide a place of hiding. Here the blindness structures the way the person thinks and acts.

The first thing I want to do in my data gathering is to locate the strongholds. Where is this person failing to see what God wants her to see? What effect does this have on the way she deals with God, self, others, and circumstances?

DEMOLISH THE PRETENSIONS

Second, Paul says that he seeks to "demolish . . . every pretension that sets itself up against the knowledge of God" (2 Cor. 10:5). What is a pretension? It is a specious allegation, something that appears to be true but is actually false. Spiritual blindness involves thinking that what is false is actually true. Spiritual blindness means believing lies.

Paul says that these pretensions set themselves up against the truth of God. When I believe a lie, I am no longer open to the truth. The lie in the Garden was not simply an alternative opinion; it set itself up *against* the truth that God had spoken to Adam and Eve. Lies are *always* against the truth. When I accept a lie, I am unable to know what I need to know as God would have me know it. My world becomes shaped by lies, rather than the life-giving, freedom-giving, and wisdom-giving knowledge of God. Paul is zealous to put an end to the rule and reign of falsehood in a person's life. He is zealous to expose unbelief and false belief and demolish them.

We are constantly dealing with pretensions in counseling, things that look and feel as if they are true but are, in fact, false. Susan's neediness was a pretense. It had the appearance of truth in that it seemed to be validated by her experiences of being sinned against, and it appeared to be reasonable because it was reinforced by the psychologized culture around her. But by believing unbiblically that her most basic problem was her neediness rather than her fallenness, Susan was *blindly willful*.

Strongholds of blindness and the self-righteousness and defensiveness that surround them rest on a foundation of plausible lies that set themselves up against the truth. That is why the second strategy in data gathering is to expose and demolish the pretensions. We work to see lies uncovered and destroyed.

TAKE EVERY THOUGHT CAPTIVE

Thirdly, Paul says that his goal is "to take captive every thought to make it obedient to Christ" (2 Cor. 10:5). This phrase pictures the instructive, corrective aspect of data gathering. Our goal is not only to help people to acknowledge that they are blind but also to help them to see biblically. Data gathering can be wonderfully corrective as the person hears our questions, learns to ask the right questions himself, and learns to think biblically about life. We are called to free people from the strongholds and pretensions of spiritual blindness so *that* we can capture them for Christ, so that their every thought is submissive to him and his truth.

Susan's mind, once controlled by lies that she actively defended, increasingly became controlled by the truth of Christ. She became more and more sensitive to subtle pretensions and more and more sensitive to her own defensiveness and self-righteousness. Data gathering was used by God to capture Susan's heart and mind. All sinners need this ministry.

HOW TO LOCATE THE STRONGHOLDS

Earlier, I listed ten ways in which people are blind. Typically they:

1. Believe they have an accurate sense of self.
2. See their primary problem as being sinned against.
3. See the difficult things in their lives as trials rather than consequences of their own choices and behavior.

4. See problems as a direct result of their neediness.
5. Think they are wise and have received much wise counsel.
6. Have analyzed their lives and believe they have insight into what is going on and why.
7. Think they have a clear sense of what is valuable and important.
8. See themselves as having a mature knowledge of Scripture and theology.
9. See themselves as holy; that is, wanting and doing the right things.
10. Already see themselves as repentant.

In each case counselees believe their assessments to be true when, in fact, they are not. However, few counselees will have *all* of these fortresses of spiritual blindness in their lives at one time.

How, then, do you locate those places where spiritual blindness is particularly strong, influential over the person's behavior, and well defended? I listen for several things.

I listen for issues in data gathering that make the counselee angry or defensive. When does the counselee feel accused by a question that is actually open-ended, that requires self-disclosure but does not attach blame? It may be that the counselee feels "set up" or accused because my question has touched a stronghold that he does not want to give up, even though he may be unaware of his defensiveness. These moments are crucial times when God is at work revealing the deceitfulness of the heart. I don't rush on with my data gathering; I stop to help the counselee become aware of his or her anger or defensiveness. I try to help him uncover what he is seeking to protect and how it fits into his life.

Susan was prickly when I asked questions about her past. Early in the questioning process she said, "Why did I expect you to be any different from the rest of my counselors? No one takes what has happened to me seriously." At this point I had not even commented on her past, and I certainly had not made an accusation. I knew, therefore, that Susan's statement revealed something important.

I stopped and pointed out to Susan that I was not making an accusation. As I asked additional questions about her defensive reaction, important counseling issues began to emerge—things I needed to know and Susan needed to see. Susan explained herself as a person who was forced to live with very significant unmet needs. This perspective did a very important thing for her: it excused her from responsibility for wrong things she had done and for their consequences in other people's lives. It was a very valuable piece of her life, and Susan actively defended herself against anyone who challenged it by saying that such a person did not love or understand her. But now, in data gathering, God began to show Susan what this stronghold really was.

As counselors, we must be good listeners and good observers as we ask questions. We need to take notice of moments of anger or defensiveness and make the counselee aware of them. Sometimes the tense and uncomfortable moments of counseling are the very best moments of change. They tend to be the moments when God is putting issues of the heart on the table where they can be seen. They are not moments to be avoided but moments of redemptive opportunity to be creatively utilized.

I look for times in data gathering when the person is closed and self-protective. Notice the questions to which you would expect a ready answer from the counselee, but instead she struggles to answer, sits in silence, tells you that she doesn't know what to say, or gives you an answer that discloses nothing about herself or her situation.

Pay attention, too, to the *way* a person tells her story. One of the most subtle forms of self-protection is the way people recount what has happened to them. It's been my observation that people are often absent from their own life story! What I mean is that their telling of the story features the behavior of others and the difficulty of the situation, but it does not disclose much about their own thoughts, desires, choices, and actions.

I often use a video analogy to highlight this for people. I'll say, "We've been watching your story on video, and I've noticed something interesting: you're not in it! The camera is on other people and on the tough situations, but it never seems to be on you. I would like to go back and talk about the same relationships and the same situations, only this time I want to put the camera on you. I want to focus on what you were thinking, wanting, and doing as these things were going on."

I have learned that it is important for me not to fill the silences when people are struggling to answer. I let them know that I am willing to wait and that it is important for them to answer. I stop and help them understand why it was difficult for them to do so. God uncovers things in these moments.

I have also learned not to be satisfied with non-answers. I lovingly let people know that their answer hasn't told me anything. I then rephrase the question and ask it again because my goal is to uncover the heart behind the self-protectiveness.

I regularly do two things when a person is not self-disclosing as he talks about his own life. First, I often give the counselee a case study to explore. I lay out a problematic situation or a difficult relationship and ask what he would be thinking if he were the person in the situation. I ask what his goals would be and how he would seek to accomplish them. I then try to build connections between the responses to the case study and the counselee's everyday life. This exercise has often been extremely helpful in uncovering the heart.

Next, I often give homework designed to reveal heart themes to me and to the counselee. I ask the person to read Scripture passages, respond to the questions, and bring a written response the next time we meet. When we get together again, I ask the person to tell me what she has learned about herself. Have any themes come up again and again? I discuss the themes I see emerging from the answers. I have found this to be very eye-opening for counselor and counselee alike. In all these ways, the counselor is seeking ways to get the person "out of the bunker" of self-protectiveness.

I look for instances when the counselee places blame for his own behavior at the feet of others. One of the most powerful strongholds of spiritual blindness is the fortress of blame. We *all* find creative ways to blame others for what we have done. From the child who says, "He did it first!" to the man who says he committed adultery because his wife didn't pay him enough attention, we sinners tend to hide in the fortress of other people's sins. And we vigorously justify our own sin in the face of another's mistreatment.

At these times I stop to ask, "Are you really saying that . . . ?" questions. I want the person to face the implications of his words. So I ask the adulterous man, "Are you saying that there is a direct connection between your wife's neglect and your unfaithfulness?" Or, "Explain the connection you see between your adultery and your wife's attitude toward you." Or, "What other responses could you have had to the hurtfulness of your wife's response?" I want my counselee to stop hiding behind the sins of others so he can do something constructive with his own actions and attitudes.

I listen for occasions when the counselee has clearly erected a logical defense of his viewpoint and actions. People who come to counseling aren't always ready to submit their attitudes and actions to biblical examination. They often come asking for help without really wanting it, and seeking counsel that they turn around and reject. Many are like the Pharisee who was in the temple praying to God but whose words actually told God that he didn't need him.

I listen carefully when a person doesn't reveal his thoughts or actions to understand himself better but instead defends himself and actively debates when he is questioned. Often people come to counseling armed with well-rehearsed defenses. They argue from past experience; they may quote a passage of Scripture or a biblical story; they may cite a book or an article; they may refer to what an expert said; or they may just argue that they have given this a lot of thought and they are convinced they are right.

I try to accomplish three things with my response. First, I try to help the person realize that debating is not usually a help-seeking activity; it's a way of defending what they have done. Second, I urge the person to be willing to hold up everything in his life for biblical inspection. God will use it as a means of blessing, not condemnation. Third, I ask questions to help him examine his thoughts and actions from the perspective of Scripture.

HOW TO EXPOSE AND DEMOLISH THE PRETENSIONS

Paul used strong language in 2 Corinthians 10:3–5 because he understood the power of the plausible lie. It is a significant part of the system of unbelief for any sinner. All of us have believed lies, and most of them tend to have a ring of truth to them. Falsehood is seductive simply because it dresses itself as truth. After all, the Enemy of our souls is called the "father of lies," and his primary work is to seduce us with well-dressed lies.

An important clarification needs to be made here. Paul does not tell us to demolish the *person* to whom God has called us to minister but the *system of lies* that has enslaved him. Exposing plausible lies does not have to be loud, harsh, or unkind. We should always speak the truth in love. At the same time, we should have a lively hatred of falsehood and its harvest of destruction in those who believe it.

The plausible lie tends to distort a person's view of life (his functional theology, if you will) at three key points: the person's view of self, his view of God, and his view of the situation. If the counselee has believed a lie in any of these three areas, it will radically affect his response to the situation in which God, in his sovereignty, has placed him. I look for evidence of functional disbelief, unbelief, or falsehood in each of the three areas. As I use data gathering to locate those places where the person is *blindly willful*, I do the following:

I seek to uncover evidence of an inaccurate view of self. Sinners don't tend to have an accurate view of who they are. They tend to think of themselves as better than they are in reality. Pride is much more endemic than self-loathing. So I look for those places where the counselee's view of self simply doesn't fit the attitudes he's expressed and the actions he's taken.

I seek to uncover these inaccuracies in two primary ways. First, I have found that a focused journal can be used by God to open the eyes of a person with a distorted picture of himself. I do not ask counselees to journalize everything that is going on; for most people this would be so intimidating that it would never get done. I keep the journal focused; that is, I only ask them to journal about certain important situations in their lives and respond in the journal to five specific questions:

1. What was going on in the situation?
2. What were you thinking and feeling as it was going on?
3. What did you do in response?
4. What did you want, or what were you seeking to accomplish by what you did?
5. What was the result?

I ask the counselee to keep the journal for two or three weeks. Then I take it back and read it through, looking for themes and patterns that emerge. Next, I take a highlighter and mark all the places where those themes are revealed. Then, in a session with the counselee, I return the journal and have him read it, right then, paying special attention to the places I have highlighted. I finally ask the counselee what he has learned about himself as he reread the journal. God has used this exercise repeatedly to open blind eyes. It seems to be particularly effective because the counselee is not responding to my opinions but to his own words!

Rachel was a very bitter woman who was completely blind to it. She believed that she was fundamentally kind, patient, and understanding. She lived with her elderly grandmother, whom she cared for, so she saw herself as a loving servant. Yet Rachel was very bitter that this duty had been put in her lap. She cursed her siblings, who never offered any help. She saw herself as patient and understanding because she had worked at the same job with the same people for twelve years. Yet she had regular run-ins with her boss and had testy relationships with most of her coworkers.

Rachel's view of herself did not include bitterness, so there were many things in her life that she had not faced. The journal was the breakthrough for Rachel. After she wrote in the journal for three weeks, I took it to read. I didn't have a highlighter with me; I had a green marker, so I underlined, in green, every instance of bitterness in Rachel's journal. The pages were literally green with bitterness. The next time I met with her, I asked her to read her journal, explaining what I had done. About halfway through her reading, Rachel began to cry. She looked up and said, "I am a very bitter lady!" The plausible lie of her inaccurate view of self had been exposed.

"Real-time" data gathering can also expose a person's inaccurate view of self. In the counseling session I get to experience the person as he or she really is. The controlling person will tend to be controlling in counseling. The angry person will tend to get angry at some point. The self-righteous person will be defensive and unteachable. The fearful person will struggle with trust. I find it very important to get counselees to examine the dynamics of their relationship with me. Here it is harder for them to hide because I have been on site with them. I ask them to be very honest about their struggles in relating to me, and I am very honest about my experience in relating to them. As we unpack the dynamics of our relationship and themes emerge, the plausible lies that the person has believed about self are revealed.

I seek to uncover functional distortions in the person's view of God. People develop an experiential theology that seems plausible because it flows out of their interpretation of what has gone on in their lives. The more this interpretation—and not Scripture—shapes their view of God, the greater the gap between their confessional (official) and their functional (actual, day-to-day) theology. Yet their functional theology will seem to have a ring of logic and truth because it fits their view of life.

For example, Joe's God was distant and uninvolved. Joe said that in his dark moments of depression, when he needed God the most, he never felt as if God were near. He said he knew that God worked miracles, but he struggled because God did not answer his prayers. Joe saw God as a harsh judge, ready to mete out consequences to anyone who "messed up." Yet in all of this Joe called himself a believer.

How did I come to know the content of Joe's functional theology and how did I help Joe see the gap between what he *said* he believed and what he *really* believed? I paid attention to the way Joe asked questions about God, and I helped Joe to understand the impact of those questions on the way he lived his life. For example, Joe would say, "I don't understand why God isn't working in my life." (This problem has been raised by many I have counseled.) The question is based on an unbiblical assumption—that for some reason God forsakes certain of his children. Such a question will not lead the questioners to a better understanding of their situation or to a further exercise of biblical faith.

My strategy was this: as Joe asked questions about God, I helped him to see the false assumptions upon which the questions were based. Some of these were: that feelings are a reliable indicator of the presence of God; that suffering is a sign of God's punishment; that if I don't see the evidence of God's hand in my life, it means he is not answering my prayers; and that God is distant rather than near. I helped Joe to see the unbiblical nature of his questions by asking the same questions, but reframing them with biblical assumptions. For example, "God declares that he is near, Joe; why does he seem so distant to you?" Or, "Joe, God is at work in your life; what are the things that keep you from seeing it?" Or, "Joe, let's look at the things for which you have prayed and see how God has answered." Each question dealt with Joe's concern, but each one was reframed by biblical assumptions. They exposed the plausible lies about God that Joe had believed, and pointed instead to true biblical faith.

Listen to the God-talk of your counselees. Listen to the questions they ask about God's person and work. Listen for plausible theological lies. Few people will suddenly reject the God of the Scriptures to become avowed atheists. However, many fall away into a cold and distant theological cynicism as the God of their functional theology becomes one who is worthy of neither worship nor respect.

I look for evidence of the person letting go of the means of grace and Christian growth, such as daily personal worship, the gatherings of the body of Christ, Christian friendship and fellowship, the teaching of the Word, and corporate worship. I seek to understand why they have withdrawn, hoping to expose and understand the lies that have led to a weakened faith in God and a loss of motivation for pursuing deeper communion with him and his people.

First Corinthians 10:13 can be the design for a helpful homework assignment to uncover lies a person has embraced about God and his work. Paul seems to address four plausible lies about God that we are tempted to believe as he makes four declarations about God and his work. I set up the homework this way:

1. Declaration: "No temptation has seized you except what is common to man."
   Question: Where have you been tempted to think that your situation is unique and that you have been singled out for particular suffering?
2. Declaration: "God is faithful."
   Question: Where have you tended to believe that God has been unfaithful to his promises to you?
3. Declaration: "He will not let you be tempted beyond what you can bear."
   Question: "Where have you thought that you have been given more than you can handle or that the extreme pressures of the situation have caused you to sin?
4. Declaration: "He will also provide a way out so that you can stand up under it."
   Question: "Where have you tended to feel trapped, with no reasonable way to deal with your situation?"

This focused assignment will reveal to both counselor and counselee the lies the counselee has believed about the person and work of the Lord.

I seek to uncover distortions in the way the person thinks about his situation. As you do data gathering, keep in mind that the person is not providing an objective, mechanical recitation of his or her situation. He is not giving pure "people, places, and events." Because every human being is an interpreter, every person tries to make sense out of what has gone on in his life. Everyone has a view of life, and everyone has a view of his present circumstances, whether he is aware of it or not. It is actually impossible for a person to give pure history or a pure summary of what is presently happening. He or she will always bare a personalized view of things; and because of this, I need to know the things for which I should be listening. Some of the most common indicators of a distorted perspective (again, the plausible lies) are given below.

I listen for **interpretations**, the times when the counselee says, "I think this means this." No counselee stops and says, "Okay, Counselor, I am now going to share with you the sense that I made out of this event." Interpretations come on the fly in endless variety. You have to be alert and listening. For example, if the person says, "I thought about it and decided that I should. . . ." she is giving you an interpretation. Stop and dig it out and seek to understand it. A person may say, "I know exactly why this keeps happening to me. . . ." Again, we are not being offered unadulterated fact but an interpretation that can reveal distortions in the way the person thinks about his life.

I also listen for **evaluations,** for all judgments of good or bad, right or wrong, true or false, important or unimportant, success or failure, possible or impossible. In fact, I constantly ask questions to draw out the person's evaluations. I'll ask, "What do you think would be the right thing to do here?" or "What was most important to you when that happened?" or "What did you think was true or false in what they said to you?" or "What made you think that this situation was impossible?" Each of these probes the evaluations that are the basis for the decisions and actions a person takes. These questions are meant to reveal the heart behind their responses.

Next, I listen for **purposes and goals**. What does the person want out of—or in the midst of—her situation? What is she really living for in the situation in which God has placed her? Listen for purpose. Listen for goals. Listen for statements that tell you what the counselee is going after. Everyone is living for something. Ask questions that get at the situational goals of the counselee. Are they the goals God has for her? For example, when a person tells us what she did or how she responded, we need to ask what she was seeking to accomplish by that behavior. Require the counselee to look at what her treasures are and how those treasures shape the way she responds. Ask questions that require her to think about motives, to answer from the heart.

I listen for **doctrine or theology**. I don't mean that I check to see if the person has read L. Berkhof's *Systematic Theology* recently! I listen for formal and informal statements of belief and the person's functional theology. I listen very carefully every time the person quotes a passage. (How was he using it? What sense did it make to him?) I listen every time a person refers to a particular doctrine. (How does he understand this biblical truth, and how is he applying it to his situation?) I listen carefully every time the counselee alludes to a biblical story. (How is he identifying his situation with the biblical account? What connections is he making?) I listen when the person quotes a Christian preacher, teacher, or author. (What meaning has he drawn that has helped him make sense of his own life?)

All people theologize about their situations, though most people are not aware that they do! And most counselees will not make direct theological observations. These will come mixed in with the telling of their stories, so we need to listen carefully and ask questions that draw this material out.

I listen for **emotions**. I take notice of the feelings expressed as the counselee talks about his situation. Joy, anger, fear, hope, discouragement, frustration, sadness, gratitude, bitterness, despair, and contentment are all windows into the heart. All need to be unpacked as they relate to the way a person interacts with the things that God has put in his life. It is my habit to stop and comment on the emotion when it is expressed and then unpack it with the counselee so that I can understand it and so that he can see how it relates to the way he is looking at his life.

As I listen for emotion, I ask myself whether or not the emotions are appropriate. That is, do these emotions flow out of biblical thinking on the situation? For example, when the Israelites grumbled about God's provision of manna and looked back longingly to Egypt, their emotions were inappropriate. They did not flow out of faith and trust in God and a view of life that was shaped by his Word. One of the easiest ways to expose the plausible lies a person has embraced is to pay attention to his emotions and to ask questions that reveal his feelings.

We sinners are people who are blindly willful. We tend to believe the plausible lie. There are pretensions embedded in each of our lives that need to be ferreted out and destroyed. This was one of Paul's fundamental ministry goals, and it should be ours as well. As we seek to know the counselee through data gathering, we should also be on a mission to bring into the light all the subtle lies of the Enemy that lure people away from God's pathway.

HOW TO TAKE EVERY THOUGHT CAPTIVE TO CHRIST

This is Paul's final summary of his ministry: "We take captive every thought to make it obedient to Christ" (2 Cor. 10:5). This should be the goal of all we do in ministry as well. When we ask good questions that flow out of a distinctly biblical view of life, we require those we counsel to think about themselves in ways that they have never thought before. In asking the questions that they have not asked, in ways they have not asked them, God can use us to break through the walls of spiritual blindness and promote biblical insight.

I remember a woman saying to me after a series of questions, "I am learning so much about myself and God and the choices I have made!" I had not gotten out my Bible to formally instruct her. Her learning was the result of data gathering. The process had confronted her spiritual blindness, and it was beginning to bring her thoughts captive to Christ.

Spiritual blindness is attempting to see without Christ, no more possible than trying to see physically without eyes. Paul says in Colossians 2:8, "See to it that no one takes you captive through hollow and deceptive philosophy, which depends on human tradition and the basic principles of this world rather than on Christ." If my thoughts about myself, others, my situation, and God aren't captive to Christ, they are captive to the hollow and deceptive philosophy of the world. When your counselees realize this and see the specific patterns in which they need a new way of thinking, they will be more receptive to teaching and confrontation. They will understand how biblical solutions truly fit the problems they face.

Notice how Paul describes the world's philosophy: "hollow and deceptive." It's deceptive. It appears to be right. It appears attractive, with good arguments and tight logic. It seems to have substance with its years of study and research. Yet it is hollow. It doesn't have substance. It doesn't offer real answers. It doesn't lead to true insight. It doesn't deliver what it promises. It is empty. Why? Because it doesn't submit to Christ. All it can ever offer is what people see—people who are sinners and struggle with spiritual blindness—and that is why it will always come up short. It will always prove in the end to be lacking.

In counseling we recognize that "all the treasures of wisdom and knowledge are hidden in Christ" and we seek to bring every thought captive to him. We recognize that all true seeing begins with Jesus, yet we also know that we counsel people who think they see but are blind; who think they understand but whose insights are hollow and deceptive.

For that reason we seek to expose and destroy the well fortified, actively defended strongholds of spiritual blindness. We seek to reveal and demolish pretensions, those plausible lies that delude every sinner. Yet, having done this, we are not done. Our ultimate goal is to bring the *willfully blind* and the *blindly willful* captive to Christ, so that they may see with biblical clarity and live in thankful obedience to him. As we depend upon him, God can use our questions to expose and invade spiritual darkness, capturing the thoughts of our counselees so that they would be obedient to Christ.

HELPING COUNSELEES BECOME AWARE
OF THEIR LIFE AGENDAS

"The purposes of a man's heart are deep waters,
　　but a man of understanding draws them out." (Proverbs 20:5)

Heart-revealing questions. The Scriptures give us many windows into the heart and what rules it. Here are a few examples of questions meant to help counselees examine personal heart themes and patterns of thought, motive, and desire. Answering them can help them begin to acknowledge the true treasures of their hearts and how those treasures shape their responses to God, others, and the situations of life.

1. When does the counselee (CE) tend to experience fear, worry, or anxiety (Matt. 6:19–34)?
2. Where has the CE struggled with disappointment (Prov. 13:12, 19)?
3. In what situations does the CE struggle with anger (James 4:1–2; Prov. 11:23)?
4. Where does the CE encounter problems in relationships (James 4:1–10)?
5. What situations of life has the CE found particularly difficult (1 Cor. 10:13–14)?
6. Where are the CE's patterns of avoidance? What things does he regularly seek to avoid?

7. Where has the CE experienced regular problems in his spiritual life or in his relationship with God (Ps. 73)?

8. Where or when has the CE tended to doubt the truths of Scripture (Rom. 1:25)?

9. What is the CE's true agenda for others? What is his definition of a good relationship? What are his expectations for others? What silent demands does he make of the people around him (James 4:1–2)?

10. Where does the CE struggle with bitterness (Eph. 4:31; Prov. 18:19)?

11. Where has the CE struggled with regret, being tempted to say, "If only . . ."?

12. What past experiences are hard for the CE to let go?

13. When does the CE experience problems in prayer and personal worship (James 4:3–4)?

14. Where does the CE struggle with envy? What does he tend to covet (Prov. 14:30)?

APPENDIX 4: DOCTRINES THAT DRIVE HOMEWORK

One methodological distinctive of biblical counseling is the regular use of homework. Good, well-tailored homework can play a significant part in the counseling and change process. Jay Adams writes, "Biblical counselors have found homework to be one of the most vital and effective forces that they can marshal in counseling."[1] Why the use of homework? There is certainly no "proof text" for it; Jesus didn't tell the rich young ruler to write down a "log list" of personal failings and return next week! Is using homework, therefore, simply a matter of stumbling upon a technique that has proven itself pragmatically?

Homework has been a consistent emphasis in biblical counseling because its use is driven by cardinal biblical doctrines. For the biblical counselor, theology is not simply a matter of the *content* of faith and practice. Biblical, exegetically derived theology also addresses the *process* of changing beliefs and behaviors: both counseling methods (from the counselor's side of the process) and progressive sanctification (from the counselee's side). The methods of biblical counseling emerge out of Scriptural theology. What the biblical counselor *does* in counseling—and has counselees do—must be as biblically consistent as what he *says*. Homework is a method that is a logical and practical extension of the beliefs that make biblical counseling distinctive.

Five doctrines drive the use of homework. After developing the rationale for the use and design of homework, we will address particular kinds of homework appropriate to various phases of the counseling and change process.

DOCTRINE OF SCRIPTURE

Sam has been a long-time church member. In recent years he has faced difficulties: his wife died after a lengthy illness; his pharmacy business has suffered from new competition; an old football injury has acted up and made him gimpy; and the congregation committed itself to a building program against Sam's vocal opposition. Sam has become increasingly sour as life has not gone his way. He is bitter, disillusioned, unhappy, full of complaints, at odds with God, neighbor, and circumstances. How do you help Sam? What part might homework play?

Biblical counselors by definition are committed to the authority and sufficiency of Scripture. They seek to look at human problems from the perspective of God's Word. For example, the Bible discusses Sam's problem at great length in many passages on the problem of "grumbling" because of what we crave or fear in situations of stress.[2] Biblical counselors want to help their counselees think biblically about life issues as well. Sam's mind needs to be renewed; he needs to process his difficulties God's way.

The biblical counselor provides much more than a listening ear and comforting words of sympathy. You listen. You sympathize with a man "tempted, tried, and sometimes failing." But you also lead Sam to understand himself and his problem in light of who Christ is: "Even when my heart is breaking, he, my comfort, helps my soul."[3] Biblical understanding leads to actions, doing what is biblically appropriate in each part of his situation. Homework? The biblical counselor works to get the counselee into the Word of God right away so that the counselee's agenda for counseling becomes increasingly biblical. Sam may want to unload complaints and prove to himself and you that life is hopeless. God wants Sam to repent of grumbling and live for his glory in the tough times.

Homework enables the counselee to mine the riches of Scripture for understanding, conviction, promises, and guidance. Biblically designed homework gives the counselor the delightful opportunity of surprising the counselee with the personal, practical wisdom of Scripture that speaks to the specifics of his life: "Let's look at people in hardship and how they were tempted to respond (Num. 11–21). Let's look at what God is up to in the midst of hardships that make people sense how fragile their lives are (Deut. 8). Let's look at what God wants you to do as you deal with your grumbling and withdrawal by turning back to him (Phil. 2:1–16)."

Biblical homework calls for commitment. At the outset of counseling it places the counselee under the authority of God in Scripture. All of God's ways are right and all of his words are true, so homework calls the counselee to test each question by Scripture. It calls for counselees to invest effort in study that leads to biblical wisdom about the issues of life. Homework asks the counselee to lay down his interpretation and pick up God's. It requires him to have a life driven and shaped by the principles of the Bible rather than by emotion and personal desire.

In short, homework practically applies the doctrine of the authority and sufficiency of Scripture to the life of the counselee. It calls for thinking and acting consistent with its teaching. Our doctrine of Scripture calls for homework that gets counselees into the Bible.

DOCTRINE OF HUMAN RESPONSIBILITY

Bill and Fran presented quite a picture when they entered my office. Bill was rigid and withdrawn while Fran was in tears before the first question was asked. I looked over their Personal Data Inventory,[4] introduced myself, and asked my first question. "Tell me," I said, "what has brought you here today? What is the problem as you see it?" Simultaneously, they each said one word to summarize the problem. Bill said, "Fran"; Fran said, "Bill"!

Now, as a counselor, I was in trouble! Neither Bill nor Fran had come intending to be a counselee. Each thought the other was the problem. Each was saying that if the other were fixed, everything would be fine. In this situation, a counselor doesn't really have any counselees in the office. Neither person was taking responsibility for the problems in their relationship or for the changes that must take place. Counseling with Bill and Fran would go nowhere unless each began to accept responsibility for existing problems and needed changes. How can homework help refocus counselees?

Obviously, the issue of responsibility is of central concern to the biblical counselor. Scripture says that each one of us stands responsible before God. Each person will give an account for every word and deed. God calls us to honest self-examination, honest confession, and honest repentance. He calls us to fully participate in his work of change. The call of Scripture is to be more concerned about my log than my neighbor's speck. God requires that people stop pointing the finger and start examining the heart.

The doctrine of Scripture calls for homework that gets counselees listening to God. This doctrine of human responsibility calls for another genre of homework: looking at oneself. Homework is designed to direct the focus of counseling. Proper self-examination takes the primary focus away from the actions of others and onto the counselee's responses to circumstances. Homework moves the focus away from the counseling "professional" and the mystique of a weekly hour and makes Bill and Fran responsible for their day-by-day participation in the process of change. Homework also directs the focus of hope. It moves people from hopes that other people or circumstances will change and make life easier. It moves people from hopes that the counselor will do powerful things to create change. Looking at personal responsibility moves hope to God and to the power of the gospel to change the counselee himself.

In the early stages of counseling, homework requires the counselee to begin to understand himself before God, to entrust himself to God, and to walk responsibly before him. Homework helps hold the counselee responsible for the changes that need to take place in relationship to God and neighbor. He does not come to counseling to sit passively before a guru. Rather, the counselor is a guide and teacher showing the counselee his part in the process of change.

Human beings are responsible, and good homework emerges out of this fact. All of this is important because the momentum of the Fall and of our culture is in the opposite direction. Bill and Fran live in a culture that has institutionalized blame-shifting. The "Inner Child," "co-dependent," "dysfunctional family," "adult-child" systems all place the blame for the counselee's attitude and behavior at someone else's feet. Not only that, but our fallen hearts' natural inclinations are to excuse ourselves and blame others while we are blind to our own wrongs. You begin to understand how important homework can be in getting the counselee active and involved in examining self and making changes out of hope and dependency on God. Our doctrine of human responsibility calls for homework that helps counselees to stop and look at themselves accurately.

DOCTRINE OF GOD

Jane had a tremor in her voice as she acknowledged her anxiety about "trying counseling one more time. I'm a nervous wreck. I've seen eight different therapists. I was hospitalized and had electroconvulsive therapy. I've been on more kinds of prescription meds than I can remember. I've tried biofeedback. I've tried New Year's resolutions. I've tried vacations. I've tried getting jobs and seeing if that would help. I've tried support groups. I've gone to inner healers to see if spirituality could heal my inner wounds. I've burned out all my friends because I'm such a drain on them. I've tried. . . ." How could homework play a part in helping Jane?

Biblical counselors stand apart from all other systems in that they believe God is the One who changes people. The distinctive of biblical counseling is its trust in a redeeming God who has the power to change the human heart. The biblical counselor sees himself not as the creator of change but as an instrument in the hands of One who can create change superior to anything a counselor or counselee could ask or imagine.

The problem is that people lose sight of God in the midst of their circumstances and the self-centeredness of their flesh. This is not a new phenomenon. Israel, camped in front of the Red Sea, was terrified as she realized that the army of Egypt was in hot pursuit. Israel lost sight of God, his loving control, and his redemptive purpose. The first few verses of Exodus 14 make clear that the situation was not out of control, that Israel had not been left to herself, and that God had a purpose for the entire experience.

The people of Israel were not unlike Jane. Like Israel, she has lost sight of God, his lordship over circumstances and his power to enable her to do all he has called her to do. Often counselees fail to interpret their circumstances in light of the Fact of facts: God IS, and he maintains his loving, redemptive control over all things. Since they fail to refer their situation to God, his character, and his work, they respond as if they are alone. This lack of God-awareness shapes their thinking and behavior.

Homework offers a wonderful opportunity to put God back in sight. Homework that points to God and his work for his people gives Jane a radically different interpretation of her circumstances. Homework that gives the counselee a God-awareness helps clarify what things in the situations are her responsibility and what things she must entrust to God. God-centered homework tends to draw the counselee away from dependency on the counselor into a deeper and more confident dependence on God. The counselee who has caught sight of God can face her own failure, weakness, and inability without fear; her hope is in God. She is able to give disciplined, anxiety-free attention to the things God has called her to do while entrusting to God the things she is unable to do.

The existence and work of God should become the main interpreter of personal experience for the counselee. Scriptural studies that begin to bring God into view are vital. These studies should include:

1. Who God is: His character and attributes.
2. How God works: His sanctifying process, sovereign control, and grace and forgiveness.
3. Counselee's relationship to God: identity in Christ and adoption as sons; how to meet God; how to serve God in the Holy Spirit.
4. Case studies from Scripture: God at work on behalf of his people; God the fulfiller of his promises.

Homework focusing on these truths about God will put the counselee's circumstances and problems in proper perspective. Truth draws the counselee's eyes away from the dilemmas of the moment to look with confidence and hope to the author and finisher of his or her faith. It is important to do more than speak these truths to counselees. They need to be involved in the process of searching the Scriptures so that God's powerful presence is indelibly stamped in their hearts. Our doctrine of God calls for homework that has counselees meet God.

DOCTRINE OF SIN

As Jim and Mary came in for marriage counseling, it was clear that their problems were not new. Their marriage had always been full of conflict. Jim was a demanding, perfectionistic workaholic who saw failure as a curse and free time as a sign of irresponsibility. His pattern was to make heavy demands on Mary and judge her harshly when her work was not a raving success. His interactions with Mary and their children were negative and cynical.

Mary was an angry woman who daily rehearsed to herself Jim's wrongs against her. She was able to recall these incidents in elaborate detail. In her own way she made daily war with Jim, striking back at him again and again. However, Mary did not see herself as an angry person. She was quite self-righteous, viewing herself as a helpless victim of a hellish life. How do we understand Mary's problem? How will homework contribute to her understanding and the counselor's understanding?

The problems of counselees run deeper than behavior. They run deeper than feelings and the labels our culture pastes on problems: low self-esteem, co-dependency, compulsion, borderline personality, impulse disorder, adult-child, and the like. There are problems that are more fundamental than habits, actions, words, and self-talk. The biblical counselor is concerned with more than exchanging behavior for behavior, feeling for feeling, cognition for cognition. The biblical counselor is concerned about the problem at its roots.

Distinctive to the biblical counselor is his concern with the "heart," as the Bible defines it. This focus is radical in a culture that doesn't even believe that the heart exists. In modern psychology the term functions only as an anachronism. In Christianized psychologies the term is loaded with all sorts of secular baggage: we hear of "wounded hearts" or "needy hearts" or the heart as a "storehouse of repressed wounds and damaged memories." None of these definitions is true. The cause of human problems is inevitably misdiagnosed when secular categories control.

If fundamental, lasting change is going to take place, the counselee must acquire a biblical definition of sin that includes a discussion of the heart.

Scripture declares that the roots of human problems are in the heart. It is the root system of the heart (Heb. 4:12; Gen. 6:5) that produces the fruit of a person's words and deeds. What controls the heart shapes behavior. What rules the heart influences each part of the person's life.

Christ put it in plain and simple language. Good comes out of good stored up in the heart and evil comes out of evil stored up in the heart. Problems of fruit are directly related to problems of root. Yet few counselees come in with an agenda to examine the heart. Most often they have an external agenda. They want the problem removed or fixed so that they can be happy again. Or their internal agenda is simply to remove unpleasant feelings.

Ezekiel 14:5 says that God has another agenda: "to recapture the hearts" of people estranged from him. He recaptures the hearts of his people so that they will serve him alone. The biblical counselor must have this heart agenda as well.

Here again homework becomes very important. Scripture functions like a mirror. As the counselee looks intently into it, he sees himself as he really is. Hebrews 4:12 says that Scripture is the great revealer of the mysteries of the heart. Scripture is able to cut through and expose the thoughts and intentions that shape the behavior of the counselee.

The counselee needs to see that his heart is interacting with all that is going on around him. If his heart is controlled by something other than God, the counselee will not respond to his circumstances in the way God has ordained. For example, James presents the cause of human conflict as the desires that battle within the heart. Because of these "encamped" desires people make war with one another. It is vital that the counselee recognizes and owns his heart's thoughts and intentions, since these shape his response to life. How does specific homework grow out of the doctrine of sin?

I asked Mary to keep a journal of her conversations with Jim. I told her that I wanted her to journal for a few weeks and then I would keep the journal for a week to look through it. I knew that anger would be a theme in her journal, and I was right. I took the journal and marked all the places where anger was evident. As Mary was journaling, I assigned her studies in Ezekiel 14:1–5, Luke 6:43–45, and James 4. Mary began to see her heart, her anger, and the way it shaped her behavior toward Jim.

A carefully assigned and organized journal coupled with biblical homework on the heart will direct the counselee to take responsibility for root change. It will correct the false cultural assumptions about the cause of the counselee's problem and cut through the blindness caused by the deceitfulness of sin.

Sin is identified in light of the alternatives: righteousness, peacemaking, love, obedience, and problem solving. As Mary identifies what is wrong (put off, as in Eph. 4), she also starts to see what God would have her do instead (put on) as she embraces the gospel of Christ. Homework gets specific with the skills of peacemaking: forgiveness seeking, learning to confront lovingly and humbly, and doing acts of tangible love even when our neighbor is acting like an enemy. Homework becomes the occasion for planning those "good works which God prepared in advance for us to do" in particular situations (Eph. 2:10). Our doctrine of sin calls for homework that helps counselees rethink the way they understand their problems and guides them into specific life changes.

DOCTRINE OF PROGRESSIVE SANCTIFICATION

Josh said, "But I've tried. I've done all the things God says to do to deal with lust, and nothing works. I've repented. I've prayed. I've yielded up con-

trol to the Lord. I've rebuked Satan. Sometimes I think I've solved the problem once for all, and then a month later I fall again." The counselor in-
quired further about several things: the circumstances of Josh's tumbles into
immorality, whether Josh had ever let any mature Christian men in on his
struggle, and whether Josh was looking for a once-for-all solution. The answers were predictable. Josh knew virtually nothing about the way the Christian life works and the means of grace God employs.

Berkhof describes the process of sanctification this way: ". . . sanctification is a work of which God and not man is the author. Only the advocates
of the so-called free will can claim that it is a work of man. Nevertheless, it
differs from regeneration in that man can, and is duty bound to, strive for
ever-increasing sanctification by using the means which God has placed at
his disposal. This is clearly taught in Scripture: 2 Corinthians 7:1; Colossians 3:5–14; 1 Peter 1:22."[5]

What are the means God employs to sanctify his children? The three
that are most prominent in the New Testament are the Word of God,
God's providence, and the edifying ministry of the body of Christ. These
are what counseling is about. Counseling is the ministry of the Word
from believer to believer in the context of what God is doing in a person's
situation. Biblical counseling at once recognizes the Word's authority,
God's sovereignty over circumstances, and the body of Christ's call to
person-to-person ministry.

What does all of this have to do with homework? Homework provides
an opportunity for the counselee to understand God's sanctifying purpose
and to participate in his sanctifying process. Homework asks the counselee
to participate in the disciplines of sanctification, particularly the study of the
Word, consistency of applying the Word in acts of faith and obedience, and
submission to the edifying, encouraging, admonishing ministry of the body
of Christ.

Homework teaches the counselee that growth in grace doesn't come by
lightning bolts and magical encounters but by humble, honest, obedient,
and practical application of God's Word to the specifics of everyday experience. In sanctification God calls his children to follow, stand fast, forsake,
trust, put off and put on, run, obey, put to death, study, flee, and resist.
Homework takes this call of God and applies it with specificity to the counselee's situation. Homework takes resistance, forsaking, following, and
putting on out of the abstract to make them concrete. Homework asks the

counselee to do, in the context of his particular circumstance, what God has called him to do as a participant in his sanctifying mercy.

Homework also fits well with the extended process of sanctification. Metaphors of sanctification in Scripture, such as running a race, growing from infancy to adulthood, and the growth from seed to mature plant, depict sanctification as a lengthy process. In reality, it is a process that encompasses our entire lives. Homework helps nudge the counselee away from the hope for a quick fix and helps the counselee to buy into God's step-by-step process of change. Homework charts the significance of each step made in God's name, erecting milestones that can be looked back upon in praise to God. A homework journal or notebook will function as an encouraging record of progress as God uses counseling to continue his sanctifying work.

Finally, homework challenges the "right to privacy" attitude that many Christians retain in the Christian experience. Often sanctification is thought of as a private matter between a person and God, but it is impossible to read Ephesians 4 and 1 Corinthians 12 and conclude that sanctification is an individual concern. The nature of homework assumes accountability and submission to a fellow believer. It calls for the counselee to be honest before God and one of his instruments of redemption, the counselor. It calls for the counselee to forsake the pride and fear that make him hide from those God has provided to help him, and to step out in honesty, thanking God for his provision. Our doctrine of progressive sanctification calls for homework that encourages counselees in the process of change and connects them to other people in an ongoing way.

SUMMARY

- ◆ Our doctrine of Scripture calls for homework that gets counselees into the Bible.
- ◆ Our doctrine of human responsibility calls for homework that has counselees stop to look at themselves accurately.
- ◆ Our doctrine of God calls for homework that has counselees meet God.
- ◆ Our doctrine of sin calls for homework that helps counselees rethink the way they understand their problems and guides them into specific life changes.

◆ Our doctrine of progressive sanctification calls for homework that encourages counselees in the process of change and connects them to other people in an ongoing way.

Homework is an essential part of biblical counseling. Using it is consistent with the doctrines that are the foundation for truly biblical counseling, as seen in the examples above. Homework provides a way for those doctrines to become practical operating principles in the life of each counselee.

APPENDIX 5: HOMEWORK AND FOUR PHASES OF COUNSELING

Fear increasingly controlled Sue's life. When she sought counseling, she told me that she had rid her house of knives because she was so afraid that she would sleepwalk and hurt her child or husband. She constantly worried that she had contracted some fatal disease. Sue irrationally distrusted her husband. She fretted that she had said or done something to hurt, anger, or alienate her few friends. She was afraid of counseling because "no one would understand what I'm going through" and "I'll be put away." How could homework penetrate this nightmare and help Sue learn to trust both God and her counselor?

Psalm 37 gives the fretful and fearful someone to trust, someone whose care runs deeper than their problems. Psalm 37 openly discusses frightening life situations. And Psalm 37 challenges fearful people to examine their own lives. At the end of our first session, I asked Sue to read this psalm several times during the next week and to ask herself, "What is God saying to me?" Over subsequent weeks Psalm 37 provided a vehicle for me to enter Sue's world of fear and build a counseling relationship with her. Further assignments from the Psalms drew out Sue's experiences of fear and set these next to the Lord's promises. She faced the cause of her destructive fears: her reactions to the sins of others revealed her own sins and unbelief.

We saw earlier that neither Fran nor Bill came to counseling to be counseled. When I asked them what they thought was wrong with their marriage, they immediately said each other's first name. Each came to counseling to tell me how to fix the other person. How could homework focus our data gathering and cut into their mutual accusations and defensiveness?

During our second session I discussed the "speck and log" principle, God's grace, and the way of repentance (Matt. 7:1–5; Luke 6:37–42). I asked each of them to construct a personal "log list": What are *you* doing that is wrong and harms the union God has ordained for your marriage? Fran and Bill did the assignment; both started to become counselees—disciples of the Lord Jesus Christ—that week. Data gathering and problem solving in subsequent sessions built on their lists and the principles of Scripture embodied in that assignment.

"You won't believe what I discovered in my homework this week!" were Judy's first words as our fifth session began. I had asked Judy to keep a journal of her encounters with her husband. Their marriage was a war zone, and Judy was convinced that it was caused solely by "Jim's typical selfish response to everything." Judy had "prayed for years, and nothing had changed." How could homework help Judy see herself biblically?

Judy's journal tracked each argument between herself and Jim, specifically noting what she was thinking, desiring, feeling, and doing in each encounter. Judy faithfully kept her journal for three weeks. On the fourth week her assignment was to read through her journal over and over, looking for patterns of thought, motive, and behavior. She compared what she found to biblical passages on relationships: James 4:1–6; Ephesians 4:25–32; 1 Corinthians 13. I *did* know what Judy had discovered that week; God's truth had broken in. I could hear new humility and new hope in her words, and I could see in her face that the words were not just words.

Bart had been estranged from his family for many years. In the course of counseling, his bitterness and cold indifference yielded to the grace of God. How could homework "put feet" on the changes in Bart's heart and attitude? For homework he wrote a letter of reconciliation to his mother, whom he had not contacted in more than ten years. I asked him not to send the letter, but to bring it to our next session where we would evaluate it together. We both wanted to make sure that Bart's letter expressed God's agenda for change in his relationship to his family, changes that flowed out of the change in Bart's relationship to God.

You see in these stories four examples of homework, each quite different, each seeking to accomplish a different purpose. My homework with Sue was a means of breaking through her walls of self-protection and building her relationship with God and with me. For Fran and Bill, homework was a major means of focusing the data gathering process. Judy's homework was self-revealing: it helped her to see herself in the mirror of Scripture. Bart's homework was an instance of applying God's agenda concretely to his everyday life.

Homework is more than guided Bible study, reinforcing the teaching aspect of counseling. Homework for the biblical counselor is not limited to a single focus and single purpose. Homework, creatively designed and appropriately used, advances each phase of counseling. Used well, homework doesn't function as an addition to the counseling process but as an integral part of it. Each step of the counseling process continues, even when counselee and counselor are not together, because good homework keeps the movement going.

The biblical counselor should ask during every phase of counseling, "What kind of homework is appropriate and helpful? What would buttress and advance what we are presently working on?"

For the purposes of this article, I want to break the counseling process into four phases. Of course, in actual counseling these phases are never as distinct as they will appear here. The four phases of counseling that will inform my discussion are:

1. Welcome: Build a godly relationship with counselees.
2. Understand: Gather data that moves toward the heart.
3. Confront and comfort: Help counselees to see themselves biblically and embrace God's promises.
4. Action: Apply God's agenda for change to everyday life.

For each phase I will give a summary goal followed by sample homework that flows from each goal. These are to whet your appetite for good homework; you will need to develop a full and diverse menu for your own counseling ministry.

WELCOME

Goal: Build a relationship of understanding and trust with the counselee while building the counselee's hope in God.

Counseling is a relationship between two (or more) people. It is a relationship that God, in his sovereignty, has brought about to accomplish his sanctifying purpose.

How important is the counselor's own life and love in counseling? Pay attention to the example of Christ, the Wonderful Counselor. He entered our world and became intimately familiar with our experience. He became a sympathetic and understanding high priest, touched by our weaknesses, temptations, and sufferings. We can approach him with confidence because we know that he will be merciful and gracious in our time of need (Heb. 4:14–5:9). Pay attention to the example of Paul. His evident love for those he ministered to and the honesty with which he lived before people gave his entire ministry of the Word integrity and persuasive force.[1]

What is *biblical* counseling in a nutshell? "Speaking the truth in love, we will in all things grow up into . . . Christ"(Eph. 4:15). Counselees need to know that you are speaking the truth from God. Counselees also need to know that they can trust you, the truth-speaker; that you are *for* them. You must, like Christ, demonstrate sympathy, understanding, and humility if counselees are to place the fine china of their lives into your hands. They need confidence that the counsel they are receiving comes from someone who understands their world and has been touched by their weaknesses. This draws counselees into confident participation in the counseling process.

How does this relate to homework? One goal of homework during the initial phase of counseling is to build relationships that are channels of transforming grace. I want the counselee to know early on, "God speaks to what I'm struggling with." I also want the counselee to know early on, "The counselor has heard me and understands what I'm struggling with."

As I begin counseling, I look for entry gate issues that will make my initial feedback and homework count. Entry gate issues are frequently those "presenting problems" a counselee describes. They may not be the core issue(s) that ultimately must be dealt with, but they open the door into a person's life. Entry gate issues must be dealt with if the counselee is going to commit to change and become a participant in the discipleship process. I ask, "What is this person struggling with right now? What homework can I give to address it?" Examples of entry gate issues include fear, discouragement, anger, bitterness, loneliness, and hopelessness.

If handled well by the counselor, entry gate issues often open the door to more fundamental problems. For example, Sue, whose life was disintegrating with fears, needed basic reassurance: her problems were understandable; she was not crazy; God cares; biblical counseling could help her. Subsequently, more basic problems emerged: anger, a demanding attitude, fear of man, selfishness, perfectionism, and unbelief. Early on we had created a context of trust and truth that then enabled us to deal with these things.

As I design and assign homework to address entry gate concerns, I want the assignments to offer hope. Frequently, counselees come to counseling with little or no hope. Hope-giving homework provides a natural entry into relationship with the counselee and stimulates confidence in God.

Sarah was a single woman in her late twenties. She described herself as an "introverted, overweight loner." Sarah hated her job, felt uncomfortable and misunderstood by her church, and was alienated from her family. She said that her closest friend was her cat! She was convinced that her life was horrible, that she was "one of God's mistakes," and that there was no way out short of death. What homework could encourage Sarah that both God and her counselor understood? I assigned her hope homework from 1 Corinthians 10:13 (see page 349).

This assignment needs to be carefully set up by the counselor before it is given. This entails working through 1 Corinthians 10:1–14 with the counselee during the session in which the homework will be assigned. The passage speaks to people in hardship; it identifies common sinful reactions to life's hardships; it speaks of how Christ is present to bless in the midst of temptation. What did this assignment accomplish with Sarah? First, it helped me enter Sarah's experience. Second, it helped Sarah see that her hopelessness had an identifiable cause. It was tied to the way she thought about God, herself, and her situation. It was tied to the way she responded. And third, it helped Sarah begin to reinterpret the struggles she faced. As she looked at her problems biblically, her sense of hope grew.

Work through this study yourself. Photocopy it to use in your own counseling, or adapt it.

Here are other examples of entry gate and relationship building homework:

1. Hope grows by seeing what God is up to in your sufferings and difficulties. For example, study Romans 5:1–11; 8:18–39; James 1:2–27; 1 Peter 1:1–2:3; Deuteronomy 8.

2. Focus on your resources and identity as a child of God. For example, study Ephesians and what it means to be "in Christ."

3. Use biblical narratives that emphasize seeing God in your situation. For example, Exodus 13–14, Numbers 11, Numbers 20, and

1 Samuel 17 all focus on whether people forget or remember the Lord. Ask the following questions of the narratives: What difficulty are they facing? What do the people in the situation think about what is going on? What are they feeling? How do they react? What do they want? What is God doing? What are the indicators of God's involvement in the situation? How would the people in the situation have behaved differently if they had "seen God" in the situation?

4. Study people in Scripture who became discouraged, e.g., Elijah in 1 Kings 19; Samuel in 1 Samuel 8; Moses in Numbers 11. Focus on three questions: What was the cause of discouragement? What was God's response to the person's discouragement? What was the solution to discouragement?

5. Deal with fear and anxiety as common human experiences; e.g., Philippians 4:4–10; Psalm 37; Psalm 46. Ask the following: What causes fear? What are the results of fear in the person's life? What are the results of fear in your life? What solutions to fear are found in these passages? How does your relationship with God affect your fearfulness? How would your life look different if you were living unafraid?

Every biblical counselor will find entry gate issues in the lives of counselees around which homework can be built. This homework says to the counselee, "I have heard your concern. I have taken it seriously. I am seeking to understand what you are dealing with. God is involved. There is hope and help to be found in him." As Sarah left the session, she felt understood and encouraged because the homework touched her where she struggled.

UNDERSTAND

Goal: Gain first-hand knowledge and refocus attention on what matters.

During the data gathering phase of counseling, it is first vital to establish a detailed understanding of the person and his/her situation. Sin and obedience are never general. They are always particular responses to the specifics of the situation in which God has placed a person. Biblical counseling aims to apply the Word of God with specificity. This is one thing that distinguishes it from public preaching. I gather data so that I understand the counselee as a person and the details of his situation well enough to make concrete application of Scripture. Data gathering is incarnational. It has to do with entering the world of the counselee, becoming familiar with the details of that world, and being touched by its realities.

Second, it is vital to focus attention on what matters. This provides me with a natural interactive teaching opportunity. As I ask questions that flow from a biblical perspective on people and their problems, counselees are required to think more biblically about themselves and their situations. My goal is to bring the counselee to a greater biblical self-awareness. As data gathering proceeds, the counselee should be learning new things before any actual instruction takes place. I am not gathering data simply to find out where change should take place; rather, data gathering done well becomes a part of the change process. Data gathering is instructional. Good questions begin to teach the counselee to organize, interpret, and explain his world biblically.

I want the homework during this phase of counseling to propel these two purposes outside of the weekly session. As previously mentioned, one of the best homework tools for data gathering is keeping a daily journal. You do not ask a counselee to write down anything and everything. That would be overwhelming and counterproductive. However, it can be useful to assign a structured, specific journal. Here is how I set it up with Judy, the counselee who thought all the problems were her husband's fault:

1. I asked her to purchase a pocket-sized notebook that could be carried in a pocket or dropped in a purse. This notebook was for jotting quick notes for later reference. I wanted Judy to have it with her all the time. She could scribble a couple of words that would help her remember the situation later in the day when she sat down to complete her journal.
2. I asked Judy to focus her journal on situations of conflict with her husband, Jim.
3. I asked her to answer five questions about each incident:
   ◆ What happened?
   ◆ What did you feel?
   ◆ What were you thinking?

- ◆ What did you want?
- ◆ What did you do?

4. I asked her to keep the journal faithfully for three weeks. After this period of time Judy read her journal as homework, looking for themes and patterns. In the following session we compared her findings with Scripture.

Judy's journal gave me all kinds of detailed data about her struggles. It also helped Judy to step back and think properly about her situation and how she interacted with it.

There are many other sorts of helpful data-gathering homework. For example, I often use lists and questionnaires that guide counselees into self-evaluation. These include:

- ◆ "Log List" (as mentioned earlier for Fran and Bill)
- ◆ "Ways I would like to see my marriage change"
- ◆ "Ways I have sought to deal with this problem"
- ◆ "If I could press a magic button and my life would be just the way I want it, what would it look like?"
- ◆ Wayne Mack's *Homework Manual for Biblical Counseling*, Volume 2 has some very useful marriage evaluation assignments.[2]

An essay evaluation is often useful to get people to describe their lives:

- ◆ I am unhappy with my life because. . . .
- ◆ The most important thing to me in my life right now is. . . .
- ◆ Growing up in my home was like. . . .
- ◆ My marriage would be better if only. . . .
- ◆ The thing I am most afraid of in life is. . . .

Use these as examples and tailor your assignments to your counselee.

For some counselees, stories and pictures allow them to communicate things they would find harder to convey in words. When I am gathering historical data, I will often ask the counselee to write about his or her family of origin in story form: "My life in the _____ family." Pictures can also be useful. For example, ask the counselee to draw a picture that depicts the relationships in his family of origin. I then ask the counselee to explain and interpret the picture for me during the next session.

One of my favorite data gathering assignments is what I call my "Big Picture" assignment (see page 350). I begin this assignment by taking counselees to Luke 6:43–45 and introducing them to the concept of "fruit and root." I tell them that I do not want counseling to focus only on the situation and its difficulties, or on other people, or on behavior alone. I want us to step back and get the big picture: situation, fruit, and root. I ask the counselee to write a response to the four questions on the homework page (feel free to adapt it to your own counseling needs or photocopy it according to the guidelines on page iv.).

Writing a letter can be a tool to help a counselee express honestly what is going on. In this case the letter that the counselee writes is not sent to anyone. It is written for the purpose of data gathering. It is a way of getting the counselee to put down his or her agenda on paper. This assignment works well when the counselee is struggling with a particular relationship. I ask counselees to "write the letter of your dreams," being honest about thoughts and feelings with regard to the relationship. It is obviously very important that this letter not be sent. It is for the use of counselor and counselee as a means of gathering data about the counselee's true desires and intentions.

John, twenty, single, and angry, wrote the letter to his mother that I asked him to write. What a letter it was—ten pages long! The letter was very useful to me; I got to know what made John tick. But John also began to know himself better. John saw himself written down on paper. The letter and the questions that came out of it began to open windows of self-awareness and conviction for John. Data-gathering homework led John into the first steps of change: "I am an angry person. How can I change?"

Homework provides opportunities to keep the data gathering momentum going outside of the counseling office. It involves the counselee in an active process of self-examination. Homework keeps counselees involved, not just being known by another, but taking responsibility for self-examination and learning to think about themselves in new biblical ways.

CONFRONT AND COMFORT

Goal: Help counselees to see themselves biblically and to embrace God's promises.

Because of the deceitfulness of sin, all of us need to be confronted. Because of the guilt, power, and misery of sin, all of us need to be comforted in Christ. We need people around us who will take up God's call to "speak the truth in love." Confrontation has been given a bad name in our culture. Confrontation has come to connote harshness. But Scripture presents confrontation as an act of love: they are words that are loving, perceptive, and candid, motivated by my neighbor's need rather than my convenience.

Similarly, comfort and encouragement have acquired misleading connotations: all-tolerant, relativistic, all-affirming, self-esteem-boosting, unconditional "support." But biblical comfort is filled with truth, with the gospel of the crucified Savior and the power of the Holy Spirit to change us.

Three aspects of biblical truth-speaking should guide your thinking about the confrontation-comfort process and how to use homework as part of it. First, engage your counselee. Second, hold up and hold out God's words to counselees. Third, probe issues of the heart as well as issues of behavior.

First, how will you engage your counselee, someone who may be resistant to the truth? Second Samuel 12:1–25 is exemplary. The prophet Nathan confronted David for his adultery and murder. Notice Nathan's confrontational methodology. He created a dialogue, rather than putting David immediately on the defensive. His story engaged David's conscience; it penetrated walls of self-deceit and hiding. Nathan then said, "You are the man." This frank and timely confrontation met with no defensiveness, no deceit, and no excuses. Psalms 32 and 51 portray the inward dynamic of David's repentant response to Nathan's skillful confrontation.

Nathan was also a skillful and timely comforter. He did not give David unconditional positive regard, blanket tolerance, or self-esteem-enhancing messages. But he did love David and brought God's hope to him: "The LORD has taken away your sin. You are not going to die" (2 Sam. 12:13). David heartily believed him. Nathan later bore another message of comfort from God to David: "The LORD loved [Solomon]"(2 Sam. 12:24–25). Therefore, Solomon gained a second name, Jedidiah, "loved by the LORD." Psalms 32 and 51 portray David's faith in the promises of grace that Nathan ministered to David. The confrontation and comfort that you offer in counseling can benefit from Nathan's interactive model.

The second aspect of biblical confrontation-comfort is found in James 1: hold up God's standard and hold out God's promises. James 1:22–24 likens

Scripture to a mirror. This passage wonderfully describes how confrontation takes place in biblical counseling. In the truth-speaking phase of counseling, I want to help counselees see themselves reflected accurately in the Word of God. Often they have been peering into carnival mirrors of self-deception and the opinions of others. They have a distorted view of themselves. Confrontation puts the mirror of the Word in front of counselees so they see themselves as they actually are. Effective biblical counselors do not always have to speak the actual words of rebuke. They hold up the mirror. They use Scripture in such a way that God's words break through blindness in order to convict. True self-knowledge leads to true repentance and confession.

James 1 also abounds in comfort (vv. 2–5; 12; 17–18; 25). Notice that the heart of biblical comfort is not human affirmation to boost self-esteem, the world's fraudulent substitute: "I'm for you. I believe in you. I think you're okay." Comfort, too, comes from God. If confrontation holds up God's mirror, comfort holds out God's promise: If any of you lacks wisdom—if your folly and sin emerge when you are tested—ask God, who gives generously and does not reproach you for needing the help only he can give. That is a promise counselees can take to heart and act on.

The third crucial aspect of the confrontation-comfort phase of counseling is also present in James 1. Verses 14 and 15 show how sinful desires give birth to sinful lifestyles, which result in the misery of God's curse. Sue, Fran, Bill, Judy, and Bart all experienced misery, confusion, and unhappiness. They all expressed specific sins in their attitudes, actions, and words. They all had defected from God in their hearts, serving false beliefs and lusts of the flesh. You must expose these issues of the heart as well as resultant behavior.

What is God's agenda in people's lives? Consider Joel 2:12–13:

> ". . . Return to me with all your heart,
>   with fasting and weeping and mourning."
> Rend your heart
>   and not your garments.
> Return to the LORD your God,
>   for he is gracious and compassionate,
> slow to anger, and abounding in love.

The prophet refers to the Old Testament custom of tearing one's clothes in a moment of grief. Rending garments was an outward sign of a heart response. God doesn't want "repentance" at the level of behavior alone. He wants repentance that flows out of a heart that returns to him. He wants to recapture and rule your counselees' hearts, thus changing the way they live. The comfort of counseling invites people to return to the merciful God with all their hearts. Truth speaking in counseling must address the heart as well as behavior.

Counseling needs to be interactive, biblical, and penetrating. How can homework help? Homework that I assign in this phase of counseling falls into two categories: instructional homework and self-awareness homework. I will discuss each of these and give examples.

I assign instructional homework because many of my counselees are poorly taught. They do not know or understand fundamental concepts, categories, principles, commands, and promises of Scripture. Understanding truth is vital if a counselee is to interpret and react to life biblically. So I must teach as I confront; I must teach as I comfort.

The assignment, "What is the Christian life?" (see pages 351–52) offers an example of homework that instructs. You can readily see that this particular homework assignment is encouraging—even inspirational—in its teaching. It also pointedly challenges counselees. Biblical counseling makes no great divide between confrontation and comfort; the two work hand-in-hand to accomplish God's ends.

Why is a study like this helpful? Many counselees do not grasp the basics of progressive sanctification: "God is up to something in your life. A disciple walks in a way of ongoing transformation, not yet perfect, still failing, but always growing in faith and obedience." Few understand that the Christian life is a process of change, neither perfection nor defeat. Many counselees look for some "secret" of the Christian life to remove the struggle. Many others simply give up and plod along in their sins and misery. Others have never heard that Christ's lordship is over all Christians, not simply over a dedicated elite who have taken some second step of consecration. Others still have not grasped that God saves us not only from the damnation of sin (justification), but also the dominion of sin (sanctification and discipleship). Luther's quotation and the Scripture passages are simultaneously a wake-up call, a challenge, and an encouragement. Study "What is the Christian life?" for yourself. Use it as is to help people you counsel, or adapt the questions to fit the people you are counseling.

Unbiblical systems of thought must be replaced with perspectives on life that are distinctly biblical. I assign the following instructional studies over and over again.

1. What does Scripture say about the heart? (Prov. 4:23; Luke 6:43–45; James 4:1–5)
2. What is idolatry? (Ezek. 14:1–6; Rom. 1:18–32; 1 Cor. 10:1–14; Eph. 5:3–7)
3. What is the counselee's identity in Christ? (Rom. 6:1–14; Ephesians, 2 Peter 1:3–9)
4. Who is God and what is he doing? (Ps. 34; Ps. 46; Isa. 40; Rom. 8)
5. How should you understand trials and suffering? (Rom. 5:1–5; James 1:1–8; 1 Peter)
6. How should you deal with being sinned against? (Matt. 5; 18:15–35; Rom. 12:9–21)

This is not an exhaustive list, but it provides samples of the kinds of instructional homework that can be assigned during the confrontation-comfort phase of counseling. These assignments allow the counseling time to be used more efficiently. The counselee comes in already having completed a guided study on critical truths that needs to be incorporated into his life and discussed in the session.

The second kind of confrontation-comfort homework I assign is self-awareness homework. These assignments focus on issues of the heart since the heart shapes behavior. The struggle with the deceitfulness of sin takes place internally; repentance and faith take place internally.

One assignment I often give comes out of James 4:1–6. James states that human conflict is caused by the desires that rule my heart. People approach others with an agenda, with spoken or unspoken demands. I ask the counselee to write down the things that are important to him or to respond in writing to the question, "What I really want out of life is . . ." or "What I really want from the people around me is. . . ." Then I ask the counselee to write down ways in which these desires have affected his relationships. "How has your heart agenda (ruling desires) shaped the way you feel and act toward those around you?" is one way to ask the question.

Obviously the goal of this assignment is to get the counselee to acknowledge the idols of heart that consistently move him away from the behavior God requires. Many counselees do not question the logic of their behavior. In fact, they don't think of behavior as having meaning; that is, that our actions portray our heart's thoughts and intentions. Because of this, counselees often think they have no choice but to do the things they do. Given their perspective on the situation and their desires, one can understand why they think they have no choice. When they understand that there is a choice, then the promise of James 4:6 becomes meaningful: "But he [God] gives us more grace. That is why Scripture says: 'God opposes the proud, but gives grace to the humble.'" Self-awareness becomes God-awareness and leads to meeting God (James 4:7–10).

I want to help counselees to think about motives. I want to help them to be able to speak from the heart. One way I do this is with the "Responding to the Situations of Life" homework (see page 353). I write a paragraph presenting a problem similar to the kinds of things that the counselee is facing. Then I ask the counselee to respond to the vignette, listing five possible responses to the situation, along with the reason someone might have for choosing each response. This part of the assignment helps him to acknowledge the strategic nature of behavior. I then ask him to characterize his response to a particular situation we have discussed and examine what it reveals about the desires and purposes of his heart.

The study of biblical narratives can be helpful here, and it can easily be incorporated into the "Responding to the Situations of Life" homework. I ask the counselee to examine a biblical character's response to his or her situation, and then look for clues as to what is motivating those responses: Jonah; Moses in Numbers 11; Gideon in Judges 6; Peter in Galatians 2; Herod in Mark 6; Esther in Esther 4–5. This assignment sets up the call to respond in godly ways out of gratitude to God and concern for God's glory.

There is one other assignment that I often use at this point in counseling. This assignment uses Matthew 22:37–40. I prepare the counselee for the assignment by discussing the passage with him during the session in which it is assigned. I ask the counselee to meditate on the two Great Commands and how they set an agenda for dealing with the situation in which he lives and the people with whom he must relate every day. Then he makes two lists with the headings, "If I truly love God above everything else, I will . . ." and "If I truly love my neighbor as myself, I will. . . ." The next week we discuss the lists and the specific changes they dictate.

The goal of confrontation-comfort is true repentance that includes thought, motive, and behavior. The biblical counselor needs to design homework that engages counselees in the process of biblical self-examination, leading to heartfelt confession to God, embracing Christ, and functional change in their styles of life.

ACTION

Goal: Assist the counselee to apply the truths learned about God, self, and others to the specifics of his living situation, making biblical corrections and instituting new biblical habits.

Counseling does not end at the point of insight. The counselee's insight into himself in light of God's Word is important as the foundation for the life change that must follow. Scripture has a functional purpose, that we would be "thoroughly equipped for every good work." The biblical counselor needs to stay on site as the counselee begins to apply what he has learned to the difficult realities of everyday life.

At this point in counseling, significant things have been learned which need to be applied. Here is the counselor's job description at this point: First, he functions as a *shepherd*, guiding the counselee as he seeks to apply truths that may be very new to him. Next, the counselor functions as a *friend*, giving comfort, support, and encouragement as the counselee seeks to deal with the old pressures in new ways. Third, the counselor functions as *pastor*, holding the counselee accountable to God's high standard when the temptation comes to turn back or give up. Fourth, the counselor functions as *watchman*, aware of the reality of temptation, warning the counselee of the Enemy's subtle attacks, and helping design a defense against the Enemy's devices. Fifth, the counselor functions as *teacher*. The course isn't over when the disciple has new biblical insight. Real life is the practicum, the lab. The teacher needs to be there, continuing to reinforce the truths that have been learned.

These five functions structure the kinds of homework that are appropriate at this phase of counseling.

1. Shepherd. Assign a biblical *Personal Agenda*. I assign this to the counselee first as homework. Then we work on it together in the next session. First, I ask the counselee to set *goals* for himself where change needs to take place. I ask him to ask, "Where is God calling for change in my daily life?" (e.g., changes in personal lifestyle and habits, changes in relationships, and changes in the living situation). Second, I ask the counselee to list under each goal specific ways to accomplish that goal. The counselee is creating a *strategic task list*. The changes are to be instituted for a reason; they move the counselee toward God's goals. Third, I ask the counselee to *prioritize the goals* and the task list under each goal. As I said, during the next session we fine-tune the plan for the counselee to put into action.

Put-off/Put-on List. Perhaps the easiest way to get the counselee started during this time in counseling is to begin with a simple put-off/put-on list. I want the counselee to ask, "What are the things in my life, my personal habits, my relationships, and my living situation, that I need to forsake?" And I want him to ask, "What have I not been doing that I now need to be committed to do?" I assign this as homework because I want the counselee to take responsibility for this kind of biblical self-examination and planning. Specific planning leads to specific obedience.

Defining responsibilities is very important. Many of my counselees are confused about what they are and are not responsible for. I assign them simple homework based around God's call to "trust and obey." This begins to clarify the issue for them (see Clarifying Responsibility on page 354). Most people who do this find it very helpful. I set it up very simply by saying, "All of us have two circles in our lives, a narrower circle of responsibility and a wider circle of concern. Our circle of responsibility contains all the things God has called us to do. Here we are called to obey. These responsibilities we can give to no one else. They are commands to us in our God-ordained situation. The second circle is the circle of concern. In this circle are things that are important to us and part of our daily concern but they are not our responsibility to produce and are not under our control. These things we must entrust to God. I want you to take the things in your life and place them in the proper circle." This has proven to be a very simple method of clarifying the issue of responsibility. It also clarifies the cause of anger, anxiety, fear, manipulation, passivity, and many other sins. Attempting to control where you are called to trust and failing to act where you are called to obey are roots of every sort of evil.

One way I set up this assignment is by taking the counselee to Romans 12:17–21. Paul discusses being sinned against; in so doing he distinguishes between God's responsibility and ours. It is not our job to repay evil for evil;

it is the job of God to avenge. Our job is to overcome evil with good. Paul says, "Leave room for God's wrath." In effect, he is saying, "Don't try to do God's job; stay out of his way. Entrust avenging evil to God and do the good he has clearly called you to do." Paul also says, "As far as it depends upon you, live at peace with everyone." Your job is to seek to make peace. But you are not responsible for actually changing any other person or turning enemies into friends. You must trust God for the outcome—whether happy or unhappy—of your efforts. This passage provides a simple way to set up the responsibility assignment. Use it or adapt it to those you counsel.

2. *Friend.* The focus here is encouraging and supporting the counselee with the gospel as she does the hard work of application. Generally, I assign guided studies of passages of Scripture that highlight one's identity as a child of God, the hope of the gospel, the promises of God, the resources that God has supplied, the power God has given one to change and obey, the present ministry of the Holy Spirit, viewing today's struggle from the vantage point of eternity, and the power of God over evil. I design each assignment for the needs of the particular counselee, have her work on it at home during the week, and then discuss it with her at the beginning of the next session.

3. *Pastor.* In Hebrews 13 the pastor is described as someone who watches over God's people as one "who must give an account." Counseling is more than dispensing advice. Counseling has a pastoral function. I am personally accountable to God for the people he has placed in my care. The pastor not only gives God's people the truth; he holds them accountable for believing and obeying it. Under this function I assign two kinds of homework. The first is assessment homework. I lay it out this way:

- Things I have learned (about God, myself, others, life, gospel, my living situation, etc.).
- Things I need to learn (areas of confusion or doubt).
- Things that have changed (list specific changes that have been made).
- Things that still need to be changed.
- Things I am doing to address these issues; places where change is needed.

The second assignment I employ here is the journal. I lay it out for the counselee in the exact manner described earlier, with the five questions. This works very well for both assessment and accountability. It is also encouraging to compare this journal work to the journaling done earlier in counseling. This leads the counselee to heartfelt praise and to recognize the need for consistency, discipline, and further change.

4. Watchman. Here the counselor functions in two primary ways. First, the watchman warns. I want to keep the counselee alert to the Enemy's attacks. Second, the watchman protects. I want to help the counselee set up suitable defenses against these attacks. I will give an example of a homework assignment under each function.

- Warning: One frequent assignment is a "pressure points" list. I want counselees to identify where their struggle is taking place. I want them to identify where they are tempted to bend the rules or cut corners. And I want them to consider why they are particularly vulnerable at these points. The discussion that comes out of this assignment is very useful for setting the agenda for the next assignment.
- Protection: What I almost always assign next is to have the counselee design a "temptation plan" for the times and places where attack is occurring. Often after counselees have done the assignment and we have fine-tuned it together, I will have them write the important elements on a 3 x 5 card to carry with them and have available at the moment temptation strikes. The plan includes three things: *Things to think* (important passages, biblical concepts, warnings). *Actions to take* (things that must be done to have victory over this temptation). A *person to call* (someone who has agreed to be "on call" as a support and encouragement when needed).

5. Teacher: Finally, I function here like a teacher moving among students gathered around the tables in a science lab. He is guiding their application work. The teacher asks questions and makes observations that students might not make. He even teaches new things when appropriate. So, as an "expert in the field," I continue to teach my counselees as they apply the things they have learned. I want to mention two kinds of teaching homework.

First is *biblical interpretation* homework. The purpose of these assignments is not only to help a counselee think biblically about his life but to teach him how to develop a valid biblical understanding and interpretation of the things he must deal with daily. We identify situations that still provoke confusion or struggle. We find relevant passages of Scripture and assign these as homework. I ask the counselee to ask four questions of each passage:

- How does God describe this?
- What is God's purpose in this?
- What does God want me to do?
- What are the resources God has given me for this?

I then take what he has learned from Scripture and help him use it to interpret what he is experiencing.

The second type of homework I assign in the teaching function is *new subject* homework. This homework goes after specific subject matter that the counselee does not understand biblically. These might include finances, sex, work and career, the church, parenting, communication, personal devotional life, etc. I design guided studies appropriate to the maturity level of the counselee. I want the counselee to do some digging before we discuss the topic together.

The final goal of counseling is taking action. This has to do with actually doing what God has called me to do in the place he has ordained for me. For the counselor, this step of action means shepherding, befriending, pastoring, protecting, and teaching. Homework is one of the tools the biblical counselor must use to accomplish these goals. The reasons for this should be clear. This phase of counseling moves toward action, and homework requires the counselee to take action. It requires him to accept responsibility for the changes in his life. It requires him to dig, study, assess, do, and redo. And he builds spiritual muscle and spiritual discipline all along.

It is difficult to overstate the importance of homework in the counseling we do with the Sues, Frans, Bills, Judys, and Barts God sends our way. Homework is not a luxury. It is not an adjunct to the normal biblical counseling process. It is a vital part of productive biblical counseling. Whether building relationships, gathering data, confronting sin, offering Christ's comfort, or making concrete application, homework is useful. It keeps the counselee active; it keeps him in Scripture; it engages his heart; it makes him responsible for his behavior. Homework makes the counselee partici-pate actively during every phase of counseling. Homework advances the work of the counselor as the counselee takes the counselor home with him in the form of practical, productive, wise, and God-honoring homework. Jay Adams, in discussing homework, says,

> From the very outset they [counselees] are required to do what God expects of them in the light of Scripture and in dependence upon the power of the Holy Spirit. The counselor does not do their work for them. He coaches them; he is a shepherd who leads his sheep. Yet they do the work. He insists that they learn to "work out their sal-vation" (solution) through obedience to God and dependence upon his aid. Homework puts the emphasis where it belongs—upon the counselee's responsibility to God and his neighbor.[3]

The Enemy's Lies	God's Truth
"Your problems are unique, bigger, and tougher than other peoples'." (List problems in your life that you have thought about this way.)	"You are dealing with common temptations." (List the daily temptations you face that are not unlike others' temptations.)
"God has forgotten you." (List the places where you have tended to feel forgotten.)	"I am faithful." (List evidences of the faithfulness of God in your life.)
"Your problems are more than you can bear." (Where have you felt overwhelmed or overburdened?)	"I will not let you be tempted beyond what you can bear." (What are the resources for dealing with your problems that are already present in your life?)
"You are trapped and there is no way out." (List the problems you are facing that seem unsolvable.)	"I will provide a way out so that you can stand up under it." (Identify changes in you that would enable you to deal with the difficulties of your situation.)

GETTING THE BIG PICTURE

LUKE 6:43-45

SITUATION:

What is going on? (Circumstances, behavior of others)

FRUIT:

How are you responding to what is going on? (Emotions, actions, reactions)

ROOTS:

What do you think about what is going on? (God, myself, others, life)

What do you want? (Goals, desires, wants, demands)

WHAT IS THE CHRISTIAN LIFE?

1. The following are different views of the Christian life:

   a. Do you think that there is a "secret" to the Christian life that ends the struggle and makes life easy sailing?

   b. Have you resigned yourself to failure as a Christian because it seems too hard to change?

   c. Have you ever become a "disciple," someone consciously changing, learning how to think and act like Jesus Christ in every situation of life?

   d. When you become aware of a shortcoming in your life, do you treat it as a great crisis, either to excuse or to despair over or to seek instantaneous perfection and deliverance?

2. Read this description of the normal Christian life:

   > This life, therefore, is not righteousness but growth
   >   in righteousness,
   > not health but healing,
   > not being but becoming,
   > not rest but exercise.
   > We are not yet what we shall be, but we are growing
   >   toward it;
   > the process is not yet finished but it is going on;
   > this is not the end but it is the road.
   > All does not yet gleam in glory but all is being purified.
   >   —Martin Luther

   a. What is this life like?

   b. What promises does this hold out, both for the present and the future?

c. Is this your view of the Christian life? Where are you challenged? How are you encouraged?

d. How specifically do you need to change?

3. Luther wrote what he wrote because he had studied the Bible. Study the following passages of Scripture: James 1:2–5; Philippians 1:6; 1:9–11; 2:12–13; 2 Peter 1:3–11. Ask of each passage the same questions you asked of Luther's quotation.

a. What is this life like?

b. What promises does this hold out, both for the present and the future?

c. Is this your view of the Christian life? Where are you challenged? How are you encouraged?

d. How specifically do you need to change?

RESPONDING TO THE SITUATIONS OF LIFE

Read the following story carefully. (Counselor writes a paragraph vignette that relates to situations in the counselee's life.)

List five ways a person could respond to the above situation and then attach a goal or purpose to each.

RESPONSE

1.
2.
3.
4.
5.

REASON

1.
2.
3.
4.
5.

How have you responded to _____?

What does that tell you about the desires and purposes of your heart?

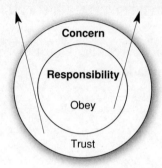

CLARIFYING RESPONSIBILITY

Things that are concerns in my life but are not my responsibility. These things I must entrust to God.

1.   6.
2.   7.
3.   8.
4.   9.
5.   10.

Things that are my God-ordained responsibility and, therefore, cannot be given to anyone else.

1.   6.
2.   7.
3.   8.
4.   9.
5.   10.

Changes that I need to make:

NOTES

CHAPTER 1: THE BEST OF NEWS: A REASON TO GET UP IN THE MORNING
1 For further study, see "Wisdom in Counseling," *The Journal of Biblical Counseling*, vol. 19.2, (winter 2001), 4–13.

CHAPTER 2: IN THE HANDS OF THE REDEEMER
1 For further study, see "The Great Commission: A Paradigm for Ministry in the Local Church," *The Journal of Biblical Counseling*, vol. 16.3 (spring 1998), 2–4.
2 See David Henderson's book, *Culture Shift: Communicating God's Truth to Our Changing World* (Grand Rapids: Baker Books, 1998), for a helpful discussion on the proper use of Scripture on p. 29ff.
3 For a further application of this principle to marriage, see "Whose Dream? Which Bread?" *The Journal of Biblical Counseling*, vol. 15.3 (spring 1997), 47–50. This article is also published as a booklet in the Resources for Changing Lives Series, entitled *Marriage: Whose Dream?*

CHAPTER 3: DO WE REALLY NEED HELP?
1 For an expanded discussion of this concept, see appendixes 1–3.

CHAPTER 4: THE HEART IS THE TARGET
1 This illustration first appeared in *Age of Opportunity: A Biblical Guide to Parenting Teens* (Phillipsburg, N.J.: P&R, 1997), 49–50.

CHAPTER 8: BUILDING RELATIONSHIPS BY IDENTIFYING WITH SUFFERING
1 I highly recommend two books for further study: *When God Weeps*, by Joni Eareckson Tada and Steven Estes (Grand Rapids: Zondervan, 1997) and *Why Does It Have to Hurt?* by Dan G. McCartney (Phillipsburg, N.J.: P&R, 1998).

2 For further study, see my article "Keeping Destiny in View: Helping Counselees View Life from the Perspective of Eternity," *The Journal of Biblical Counseling*, vol. 13.1 (fall 1994), 13–24. This article is also published as a booklet in the Resources for Changing Lives series, entitled *Suffering: Eternity Makes a Difference*.

CHAPTER 12: THE PROCESS OF SPEAKING THE TRUTH IN LOVE

1 For more reading on the use of homework in each stage of personal ministry, see appendixes 4–5.
2 For further discussion, see "Speaking Redemptively," *The Journal of Biblical Counseling*, vol. 16.3 (spring 1998), 10–18, and "Grumbling—A Look at a 'Little' Sin," *The Journal of Biblical Counseling*, volume 18.2 (winter 2000), 47–52.

CHAPTER 14: INSTILLING IDENTITY WITH CHRIST AND PROVIDING ACCOUNTABILITY

1 This hymn, with lyrics by Heinrich T. Schenk, is taken from *The Trinity Hymnal* (Philadelphia, Pa.: Great Commission Publications, 1990), #542.

APPENDIX 4: DOCTRINES THAT DRIVE HOMEWORK

1 Jay Adams, *Ready to Restore*, (Phillipsburg, NJ: P&R, 1981), 72.
2 Numbers 11–21; Philippians 2:14–16; etc.
3 Quotes are from the second and third verses of the hymn "Jesus, What a Friend for Sinners!"
4 An example of a Personal Data Inventory (PDI) may be found in Jay Adams's *The Christian Counselor's Manual* (Grand Rapids: Zondervan, 1973), 433–435.
5 L. Berkhof, *Systematic Theology* (Grand Rapids: Eerdmans, 1941), 534.

APPENDIX 5: HOMEWORK AND FOUR PHASES OF COUNSELING

1 See 2 Corinthians 1:3–2:4, 1 Thessalonians 2:1–20, and Acts 20:17–38 for three extended passages in which love and personal honesty set the stage for effective ministry of the Word. Paul continually builds on his relationship with his hearers, even in those epistles that are relatively more "impersonal" and "objective" (e.g., Ephesians, Colossians, Romans).
2 Wayne Mack, *A Homework Manual for Biblical Counseling*, vol. 2 (Phillipsburg, N.J.: P&R, 1980).
3 Jay Adams, *Christian Counselor's Manual* (Grand Rapids: Zondervan, 1973), 306f.

INDEX OF SCRIPTURE

Booklet Series: A.D.D.; *Anger; Angry at God?; Bad Memories; Depression; Domestic Abuse; Forgiveness; God's Love; Guidance; Homosexuality; "Just One More"; Marriage; Motives; OCD; Pornography; Pre-Engagement; Priorities; Procrastination; Self-Injury; Sexual Sin; Stress; Suffering; Suicide; Teens and Sex; Thankfulness; Why Me?; Worry*

For a complete catalog of titles from P&R Publishing, call (800) 631-0094 or visit www.prpbooks.com.

Paul Tripp is the president of Paul Tripp Ministries, a nonprofit organization whose mission statement is "Connecting the transforming power of Jesus Christ to everyday life." This mission leads Paul to weekly speaking engagements around the world. In addition to being a gifted communicator and a sought-after conference speaker with Paul Tripp Ministries, Paul is on the pastoral staff at Tenth Presbyterian Church in Philadelphia, Pennsylvania, where he preaches on Sunday evenings and leads the Ministry to Center City. Paul is also the Professor of Pastoral Life and Care at Redeemer Seminary in Dallas, Texas, and the Executive Director of the Center for Pastoral Life and Care in Dallas/Fort Worth, Texas, and has taught at respected institutions worldwide. As an author, Paul has written ten books on Christian living that are read and distributed internationally. He has been married for many years to Luella, and they have four grown children. For speaking engagements and other information see www.paultrippministries.org.

RESOURCES FOR CHANGING LIVES

Addictions—A Banquet in the Grave: Finding Hope in the Power of the Gospel. Edward T. Welch shows how addictions result from a worship disorder—idolatry—and how they are overcome by the power of the gospel. 978-0-87552-606-5

Age of Opportunity: A Biblical Guide to Parenting Teens, 2d ed. Paul David Tripp uncovers the heart issues affecting parents' relationship with their teenagers. 978-0-87552-605-8

Blame It on the Brain? Distinguishing Chemical Imbalances, Brain Disorders, and Disobedience. Edward T. Welch compares the roles of the brain and the heart in problems such as alcoholism, depression, ADD, and homosexuality. 978-0-87552-602-7

Instruments in the Redeemer's Hands: People in Need of Change Helping People in Need of Change. Paul David Tripp demonstrates how God uses his people, who need change themselves, as tools of change in the lives of others. 978-0–87552–607–2

Seeing with New Eyes: Counseling and the Human Condition through the Lens of Scripture. David Powlison embraces, probes, and unravels counseling and the problems of daily life with a biblical perspective. 978-0-87552-608-9

Step by Step: Divine Guidance for Ordinary Christians. James C. Petty sifts through approaches to knowing God's will and illustrates how to make biblically wise decisions. 978-0-87552-603-4

War of Words: Getting to the Heart of Your Communication Struggles. Paul David Tripp takes us beyond superficial solutions in the struggle to control our tongues. 978-0-87552-604-1

When People Are Big and God Is Small: Overcoming Peer Pressure, Codependency, and the Fear of Man. Edward T. Welch exposes the spiritual dimensions of pride, defensiveness, people-pleasing, needing approval, "self-esteem," etc. 978-0-87552-600-3